THE WORLDS OF THE MOCHE

ON THE NORTH COAST OF PERU

THE WILLIAM & BETTYE NOWLIN SERIES
in Art, History, and Culture of the Western Hemisphere

The Worlds of the
Moche on the
North Coast of Peru

ELIZABETH P. BENSON

 UNIVERSITY OF TEXAS PRESS
Austin

ON THE TITLE PAGE: Gilded copper banner from Sipán. *Museo Tumbas Reales de Sipán, Lambayeque.*

Copyright © 2012 by the University of Texas Press
All rights reserved
Printed in the United States of America
First edition, 2012

Requests for permission to reproduce material from this work
should be sent to:
 Permissions
 University of Texas Press
 P.O. Box 7819
 Austin, TX 78713-7819
 www.utexas.edu/utpress/about/bpermission.html

(∞) The paper used in this book meets the minimum
requirements of ANSI/NISO Z39.48-1992 (R1997) (Permanence of
Paper).

LIBRARY OF CONGRESS CATALOGING-IN-PUBLICATION DATA
Benson, Elizabeth P.
 The worlds of the Moche on the north coast of Peru / by
Elizabeth P. Benson.
  p.   cm. — (The William and Bettye Nowlin series in
art, history, and culture of the western hemisphere)
 Includes bibliographical references and index.
 ISBN 978-0-292-73759-4 (cl. : alk. paper)
 1. Mochica Indians—History. 2. Mochica pottery.
3. Mochica architecture. 4. Pacific Coast (Peru)—Antiquities.
I. Title.
 F3430.1.M6B42   2012
 985'.3—dc23   2012008955

Dedicated to the memories of

Robert Woods Bliss

and

John Seymour Thacher.

Had it not been for them,

I would never have written this book.

CONTENTS

PREFACE AND

ACKNOWLEDGMENTS

THE PEOPLE KNOWN AS MOCHE, or Mochica, the dominant people of their time on the north coast of Peru, achieved one of the great pre-Hispanic civilizations. When I wrote my first book about them (*The Mochica: A Culture of Peru* [1972]), Moche archaeology was quite simple. Writing the book was mostly a matter of describing the environment; summarizing fieldwork (the archaeological literature could be read in a week); illustrating the visually various ceramic art, collections of which had been known and published for decades; and making some reasonably intelligent guesses about the meaning of the art in the context of the environment and the fieldwork.

Since then, the material to consider has grown enormously; the literature about, and relevant to, the Moche has increased a hundredfold. Ethnohistoric and ethnographic sources are now available for comparison and complementarity, as they were not in the past. Knowledge about El Niño and other geographic and climatic information has increased our understanding of the physical worlds of the Moche. Most relevant, the last three decades of archaeological excavation in a number of sites have literally opened up new corridors and vistas, as well as a new corpus of objects and murals, and new evidence for patterns of building. Discoveries in archaeology often explain material that was previously known only visually. Walter Alva (2001:242), who has excavated the rich site of Sipán, writes: "Time and again, types of items found in the tombs at Sipán are represented in the fine-line paintings on Moche vessels." The late Donna McClelland's superb roll-out drawings of complex Moche ceramic scenes, many of which appear in her and Christopher Donnan's publications (and many of

which appear here), are a great contribution, as is the Archive of Moche Art, established by Donnan, which he has now given to Dumbarton Oaks. Many images have now been put on the Internet, notably by the Museo Arqueológico Rafael Larco Herrera in Lima. For years, images on ceramics and other artifacts provided most of the working material for Moche studies, and interpretation of that imagery is still a major part of Moche studies. The ceramic iconography and its changes give clues to developments in Moche history.

This is a general book on the Moche, but it is even more an adventure of trying to comprehend a fascinating ancient culture. With new data emerging—particularly from excavations—concepts are changing. Some new excavations confirm old notions; others offer new findings that challenge old ideas. With more information, there are more questions. We tend to ask either/or questions and set up monolithic models, but lives and histories are not that simple: there is always input from causes that we cannot know. We will never understand or reconstruct the Moche worlds completely or accurately, yet we are compelled to marshal all possible resources to attempt a description of the life of these complicated people who lived in a complex environment.

Those now striving to interpret the Moche culture agree generally that the art is, to a large extent, narrative; that it provides many realistic depictions; that the reality is pervaded by ritual and mythic meaning; that some portrayals are supernatural; and that although the images appear to be richly various, only certain themes are played, replayed, and developed. Those who decipher Moche iconography, however, have different ways of lumping and splitting, and no two people agree completely on what elements belong in what rite, nor which portrayals are human and which are divine—even which are male and which are female. Eventually, we should arrive at some valid general conclusions. Meanwhile, we thrive on the detective work of putting Moche puzzle pieces together. In this book I have gone into detail on some subjects because they interest me particularly, because I feel that I have something new or contradictory to say, or because I do not think that they have been properly considered, or they have come to light recently and have been little discussed. Where there is general agreement and/or I have no new case to make, I have not elaborated.

The naming of the culture has gone through many changes: Max Uhle had called it "Proto-Chimu" (Chimu was a later North Coast culture); Julio C. Tello used "Muchik" and "Chimu"; "Mochica" was employed by Alfred Kroeber in 1926; in 1930 he used "Early Chimu," which Gerdt Kutscher (1951) also favored; Rafael Larco Hoyle, in 1938, called it "Mochica," as did other scholars, including Duncan Strong and Clifford Evans in 1952; John Rowe introduced "Moche" in the 1960s. The best-known site, near the modern city of Trujillo, is often called Moche, the name of the river and the adjacent modern village, but it is officially known as the Complejo Cerro Blanco, or Cerro Blanco Complex, which will be used here. Cerro Blanco, an imposing hill, is the focal point of the site and its landscape. The use of the term *Moche* for the site, the valley, the culture, and the people can be confusing; Cerro Blanco Complex is a clear reference.

Some words in this book, in common use in the Andes now, are from the Quechua language of the later Incas. These appear here in traditional Spanish spellings, out of respect for the views of the late Peruvian ethnohistorian Franklin Pease. Little is known of the language that the Moche people might have spoken. Spanish reports of languages on the North Coast in the sixteenth and seventeenth centuries are confusing and sometimes contradictory (Netherly 2009).

I owe many people for many kinds of help, for information and discussion, for hospitality and opportunity, and for work on my behalf. In my early days of study, I was—and still am—grateful to the late Alex and Margarita Ciurlizza, from whom I learned that Peruvians will stop whatever they are doing to

take you to what you want to do, and to the late George Kubler, who introduced me to the Ciurlizzas; Alejandra Ciurlizza Mellon has continued the family tradition. Among others from whom I learned early the graciousness of Peruvians were María Rostworowski de Díez Canseco, Guillermo Ganoza, André Garde de Ste. Croix, Federigo Kauffman Doig, Jorge Muelle, Victor Antonio Rodríguez Suy Suy, Jorge Zevallos, and Hernán Amat. More recently, I am in debt to Walter Alva, Nestor Ignacio Alva, Miguel Asmat, Marco and Marina Aveggio, Jesús Briceño, Cristóbal Campana, Marco Curatola, Régulo Franco, César Gálvez, Jorge Gamboa, Ulla Holmquist, Peter Kaulicke, Krzysztof Makowski, Ramiro Matos, Luis Millones, Ricardo Morales, Juan Antonio Murro, Humberto Rodríguez-Camillioni, Carol Rojas, Julio Rucabado, Abelardo Sandoval, Moisés Tufinio, Santiago Uceda, Segundo Vásquez, Juan Vilela, and staff members of the Museo Arqueológico de la Universidad Nacional de Trujillo, who have given me time, stimulation, permissions, papers, pictures, and books. I am grateful to three Montrealers—Steve Bourget, Claude Chapdelaine, and Jean-François Millaire—who are as gracious as Peruvians; to Anne-Marie Hocquenghem, Izumi Shimada, and James Vreeland, who are practically Peruvian; and to my knowledgeable driver in Chiclayo, José Oliden.

I have had good exchanges with Catherine Allen, Patricia Anawalt, Lloyd Anderson, Jorge Angulo, Yuri Berezkin, Susan Bergh, William and Barbara Conklin, Lisa Deleonardis, Dieter Eisleb, Blenda Femenias, Mary Frame, Patricia Lyon, Carol Mackey, Susan Milbrath, Patricia Netherly, Susan Niles, Joanne Pillsbury, John Rick, Ann Rowe, Frank Salomon, Anne-Louise Schaffer, Karen Stothert, John Topic, Constantino Torres, John Verano, and the late Anne Paul, John Rowe, Alan Sawyer, Immina von Schuler, and Henry Wassén. I would also like to thank Julie Jones, with whom I have traveled happily in Peru and had good discussions, and who has helped me in many ways. I appreciate aid from Bridget Gazzo and Emily Gulick. Alana Cordy-Collins made useful comments on this manuscript, and I'd like to acknowledge those who provided illustrations, especially Donald McClelland, Isabel Collazos Ticona, Christopher Donnan, Steve Bourget, Manuela Fischer, and Doris Kurella. I am endlessly grateful to Jeffrey Splitstoser, who contributed both intellectually and electronically to this publication.

Michael Coe asked me to write my first book on the Moche people; I am indebted to him for that and other things. I am grateful to Kathleen Berrin for inviting me to work on the exhibition from the Museo Arqueológico Rafael Larco Herrera at the M. H. de Young Memorial Museum of the Fine Arts Museums of San Francisco. I especially appreciate the Moche symposium in my honor organized by Bourget at the University of Texas at Austin (Bourget and Jones 2008), and the one honoring me and Christopher Donnan, arranged at the Museo Arqueológico Rafael Larco Herrera by that museum and Dumbarton Oaks, which was organized by Jeffrey Quilter, with Andrés Álvarez-Calderón of the Museo Larco and Luis Jaime Castillo of the Pontificia Universidad Católica del Perú (Quilter and Castillo 2010). All have also been helpful on other occasions. Isabel Larco de Álvarez Calderón and Augusto Álvarez Calderón have been particularly generous. I am grateful to Anita Cook and Joan Gero for the dedication of the Northeast Conference on Andean Archaeology and Ethnohistory to me and Betty Meggers in 2005. I would like to acknowledge also the enthusiastic Mochephile members of the Pre-Columbian Society of Washington and express appreciation for the symposium they organized for me in 2006, which has been published in a beautiful volume designed by other helpful friends, Barbara and Justin Kerr (Jones 2010).

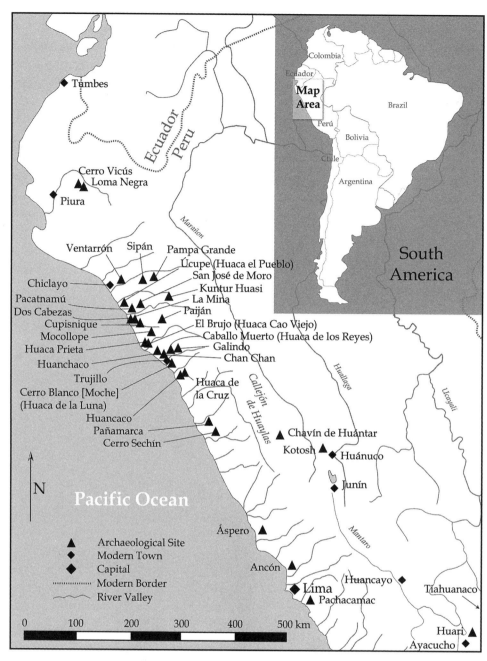

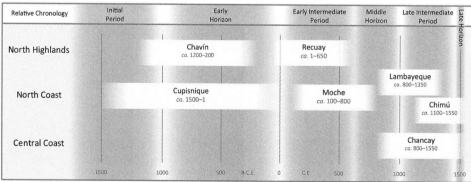

FIGURE 1.1 Map of the north coast of Peru, and a date scale for the North Coast region. *Kindness of Jeffrey Splitstoser.*

CHAPTER ONE   # Approaching the
Moche Worlds

THE PEOPLE NOW CALLED "MOCHE," or "Mochica," created an extraordinary civilization on the north coast of Peru circa AD 100–800. To understand it, one must call to mind the environment in which the Moche achieved their success in livelihood generally and, specifically, in architecture, mural painting, metallurgy, ceramics, and other arts and occupations.

THE ENVIRONMENT

One of the driest deserts in the world, the coast of Peru is a sandy strip, in some places very narrow, between the vast, deep expanse of the Pacific Ocean and some of the world's highest mountains. The Peruvian Andes rise steeply to snow-capped peaks not far south of the Equator and within a short distance from the sea. East of the mountains lie the lush rain forests of the Amazon Basin. On a flat map the distance across these extremes of climate and topography, from sea over mountains to rain forest, is roughly the distance from New York to Boston, or London to Paris.

The North Coast region lies within the tropics, but the Humboldt, or Peru-Chile, Current flows north from Antarctica in a deep, offshore trough. Air moving eastward across the Pacific normally gathers moisture, is cooled by the upwelling current, and is heavy when it reaches warm continental land. Some water is released before the air mass comes to land; some air rises and drops water in the highlands. The coastal plain is foggy but arid. Normal average annual precipitation on the north coast is about a centimeter, most of which is moisture from mist. Because of the

cold current, winds, and fog conditions, the climate is relatively cool. Moist, easterly winds that blow from the Atlantic to the Amazon rain forest are blocked by the Andes, so that they deposit heavy rainfall on the eastern mountains but leave the western heights dry and barren.

In the coastal desert the sand is sometimes wind-blown into sculptural forms (Figure 1.2). Hills and mountains that rise from the sands are bare, but scrub growth may dot the pale valleys. The landscape changes slightly in some areas but remains stark. Where the desert is crossed by rivers flowing from the highlands, water permits irrigation and crop cultivation, and the sands are slashed with patches of green. North Coast rivers generally have a larger volume than other Peruvian rivers, are located near each other, and are more or less perpendicular to the coastline. Algarrobo (*Prosopis* spp.) and other scrub trees and growth, usually called *monte*, often appear in the margins of cultivation, and cane and marsh grass grow near rivers. Some valleys have places with high water tables, underground aquifers, or springs, and there is vegetation, even cultivation. Sunken gardens can be developed where there is groundwater; sometimes wells are dug; and occasionally there is a lagoon. During winter (July-August), certain areas of the coast, especially upper slopes (250–800 m) near the sea, are enveloped by sea fogs that precipitate enough moisture to sustain seasonal plants; in very moist years these *lomas* support cultivated crops. In the past, guanacos—wild camelids, relatives of the llama—grazed and were hunted on *lomas*. Sheltered *yunga* (warm valley) zones, at 500–2,500 m, are warmer and sunnier than the coast and good for certain crops.

FIGURE 1.2 *The desert along the north coast of Peru. Photograph by the author.*

Today the common crop of the lower North Coast is sugarcane, an introduced plant. More of the landscape was once green with varieties of flora. Animals were attracted, notably foxes and deer, both of which are significant in Moche art and can still be found in the area. Monkeys, jaguars and pumas (and other, smaller felines), boa constrictors, iguanas, parrots, and macaws were common in some places. There is still an occasional constrictor or parrot. Writing in the sixteenth century, the Spaniard Pedro de Cieza de León (1959 [1550, 1553]:316–321) remarked on the lushness of irrigated valley environments that began to be destroyed soon thereafter by Spanish demands for charcoal and other needs, and by imported European animals and crops (see also Briceño 1999a; Dillehay and Netherly 1983; Shimada 1994a:36–44). These regions are now mostly desert, with some exceptions: central La Leche Valley, for example, has some subtropical, thorny evergreen forest (part of the valley is now a nature preserve, Reserva Nacional de Laquipampa), as does the upper Piura Valley, which gets significant rainfall; in the upper Zaña Valley, an unusual climatic pocket has remnant subtropical and temperate evergreen forest.

Along the coast, trade was moved by water on rafts, usually made of bundles of rushes, or on land by men with tumplines or llamas with saddlebags. Human and llama traffic journeyed between coast and mountains. The microenvironments of the highlands, which change dramatically with altitude, offered additional resources. Most important, mountains provided water for agriculture, which was critical to subsistence on the coast. The sun rising beyond the mountains added mythic and religious meaning: mountains, sun, and water are vital elements in Andean cosmology. The fact that rivers originated in other people's lands added pragmatic political implications.

The cold waters of the Humboldt Current normally constitute one of the world's richest fishing grounds, perhaps the richest, for fish thrive in cold water. Peru has supplied a fifth of the world's catch for both food and fish-meal fertilizer (Richardson 1994:10–12; see also Murphy 1936, I:286–295). In the low temperatures of the current, mineral salts and nitrogen compounds support a vast quantity of phytoplankton; organisms that feed on this minute vegetation provide food for fish, notably vast numbers of anchovetas, on which seabirds and sea lions feed.

EL NIÑO AND OTHER DANGERS

The coast of Peru is the epicenter for the sporadic El Niño, which has deeply affected it many times, as is evident in the archaeological record (Dillehay 2001:268–270; Moseley, Donnan, and Keefer 2008; Morales Gamarra 2000a; Sandweiss and Quilter 2008). The ravishings of mega-Niños between AD 450 and 750 were surely a factor in the decline of Moche civilization.

El Niño was named by Peruvian fishermen for the Christ Child because it normally arrives around Christmas every three to seven years with varying intensity and duration. Long explained as a warm countercurrent running south from Ecuador and intruding into the Humboldt Current, a strong El Niño is now known to be part of a much larger and more complex climatic pattern (Glantz 2001; Suplee 1999). When it is severe, local warming of waters off the Peruvian coast coincides with sea-surface anomalies over the entire eastern equatorial Pacific, where there is an increase in sea-surface temperature and in near-surface air temperatures. The combination is known as the El Niño/Southern Oscillation (ENSO) cycle/phenomenon. El Niño is usually brief and its effects minor, but it can last for a year or more with varying intensity, duration, and pattern, and when intense, it can have calamitous impact. The worst twentieth–century ENSO events occurred in 1925–26, 1982–83, and 1997–98. The north coast is most severely afflicted, but the entire coast can be affected. Indeed, El Niño events can alter weather worldwide, even slowing Earth's rotational momentum.

The Mexican novelist Carlos Fuentes (1989:15) describes El Niño as "beating against the Peruvian coast, suffocating the anchovies and algae . . .; hurling dead fish against the walls of the continent . . . water sinking water . . . the cold ocean drowned by the hot ocean." El Niño–warmed water kills phytoplankton, forcing fish, birds, and sea mammals to migrate or starve. Sea lions raid fishing nets, competing with fishermen. Horrendous photographs from the 1997–98 event show bays choked with millions of dead fish and offshore islands littered with sea lion skeletons. The 1972–73 El Niño event was not a major one, but it ravaged North Coast fishing (El Niño can shift fishing grounds), and Peru has not fully regained its role as a major fishing nation.

The differences in atmospheric pressure and temperature may cause torrential rains on the coast and in the western highlands, bringing devastating floods and inundations of sediment, sand, and mud; carrying off people, animals, and houses; washing out cemeteries, fields, canals, and roads; and destroying settlements and crops. Damage in the North Coast region in 1982–83 was caused largely by rain. In 1997–98 the far north had heavy rain—as much as 15 cm a day around Piura—but in most valleys high water did not come from the sky but from flooding rivers racing down the mountains, rushing through normally dry beds, and ripping out bridges and irrigation systems. A long-term effect of ENSO events is the deposit of massive amounts of sand and the altering of shoreline. Wind-blown over fields and canals, sand can do severe damage and destroy farming areas. The Early Moche site of Dos Cabezas was abandoned because of the accumulation of aeolian sand, independent of immediate El Niño conditions (Donnan 2007; Moseley, Donnan, and Keefer 2008:83–85).

Some benefits come from El Niño. Where there is water, the desert turns green, allowing farmers to produce short-term, floodwater cultivation in normally dry places, and providing vegetation for animals to graze. In the 1982–83 and 1997–98 events a lake with waterfowl engulfed much of the Pampa de Paiján, and another lake virtually covered the Sechura Desert, a normally waterless, 125 km coastal expanse to the north (Briceño 1999a:23; Gálvez and Briceño 2001:144; Makowski 1994b:101; Murro 1994:20; Suplee 1999:77–80). Mosquitos breed, however (there have been outbreaks of malaria), and other insects and diseases can appear.

Scientific techniques for predicting El Niño are now being developed, but ancient coastal peoples would have recognized signs of a coming Niño event. Winter weather would have been warmer, and some plants and sea life would behave differently. Sharks, warm-water fish, are prevalent in El Niño waters, and sea turtles and manta rays also show up. Shrimp can be harvested offshore, where it is normally too cold for them. Anchovetas are dispersed by the warm waters, but the dispersal is preceded by a greater than usual concentration of the small fish. In 1997, months before the full impact of the ENSO event, exotic fish appeared in coastal markets, replacing the usual species. After the 1997–98 El Niño was predicted, preparations on the north coast included storm drains and roofs so that excavations at important archaeological sites would not be flooded. Current excavations were saved, but damage was severe in many places.

Other natural events also disturb the North Coast world. Water from the highlands may be too little for crop cultivation—there have been disastrous droughts (Bawden 1996:267–269; Sandweiss and Quilter 2008; Shimada et al. 1991)—or so much that it causes floods and landslides. Mountains are still forming in this volatile region, and earthquakes occur. A quake in 1970 that caused tragic calamity in the mountains also leveled half of the coastal town and fishing center of Chimbote (Casma Valley). The quakes that rumble mountains and valleys may also bring about rough seas, causing further damage and loss of human life.

Environments have assets, gifts, demands, and dangers that inhabitants factor into systems of livelihood and belief. Trying to understand the world that the Moche people lived in, we question what they would have responded to, benefited by, or feared, and how they would have dealt with these elements.

FIGURE 1.3 The Cerro Blanco Complex. Huaca del Sol is the large shape to the right, beyond the field and river trees. The long form behind it is Huaca de la Luna. Cerro Blanco rises at the left. *Photograph by the author.*

MOCHE ACHIEVEMENTS

Moche culture belonged to what archaeologists call "the Central Andean tradition." The Central Andes was one of two pre-Hispanic areas of high culture, the other being Mesoamerica (which includes parts of Mexico, Guatemala, Belize, Honduras, and El Salvador). Both are regions of great geographical diversity with some cultural unity. The Central Andes, which produced notable development from the fourth millennium BC until the Spanish conquest in the sixteenth century, includes the western part of what is now Peru and the adjacent parts of Ecuador and Bolivia, as well as northern Argentina and parts of Chile; the peripheral regions lacked significant architecture but had other outstanding achievements and some contact with the core region.

Moche remains are found for some 600 km along the Pacific coast of Peru from the Huarmey Valley north to the Piura Valley. At the approximate center of the Moche world, in the Moche Valley, lies the best-known and most explored site, the Cerro Blanco Complex, known also as Moche or Huacas de Moche, with two massive *huacas* at the foot of a hill (Figure 1.3). A *huaca* (from the Quechua language

of the later Incas) is a sacred place, object, or ancestor—an entity with spiritual power and life; the word is often applied to ancient structures.

The Moche Valley and the next valley to the north, the Chicama, are separated from the more northern Jequetepeque Valley by the Pampa de Paiján. North of the Jequetepeque Valley, a complex of valleys—La Leche, Reque, and Zaña—leads to Lambayeque, which is separated by the Sechura Desert from the Piura Valley in the north. South of the Moche Valley, some evidence for Moche presence occurs in the Virú, Chao, Santa, Nepeña, Casma, and Huarmey Valleys, which are smaller than the northern ones. Cultural and stylistic variations are evident between the valleys north of Chicama, and the Chicama Valley and south.

In many of these valleys the Moche people used thousands of sun-dried adobe bricks to build enormous ceremonial edifices with mural paintings and reliefs. With skill and innovation, Moche artisans, surely the most extraordinary of their era in the Andes, worked gold, silver, and copper—often inlaid with shell and stone—to make handsome, symbolic ornaments, and they wove textiles in complex techniques and designs. The ceramic vessels that they produced with skill and artistry reveal a great deal about the Moche; the only other peoples whose ceramics are so informative are the Classic Greeks and the Maya of Mesoamerica.

ARCHAEOLOGY AND IMAGES

The Greeks and the Maya had writing; the Moche, like most New World peoples, did not. The Greeks and the Maya had three-dimensional sculpture; the Moche people had virtually none. The Moche expressed, with symbolic language in metal and clay, what the others presented in writing on paper and stone. Images on Moche ceramics, published from collections worldwide, have long been a source of information to be interpreted. Recently uncovered murals have added striking images to the visual evidence. The garments that figures wear, the objects they hold, the gestures they make, and the contexts in which they appear all offer clues to the culture. Some images are quite realistic, but in other instances, myth is obviously depicted, and some images seem to combine myth and ritual; others show ritual without evident reference to myth.

Most known Moche objects with rich iconography come from unofficial digs by *huaqueros* (those who loot huacas). Conjectures can be made about these objects, but an enormous amount of information about their use and the places they were found has been lost through extensive and continuing looting of Moche sites. Huaquero pits are mentioned in virtually every modern account of scientific excavation, which provides firsthand, contextual information on the people and the reality behind the ceramic scenes. Excavating the remains of cities reveals the spaces in which people lived, worked, worshiped, and were buried, as well as the ritual and practical objects they used. Archaeological material indicates social structure and relationships, and also trade, social intercourse, and conflict. An important aspect of archaeology is the evidence for burial customs, which reveal beliefs, activities, and the diversified structure of society.

A fruitful period of legitimate Moche excavation began in 1987, when, in a rescue operation after finding looters in the Huaca Rajada, a burial platform at Sipán (in the Lambayeque drainage), Walter Alva began work on a tomb that was the richest yet

excavated scientifically. Continuing work there, under Alva and Luis Chero Zurita, has found other graves with remarkable metal objects and other material providing rare information. At the time of the Sipán discovery, other Moche excavations were under way. Christopher Donnan was ending a project with Guillermo Cock and others at Pacatnamu (begun in the 1980s) before starting work with Luis Jaime Castillo at San José de Moro, both sites in the Jequetepeque Valley. Castillo continues to excavate at long-occupied San José, and Donnan and Cock have since excavated at the Jequetepeque site of Dos Cabezas.

In 1991 a project began at Huaca de la Luna, in the Cerro Blanco Complex, under the direction of Santiago Uceda and Ricardo Morales. That same year Régulo Franco, César Gálvez, and Segundo Vásquez began work in the Chicama Valley at Huaca Cao Viejo. Both of these undertakings, and others, are unearthing remarkable architecture, murals, burials, and offerings. Steve Bourget, after working at Huaca de la Luna, excavated at Castillo de Huancaco, in the Virú Valley; at Huaca el Pueblo, near Úcupe, in the Zaña Valley; and, more recently, at Dos Cabezas. Spaces like those inhabited by lords depicted on ceramic bottles are being found in actual architecture, and evidence for sacrificial rites uncovered by Bourget and others at Huaca de la Luna may explain certain ceramic scenes. Material from recent excavations—for example, the magnificent burial of the Lady of Huaca Cao Viejo (Chapter 12)—is constantly modifying our ways of perceiving the Moche culture.

THE EARLY QUESTIONERS

Moche remains have long attracted archaeologists and other scholars as well as travelers and collectors (Arsenault 1995a, 1995b; Moseley 1992:16–21; Shimada 1994a:13–34; Uceda and Mujica 1994). Interest began in the nineteenth century as people became curious about other, exotic worlds. The Cerro Blanco Complex was described in 1855 by two serious, adventurous Europeans, Mariano Eduardo Rivero and Johann Tschudi, and by the American Ephraim George Squier in 1877. It was the setting for some of the earliest archaeology in the Americas when, in 1895, the German archaeologist Max Uhle explored the complex for the University Museum (of the University of Pennsylvania) and then excavated, for the University of California in 1899–1900, the two large structures there, Huaca del Sol (Pyramid of the Sun) and Huaca de la Luna (Pyramid of the Moon), and the summit of Cerro Blanco (Menzel 1977; see also Benson 1997a, Donnan 1965, Kroeber 1925, Morales Gamarra 2000b, J. Rowe 1954). The "Sun" and "Moon" designations, used by Squier, are of unknown origin; in an early reference Huaca del Sol is called "Huaca Capuxaida" (Zevallos 1994:18). Uhle, one of the first to explore temporal sequences of style and culture, also worked at Pachacamac, a major Central Coast site, and at Tiahuanaco, in the Bolivian highlands. He wrote that of all the cultures that developed in the Americas, none achieved greater distinction than that of the Moche.

The Humboldt Current was named for German scientist Alexander von Humboldt, who traveled in the Americas around 1800 and published descriptions of antiquities he saw. A strong German interest in pre-Hispanic America is attested by splendid collections of artifacts, many of them Moche, begun in the nineteenth century by travelers and businessmen and now housed in German museums. Hans Heinrich (or Enrique) Brüning went to Peru in 1875 and spent 50 years there, mostly in the North Coast region, photographing flora and fauna, and studying the life of native peoples and the remains of the local language (Schaedel 1988; see also Larco Hoyle 2001, I; Salas 2002; Zevallos 1946). Brüning discovered Huaca Fortaleza at Pampa Grande (in the Lambayeque drainage of the Reque Valley), and he founded what is now the Museo Arqueológico Nacional Brüning de Lambayeque with a fine collection of North Coast objects. In 1902–3 Adolf Baessler, whose collection of Moche ceramics forms part of the large American collection of the Ethnologisches Museum (formerly Staatliches Museum für Völkerkunde) in Berlin, published drawings of Moche pottery by Wilhelm von den Steinen (see Figure 9.1). Gerdt Kutscher, a major contributor to Moche iconographic studies at midcentury, described ceramic scenes and provided drawings that are rich visual resources. Excavations in the 1950s by Hans Dietrich Disselhoff and Heinrich Ubbelohde-Doering are also important to the archaeological record.

In Peru the Larco family has added greatly to the knowledge and appreciation of Moche art. Victor Larco Herrera formed a pioneering collection of ancient Peruvian art and founded a museum in Lima with a publication, *Revista de Arqueología*, begun in 1923; the collection went eventually to the Museo Nacional de Arqueología, Lima. In 1903 Rafael Larco Herrera had begun collecting Moche objects at Hacienda Chiclín, his sugarcane plantation in the Chicama Valley. In 1920 he gave most of his objects to the Museo del Prado, Madrid; they are now in the Museo de América, Madrid. In 1925 he acquired two other collections and gave them to his son, Rafael Larco Hoyle, who developed an avid interest and began to collect artifacts, do fieldwork, and publish definitions and interpretations of Moche and other North Coast cultures. (Larco Hoyle's 1938 and 1939 publications were sumptuously republished in 2001; see also Berrin 1997; Castillo and Donnan 1994a:147–148; Salas 2002; and Uceda and Mujica 1997:11–12). Larco Hoyle was a pioneer in formulating the prehistory of the southern North Coast valleys and re-creating the life of ancient Peruvian peoples, especially the Moche. He defined Moche and other North Coast styles, and used ethnographic and other sources to identify human physical types, fauna, and flora. In 1926 he inaugurated the Museo Rafael Larco Herrera at Chiclín, and in 1949 he moved the collection to Lima to establish the Museo Arqueológico Rafael Larco Herrera, where, after his death, his daughter, Isabel Larco de Álvarez-Calderón, continued work with the collection. His grandson Andrés Álvarez-Calderón Larco is now the very active executive director. The Larco collection is probably the most important collection of Moche art.

Larco Hoyle excavated in the Chicama, Santa, Virú, and Jequetepeque Valleys and at the Cerro Blanco Complex. Using stratigraphic and associative data from Moche burials—along with comments on style, shape, and technical changes—he established a sequence for the finely made and decorated Moche ceramics found mostly in the Chicama and Moche Valleys and valleys to the south (Larco Hoyle 1948; see also Benson 2003, Donnan 1978, Sawyer 1966:24–33). Larco Hoyle's sequence is based largely on pottery shapes, particularly the stirrup-spout form, and is designated Phase I–V, or Moche I–V. This is still the standard designation for ceramics from Chicama south, and the phase designations are often applied to Moche culture generally.

FIGURE 1.4 Early Moche (Phase I) stirrup-spout effigy bottle portraying a seated man with a fox head and paws on his headdress, and the Crested Animal repeated on his garment. Ear ornaments were probably attached. *Courtesy Museo Larco, Lima, Peru, XSC-006-002.*

FIGURE 1.5 Phase III bottle depicting a coca ritualist holding a stick and a container for lime. He has around his neck the string of a bag for coca leaves. His face has inlays of turquoise or chrysacolla. *Courtesy Museo Larco, Lima, Peru, XSC-007-004.*

Ceramics of Phases I and II, fairly closely related to the earlier Cupisnique style (Chapter 2), are frequently modeled in a compact, sculptural manner, and sometimes inlaid with shell or stone (Figure 1.5). Phase I has slightly more thickness at the end of the spout than Phase II does. Phase III, with a slightly flared spout end (Figure 1.5), sometimes deliberately evokes an earlier style; it also presents new techniques and motifs that will be put together in Phase IV to form a group of fairly standardized themes. Phase IV is the best-known, best-represented phase (Figure 1.6). Phase V displays changes in style, with some new subject matter and old motifs mixed in new ways in a particularly dense drawing style (Figure 1.7). The alterations show the evolution of southern style and subject matter, and reflect social, political, and religious changes (Benson 2003).

The Larco sequence does not work in the northern valleys, where change took a different pattern, and art had a somewhat different expression. The sequence

itself does not need revision, but alterations must be made in its application; it cannot be used for a strict chronology because phases lasted longer in some places and started sooner in one place than in another. Larco Hoyle was aware of such limitations, although when he developed the sequence, little was known of the Moche presence in the north, and modern dating techniques were not yet in use. Uhle had not known of Moche sites north of Chicama. Larco Hoyle did know something of the Jequetepeque and Lambayeque Valleys, but not as integral parts of the Moche world; the far north began to be known before his death, and he wrote on Vicús, the style found with the Moche style in the Piura Valley. With increased knowledge, the picture has become complex (Castillo and Donnan 1994a:148–153; Castillo and Uceda 2008; Donnan 2001; Donnan and McClelland 1999:20–22; Jiménez 2000:78–84; Kaulicke 1992, 1994, 2000; Makowski et al. 1994). Early Moche (southern Phases I and II), Middle Moche (southern III and early IV), and Late

FIGURE 1.6 Phase IV bottle depicting warriors, captives, and weapons. *Museo Nacional de Arqueología, Antropología e Historia del Perú. Photograph by Christopher B. Donnan.*

FIGURE 1.7 Phase V bottle with full-round monkeys and a weapons bundle on the spout shows a supernatural paddler in a raft with bottles beneath him. *Private collection. Photograph by Christopher B. Donnan.*

Moche (southern late IV and V) are designations now used for the north, paralleling Larco's sequence. Recent excavations indicate that northern sites continued to produce Early Moche after those in the south had begun to produce III and IV. It is now clear that Phase IV was essentially a southern phenomenon, and V, or Late Moche, was largely northern.

The well-known Peruvian archaeologist Julio César Tello visited North Coast ruins and excavated at the early sites of Cerro Sechín (Casma Valley) and Chavín de Huántar (eastern highlands). His 1938 volume of photographs of Moche art in Lima museums is still a useful corpus. Tello wrote of Moche and other cultures in a 1923 publication based on Wira Kocha, a major god or supernatural being in Inca times. Tello was among the first to correlate ethnohistory and folklore with images and archaeology to postulate the Andean mythic world. Another Peruvian who studied and also made drawings of Moche ceramic art was Arturo Jiménez Borja.

For the University of California, Alfred Kroeber investigated the Cerro Blanco Complex in 1925 and 1926, and published Uhle-excavated objects. Wendell Bennett's excavations, for Yale, in the Lambayeque and Virú Valleys were published in 1939. The first large-scale enterprise that included Moche culture was the Virú Valley Project, 1946–48. It coordinated the work of archaeologists from six institutions working independently under the aegis of the Institute of Andean Research and the Viking Fund (Bennett 1948, 1950; Collier 1955; Ford and Willey 1949; Strong and Evans 1952; Willey 1953; see also Arsenault 1995b:446–447). The aim of the project was to determine "the exact nature of the relationship between man, a biological and cultural being, and a favorable but definitely circumscribed environment, the Virú Valley, from man's earliest advent to the year 1956" (Strong and Evans 1952:3). The undertaking did not achieve this vast ambition but did produce valuable results. For instance, the Tomb of the Warrior Priest, excavated by Duncan Strong and Clifford Evans in the Huaca de la Cruz, was the first rich, unlooted Moche tomb that archaeologists had found.

The Chan Chan–Moche Valley Project, 1969–75, directed by Michael Moseley and Carol Mackey, and sponsored by the National Geographic Society and the National Science Foundation, set out to reconstruct the prehistoric occupation of the valley and establish continuity or discontinuity, an ambition only somewhat more modest than that of the Virú Valley Project (Bawden 1982, 1983; Donnan and Mackey 1978; Hastings and Moseley 1975; Mackey and Hastings 1982; Moseley 1975a, 1975b, 1975c; Moseley and Day 1982; S. Pozorski 1976, 1979a, 1979b; S. Pozorski and Pozorski 2003; T. Topic 1977; see also Arsenault 1995b:448–450).

Izumi Shimada (1994a) began excavations at the northern site of Pampa Grande in 1973, and work has continued there on and off since then. More recent discoveries and developments will be discussed in succeeding chapters.

New museums have also come into being. The Museo de la Nación, in Lima, has a fine collection, and the Museo Tumbas Reales de Sipán, in Lambayeque, has exhibited treasures from Sipán for some years; there are also new site museums at Sipán, Huaca Cao Viejo, and the Cerro Blanco Complex, and a regional museum is planned for the Zaña Valley, which will show remains from Huaca el Pueblo, which are fewer than, but as fine as, those from Sipán.

UNDERSTANDING THE MOCHE WORLDS

With no written Moche texts, we sort through not only Moche remains, but information from other times and places that might help us understand the Moche, always keeping in mind that although there are general similarities among many cultures, variations are infinite, other sources can rarely provide entirely satisfactory explanations, and our very different worldview precludes our exact understanding. The use of these sources must be a highly selective process.

Andean peoples, however, are very conservative and have retained customs and beliefs over long periods of time; moreover, certain concepts, such as ritual and the importance of supernatural beings, seem to be fairly general throughout the ancient New World. In the Andes a dualistic perception of nature, human behavior, and social structure has had continuing importance. Dualism is inherent in the Andean landscape—in mountains and sea, agriculture and fishing, drought and El Niño—and it seems also to be inherent in social structure, reflecting the natural world.

Ethnographic data from the North Coast and farther afield, recorded in the last hundred or so years, can be consulted for patterns of myth, ritual, and conventions of behavior. Ethnologist John Gillin's work in the 1940s at the modern town of Moche has been useful in reconstructing daily life at the ancient site there. Alfred Narváez's recent volume on Lambayeque oral traditions is a valuable contribution. Findings on North Coast shamanism by Bonnie Glass-Coffin, Donald Joralemon, Laura Larco, Susan Ramírez, Douglas Sharon, and others can be consulted when interpreting Moche grave goods and ceramic scenes. Contributions of ethnographers working in the humid lowland forests of Amazonia (Peter Roe, Henry Wassén, and others), and the high altitudes (Catherine Allen, Peter Gose, Gary Urton, and others) can also relate to the Moche world because of long-lasting, widespread practices.

Chronicles from the Spanish Colonial era can be helpful (see Pillsbury 2008), even though they were written nearly a thousand years after the Moche florescence. Of course, the Spanish conquistadors, priests, and administrators who wrote them had their own agendas and prejudices, and did not always ask the questions that we would like answered, or may not have interpreted with complete accuracy what they observed in the meetings between two very different worlds. Even if the information were always valid, it cannot be applied directly. In addition to time difference, the information concerns a culture dominated by a highland people, the Incas, and there are basic contrasts in mindset between coastal and highland cultures. Nevertheless, Guaman Poma de Ayala's (before 1615) illustrations and descriptions of people and customs are valuable, as are the North Coast experiences of Antonio de la Calancha (1638) and Pablo José de Arriaga (1621), and the rich information of Pedro de Cieza de León (1550, 1553), Juan de Betanzos (1551), Cristóbal de Molina (1575), and Bernabé Cobo (1653) (see also J. Rowe 1946, 1948).

Important for the Andean tradition is the Huarochirí manuscript, from the Central Coast, ca. 1600, which comprises information gathered by Francisco de Ávila (Salomon and Urioste 1991). Other sources include Miguel Caballo Balboa's *Miscelánea antarctica* (1586), from Lambayeque, and several later manuscripts (see J. Rowe 1948; Lizarraga 1968 [before 1615]; Narváez 2001). A late-eighteenth-century compendium of watercolors of North Coast flora, fauna, geography, and people was sponsored by Baltasar Jaime Martínez Compañón (1978, 1985, 1994; see also Pillsbury and Trever 2008), Bishop of Trujillo, who also commissioned the mapping of ancient monuments, including Huaca del Sol at the Cerro Blanco Complex.

Ethnohistoric sources have been used by many Moche scholars, from Tello on. Anne-Marie Hocquenghem's book on Moche iconography includes an admirable compendium of material from ethnohistory and ethnography. Peruvian ethnohistorian María Rostworowski, in her extensive work on Inca and Colonial matters, has used little-known early sources to interpret Moche scenes. Patricia Netherly cites Colonial sources in her studies of the Chimu, the later North Coast people who founded Chan Chan, across the Moche Valley from the Cerro Blanco Complex. Her work, especially descriptions of regional ecology and Andean social systems, is valuable for Moche studies.

Knowledge of other Andean archaeology can be useful. Indeed, similar themes recur throughout the Americas, with rough parallels among contemporaneous cultures: Olmec (in Mesoamerica) and Chavín (in Peru), for example, and Aztec and Inca. Some years ago I began to notice traits shared by the Moche and the contemporaneous Maya of Mesoamerica (Benson 1976a, 1978, 1983, 1988a, 2004, 2010; see also Quilter 2002; Uceda 2004). The environments and accomplishments of the Moche and the Maya were very different: the Maya lived in lowland forest, erected stone buildings and sculpture, and did not work metals, but both peoples achieved high development and may have shared some ways of thinking. Both constructed enormous sacred buildings and placed rich burials in them. For both, rulership was a major subject of iconography; military and sacrificial imagery was prominent; and art was focused on an elite world integrated with the "other" world. I make no case for diffusion (but see Cordy-Collins 2001c); however, since the Maya were the only truly literate people in the Americas and the most intensively excavated, it seems worthwhile to examine comparisons for questions about the Moche and the kinds of answers to expect.

Every documented culture has creation stories, supernatural beings, a god concept, and something like a sacred ancestor or culture hero. Virtually every known culture has a ritual calendar and liturgy, and a history of ritual sacrifice and mortuary practices. Andean thought is based on continuity and conservatism, yet changes in politics and religion, in themes and emphases, obviously occurred within the Moche period. What we know of Moche archaeology and imagery should be evaluated in terms of what all people at a certain stage are concerned with—basically, feeding a growing population in a developing culture—and the endless variations that exist in the problems to be approached and solved.

CHAPTER TWO

Precursors and Neighbors

DESPITE ENVIRONMENTAL RIGORS, the northern Peruvian desert has long been a viable habitat for people with social organization, communal labor forces, and tenacity. For millennia, the coastal valleys have been inhabited by successive populations. The Moche people had notable predecessors who lived in many of the same places and shared certain traits.

Distinctive projectile points, stone tools, and other remains from early hunters and gatherers of the Paiján traditions of the central northern valleys date to ca. 10,000 BC; there are also remains of the more widespread Fishtail point tradition of the era (Briceño 1999a, 1999b; Chauchat et al. 1998; Dillehay 2000:138–151; Richardson 1994:17–18, 33–38; Sandweiss 2009; Zevallos 1995:23–27). The coastline was at least 35 km farther out than it is now; most early sites known today are inland, often in the foothills, sometimes on rises of ground and often near springs. Sites tend to be quarries, lithic workshops, or short-term camps; some have large trash middens. In and around encampments and in separate burial grounds, there are burials and remains of human occupation. Moche Valley sites include La Cumbre (Donnan and Mackey 1978:13–14) and, quite far upvalley, the Quirihuac Rockshelter. La Cumbre, now near the sea on the northern end of the valley, was a quarry and workshop. The Paiján site, in the northern Chicama Valley, lies inland; some other Early Chicama sites are upvalley. To the north, in the Cupisnique, Jequetepeque, and Zaña regions, there are also early remains. Squash cultivated ca. 7000 BC has been found by Thomas Dillehay and others (2007) in the Ñanchoc (Zaña) Valley.

Mollusks, fish, and plants were gathered from rivers and their borders, and from the seashore. There was clearly some early dependence on the sea (Moseley 1975a; Sandweiss 2009). Anchovetas were a critically important food, and sea mammals and birds were hunted; remains of terrestrial creatures have also been found. Land snails appear in quantity in middens, and remains of lizards, birds, foxes, and viscachas (a rabbitlike rodent now usually found at higher altitudes) have been recovered, as have deer bones and remains of lithic points.

Sedentary life had begun before 6000 BC, and by 3500 BC villages had grown and increased. Societies with sizable populations, developing agriculture, and ceremonial structures were present before 2500 BC, and before the appearance of pottery. The Peruvian coastal desert, along with a few sierra sites, has the earliest large ceremonial architecture known in the Americas (Donnan 1985; see also Billman 1999; R. Burger 1992; Moseley 1992:98–121; Moseley and Deeds 1982:28; T. Pozorski and Pozorski 1993; Shady and Leyva 2003). Large-scale mobilization of labor was achieved before social stratification and state apparatuses were fully developed, a point made by Richard Burger (1992:37); Richard Keatinge (1981:173, 176) has emphasized that labor serving religion was established early, because religion was already a catalyst for manipulation of people and control over strategic resources. Monumental buildings were constructed, often of river cobbles with mud or clay mortar. Sun-dried mud bricks might be used with stone; some buildings were entirely of these adobes. Floors were often of clay, and clay sculpture decorated certain buildings. Characteristic of the period are large, U-shaped structures—usually a pyramidal building facing a walled, sunken courtyard—which imply a fairly sizable and organized population, as do irrigation systems, which began at about this time. Alto Salaverry (S. Pozorski and Pozorski 1979), in the Moche Valley, dates from this era, as does Salinas de Chao (Alva 1986b), a large ceremonial site and an important salt source to the south.

In 2007 excavation was begun by Walter Alva and his son Ignacio at a previously unknown site, Ventarrón, near the Moche site of Sipán; Ventarrón has dates ca. 2000 BC, but earlier, Preceramic levels are being found there. The site has notable architecture and a very early mural painting of a deer caught in a large hunting net (Alva and Alva 2008; *El Comercio*, 11 November 2007). Deer hunting was an important theme of Moche ceramics in Phase IV, and a net is prominent in many of these scenes.

Cotton domestication has marked the start of the Late Preceramic, or Late Formative, period at 3000–2000 BC, but Dillehay's recent work puts the earliest cotton cultivation at 3500 BC (Dillehay et al. 2007; see also Vreeland 1992b). *Gossypium barbadense*, a cotton plant commonly used at this time in northern Peru, was native there. An ideal plant for North Coast cultivation, it grows in marginal soil conditions, resists drought and flood, and needs relatively little water or maintenance. Ignacio Alva (personal communication, 2010) points out the importance of cotton in the development of coastal civilization. Cotton may have been cultivated in Peru initially for net-fishing and diving for shellfish; it was also used for hunting nets and bags for carrying food and objects. More than 6,000 fabrics and fabric fragments of cotton and other plant fibers, made by twining, weaving, and other techniques (2500 BC), were found by Junius Bird at Huaca Prieta, Chicama Valley, where he excavated 33 Preclassic burials (Bird 1948; Bird, Hyslop, and Skinner 1985:101–218; see also Fernández 2001). Other early twining is known, but Huaca Prieta textiles are the best recorded and perhaps the most varied technically. Their designs, expressed through transposed warp construction and other techniques, include a condor with a snake in its stomach, crabs with snake-head tails, and two-headed birds. Recent, unpublished excavations at the site, under Dillehay, have revealed additional textiles.

Among other plant remains in Preceramic levels at Huaca Prieta, the most common were cultivated squash (*Cucurbita* spp.) and gourds (*Lagenaria siceraria*); the latter were made into bowls, utensils, and floats for fish nets (Bird, Hyslop, and Skinner 1985:229–237; see also R. Burger 1992:28–33; S. Coe 1994:21–24, 37–40; S. Pozorski 1979b; Towle 1961). There was also early cultivation of beans (*Phaseolus lunatus* and *P. vulgaris*) and chile peppers (*Capsicum* spp.). The foot plow, or digging stick—for millennia the most common agricultural tool on the coast—appeared in the Preceramic period. Food was transported between coast and highlands: some upland vegetables—the potato (*Solanum tuberosum*), for example—have been encountered in Late Preceramic contexts on the coast, Alto Salaverry being one. Marine fish are found in highland sites. Salt was surely a trade item, although salt exists in places in the sierra.

Llamas and alpacas, two of the four New World relatives of the camel, had been domesticated in the highlands before 2500 BC; the related guanaco and vicuña are still wild. Camelid remains found on the coast date from between 2000 BC and the beginning of the modern era, occurring in substantial quantities from 500 BC on (Chapter 3).

THE INITIAL PERIOD: CUPISNIQUE AND CHAVÍN

The earliest pottery reported in the Americas comes from the northern Andes—the Caribbean coast of Colombia and the coast of Ecuador—and from the mouth of the Amazon, dating from ca. 3500–3000 BC (Bruhns 1994:116–121; Dillehay 1999; Meggers, Evans, and Estrada 1965; Reichel-Dolmatoff 1965, 1985; Roosevelt 1991:98). Pottery production began on the North Coast and elsewhere in the Central Andes early in the Initial period, ca. 2000–1500 BC, and ceramics with distinct styles and iconographic elements began to develop. An impressive North Coast style is known as Cupisnique (ca. 1200–200 BC), identified and named by Rafael Larco Hoyle for a *quebrada* between the Chicama and Jequetepeque Valleys where he first found it (Larco Hoyle 1941, 1946, 1948, 2001, I; see also Alva 1986a; Briceño 1999b; R. Burger 1992; Chauchat et al. 1998; Cordy-Collins 1992, 1998; Elera 1983, 1993; Kaulicke 2000; T. Pozorski and Pozorski 1993; Quilter 2001; Roe 1982; Salazar and Burger

2000; Salazar-Burger and Burger 1996; Tellenbach 1986, 1998; Zevallos 1995). Puémape, a Cupisnique cemetery in the quebrada, was excavated by Carlos Elera and José Pinilla (1990); Paiján remains also come from this quebrada.

Cupisnique potters used the stirrup-spout bottle, a widely produced early form, later predominant in fine Moche ceramics. With intricate incising and/or modeling, Cupisnique effigy bottles, and those of certain related styles, take the shape of a vegetable, shell, animal (usually a powerful predator such as a jaguar, cayman, harpy eagle, or snake), a human figure, or a supernatural being, subjects similar to those of later, Moche wares, with a similar mixture of realism and seeming fantasy (see Ayasta 2006; Campana 1995; Tellenbach 1998). Steatite cylindrical cups and shallow bowls were carved with intricate designs, notably a spider deity bearing severed heads (Figure 2.1), often referred to as "trophy heads," although they were likely not war trophies but offerings in sacrificial rites. These were also to be a theme of Moche art. Other carvings present a creature with mixed feline and eagle traits; creatures of such mixed ancestry are common in Andean art. The Cupisnique style varies somewhat according to where it was made, but it is generally of high quality and impressive style. Cupisnique artisans also produced sophisticated hammered goldwork with complex designs, some of the earliest goldwork in the New World (Ayasta 2006).

Research since Larco Hoyle's time has confirmed his belief that the Cupisnique style appeared over an area later occupied by the Moche people, from the Moche Valley north to the Lambayeque Valley (the Cupisnique quebrada is at midpoint), and there may have been a Cupisnique presence as far north as Piura. The Piura Valley, the widest coastal region in Peru, thrived in the Initial period and was surely known to the people who produced the Cupisnique style; the upper valley was possibly a place for contact between coastal, mountain, and tropical forest peoples. Although important sites in the Piura Valley are inland, *Spondylus* shell—the thorny oyster from the deep, warm waters off Ecuador—has been found in Initial period remains in midvalley at Cerro Ñañañique, a possible gateway for movement of goods through lower mountain passes; it is also on an easy route to the Lambayeque Valley.

FIGURE 2.1 The underside of a Cupisnique shallow steatite bowl showing a spider anthropomorph with trophy heads in the web. *Courtesy Dumbarton Oaks Research Library and Collection, Washington, DC, B-580.*

The Cupisnique style has some relationship with what is often considered to be a religious cult known today as Chavín (Bennett 1944; R. Burger 1992; Campana 1995; Chauchat, Guffroy, and Pozorski 2006; Conklin and Quilter 2008; Kembel 2008; Kembel and Rick 2004; Lumbreras 1993; J. Rowe 1962; Salazar and Burger 2000; Tellenbach 1998; J. Tello 1960). The latter part of the Initial period is often called the Early Horizon because of the wide spread of the cult and its influence, but it may be that numerous influences, including the Cupisnique style and subject matter, met to form the Chavín phenomenon; related architecture, sculpture, metallurgy (Figure 2.2), and ceramics are found along the north and central coasts and in the highlands.

The main temple site lies on the eastern slopes of the Andes, adjacent to the modern town of Chavín de Huántar, where the Mosna and the Huachecsa Rivers meet in the drainage of the Marañón, which empties into the Amazon. The temple and its sunken

FIGURE 2.2 Chavín gold plaque with a supernatural figure hammered in relief. *Courtesy Dumbarton Oaks Research Library and Collection, Washington, DC, B-604.*

Cupisnique ceramic figures, Chavín figures can be basically a human body with an animal head or other transforming traits. Some Chavín designs, however, are dense conglomerations of symbolic motifs with little resemblance to a human body.

The temple at Chavín de Huantár, which seems to present a synthesis of architectural elements found in other places, may have been a special ceremonial center (Kembel and Rick 2004; Conklin and Quilter 2008). This is suggested by passageways and stairways that may have been settings for ritual, by shafts that seem to have been intended to transmit light, and by passages for water drainage through the building, as well as by the complications of the architecture and the masterful and complex sculpture with supernatural themes. Several chronologies have been published because dating of the Chavín site has proved difficult. Recent work by John Rick (2008) and others suggests that the older part of the structure may be pre-1100 BC.

The Cupisnique site of Caballo Muerto was partially excavated in the Chan Chan–Moche Valley Project (T. Pozorski 1980, 1982; see also R. Burger 1992; Chauchat, Guffroy, and Pozorski 2006; Conklin 1985; Moseley and Watanabe 1974; T. Pozorski and Pozorski 1993). Well up the Moche Valley, it is a complex of eight structures, of which the best known is the U-shaped Huaca de los Reyes (T. Pozorski 1980, 1982), with architectural sculpture showing supernatural beings much like those at Chavín de Huántar. Carbon 14 dates for Caballo Muerto average ca. 1500 BC. The Chavín and Cupisnique styles were generally contemporary, but the dates of both may still be adjusted.

Other notable sites of this period are more or less related to the Chavín phenomenon (Alva 1986a, 1986b; R. Burger 1992; Millones and Onuki 1993; Proulx 1982). Sechín Alto, in the Casma Valley, where Shelia and Thomas Pozorski (S. Pozorski 1987; T. Pozorski and Pozorski 1993) have worked, was a large ceremonial center with an immense structure. In the same valley, Cerro Sechín (Samaniego, Vergara, and Bischof 1985) and Pampa de los Llamas/Moxeke (S. Pozorski and Pozorski 1987; J. Tello 1956) are important sites with notable sculpture. In the Nepeña Valley, sculpture of the period comes from Cerro Blanco (not to be confused with the complex in the Moche Valley), where Henning Bischof (1997) has worked. Kuntur Huasi, up the Jequetepeque Valley,

plaza form a complex, U-shaped structure, the result of many building stages. Its smooth stone walls and columns are decorated with the most splendid and complex architectural sculpture in ancient Peru, relief surfaces depicting enduring religious motifs in a sophisticated, recognizable style and iconography. A standing, frontal figure with feline fangs and bird feet may hold a symbolic object in either hand; other creatures combine traits of raptor, feline, and snake; at times, details of these creatures are repeated as patterns.

The mixed motifs reflect the long Andean history of otherworldly creatures that combine symbolic traits to express beliefs, descriptive qualities, and an attitude toward the interrelationship of the natural and supernatural worlds. Like many Moche depictions, and like had architecture, sculpture, and rich burials indicating significant differences in social rank (Kato 1993; Onuki 1997). Montegrande, Jequetepeque Valley, was large and complex (Tellenbach 1986), and extraordinary gold objects were found at Chongoyape, in Lambayeque (Lothrop 1941, 1951). The burial ground of Morro de Etén, on the littoral of the Lambayeque drainage, yielded Cupisnique- and Chavín-related pottery and some gold objects (Elera 1983). Pacopampa, near the city of Cajamarca, was the northernmost important ceremonial center in the sierra at this time (Kaulicke 1976).

Copper technology probably began ca. 1000 BC, according to evidence from Mina Perdida, a large site in the Lurín Valley on the central coast (R. Burger 1992; Shimada and Merkel 1991; see also R. Burger 1996; Jones 2001; J. Rowe 1962). Cupisnique and Chavín people hammered gold and silver to produce objects with low-relief portrayals of supernatural beings (Figure 2.2). Judging from the available sample, Cupisnique goldsmiths were the most skillful of the era, beginning a tradition of North Coast metallurgy that Moche smiths carried to remarkable successes.

Cupisnique-style ceramics appear at Chavín, and there seems to be Cupisnique influence on ceramics of Chavín and other sites; also, Chavín-style objects are found in Moche territory (Lumbreras 1993; Morales Chocano 2008:147). The Cupisnique-Chavín inheritance in Moche art and culture suggests the possibility of Moche pilgrimages to the Chavín site (see Chapter 10).

FROM CUPISNIQUE TO MOCHE

As Cupisnique/Chavín waned, the Salinar culture, also named by Larco Hoyle (1944, 1946:155–161, 1948:220–222), became prominent in the Chicama–Moche–Virú area ca. 450–150 BC. It generally produced small sites with adobe-brick mounds, but Cerro Arena is a large Salinar site of 2,000 quarried-stone structures (some with 20 rooms) on a ridge in the southern Moche Valley (Brennan 1980; Mujica 1984). More than 100 Salinar sites have been located in that valley, many of them found by Brian Billman (1999:146–153). Structures identified as Salinar were found on Cerro Blanco and at the Cerro Blanco

Complex, and Salinar burials were excavated at Caballo Muerto (Bourget 1997b; Elera and Pinilla 1990; see also Bawden 1996:184–186; Donnan and Mackey 1978:25–44; Shimada 1994a:63–66; Willey 1953). Salinar pottery sometimes used Cupisnique themes with simpler forms and designs. Bottles may have a stirrup spout, a strap-handle cylinder spout (Figure 2.3), or a double spout with a bridge.

The Salinar style was still present in the middle and upper Virú Valley in the first century AD, when a new style appeared in the lower valley. Named "Virú" by Larco Hoyle (1945a, 1948:22–24, 1966:104) and "Gallinazo" by Wendell Bennett (1939, 1950), who, excavating in the Virú Valley Project, used the name of a group of elite structures there, the style has commonly been called Gallinazo in U.S. publications (Millaire with Molion 2009; see also Billman 1999:152–158; Collier 1955; Daggett 1985; Donnan and Mackey

FIGURE 2.3 Salinar architectural bottle. *Courtesy Museo Larco, Lima, Peru, XXC-000-815.*

FIGURE 2.4 Gallinazo stylized feline effigy bottle with resist painting and a strap-handle cylinder spout. *Courtesy Museo Larco, Lima, Peru, XSC-008-004.*

1978:45–54; Kaulicke 1992; Kroeber 1930:77,80; Moseley and Mackey 1972; Shimada 1994a:66–75; Shimada and Maguiña 1994; Strong and Evans 1952:60–128; J. Topic and Topic 1983; Willey 1953; Wilson 1988:151–198). Sometimes the two names are used in somewhat different ways, which increases confusion in the literature. The style is distributed on the coast, perhaps as far south as the Casma Valley and as far north as the Piura Valley. Gallinazo sites are found in various parts of the Moche Valley but are densest in the central part. One of these sites, Cerro Oreja, fairly far upvalley, also had a Cupisnique occupation and a long history.

The people whose culture is identified as Gallinazo built monumental architecture and impressive irrigation systems, indicating a sizable population and a degree of urbanization. Their pottery often combines modeled forms with resist, or negative, painting in which a waxy substance was applied to surfaces and burned off in the firing, leaving designs in its place. The subjects are often those of Moche ceramics—warriors, felines (Figure 2.4), birds, sea life, and houses—but the style is distinct. Plain domestic wares with a

coarser temper, often face-neck jars with a lug at either side, also appear at Gallinazo sites. Indeed, a kind of relatively simple pottery was made in both Gallinazo and Moche workshops (Donnan 2007:8–9, 2009).

The Moche began their rise to prominence in the early centuries AD, at the onset of the Early Intermediate period (also known as the Florescent, Regional Development, or Mastercraftsman period). They moved into the Cerro Blanco Complex and consolidated their power in the Moche Valley. The nucleus of Huaca de la Luna, one of two huge structures at the Cerro Blanco Complex, may have been built by Gallinazo craftsmen, as was, apparently, the oldest sector of the site, at the foot of the Huaca del Sol (Hastings and Moseley 1975; Ramírez-Gamonal and Herrera 1994; T. Topic 1982:265; Uceda, Gayoso, and Gamarra 2009).

The Gallinazo style was long considered simply earlier than the Moche, but then many excavators found that the Gallinazo stylistic tradition, especially in domestic pottery, continued in many places unsubdued by the Moche people, and in some cases it lasted as long as Moche or longer (Castillo and Uceda 2008; Kaulicke 1994:330; Narváez 1994:79–80). The two groups seem to have been contemporary occupants of the Lambayeque region, with a Gallinazo population in the central area. The Gallinazo people may often have been relegated to secondary position, but near Huaca La Merced, at Batán Grande (La Leche Valley), a probable ceramic workshop contained Middle Moche and Gallinazo sherds together (Shimada and Maguiña 1994). There is an Early Moche presence in parts of this region, but Middle Moche occupation of central La Leche and the Lambayeque coast seems to have been the result of southern Moche expansion. Moche and Gallinazo styles appear jointly at Pampa Grande in late times, with Moche dominant (Shimada 2001:181–183, 198, 200). At one time the two groups apparently used Pacatnamu (Jequetepeque Valley) jointly (Donnan and Cock 1997; Ubbelohde-Doering 1967:22). San José de Moro (Jequetepeque Valley) had a Gallinazo presence (Castillo 2001:313), and there is an apparent Gallinazo influence at Huaca Cao Viejo (Franco and Gálvez 2009). Huaca Licapa (Chicama Valley) is a high, large, terraced construction with both Gallinazo and Moche associations (Bonavia 1985:43; Gálvez and Briceño 2001:145; Reindel 1993:253–261).

Christopher Donnan (2009a), based on his excavations at Pacatnamu and Dos Cabezas, thinks that the Gallinazo presence has been exaggerated. He now argues that Gallinazo sites should be identified only by the fine pottery, Gallinazo Negative, because the everyday pottery can be Moche as well as Gallinazo and should not be used as a criterion for Gallinazo presence; other writers are also thinking in similar ways (for example, Uceda, Gayoso, and Gamarra 2009). The Gallinazo position should therefore be reconsidered, for the domestic ware is often associated with Moche fine ware with no Gallinazo Negative present. Sites with only domestic ceramics could be Gallinazo or Moche.

If Moche and Gallinazo groups were inhabiting the same valleys at the same time, the balance of power may have varied from valley to valley with differing interactions. In some cases they apparently settled in different parts of a valley or lived side by side. The complicated relationship is only beginning to be sorted out (Shimada et al. 2008). The producers of the Gallinazo style have been considered a people different from the Moche, but they may have been part of the same ethnic group with different cultural patterns. The two cultures appear at roughly the same time, and as Garth Bawden (1996:198–209, 220–221) has pointed out, they shared similar burial practices and seem to have made very similar domestic pottery.

Heavy looting of rich tombs in the Piura Valley began ca. 1960. In 1963 Ramiro Matos Mendieta (1965–66) was asked by the Patronato Nacional de Arqueología to inventory the region where looters had been active, and he documented 40,000 *huaquero* holes around a single town (see also Diez Canseco 1994; Makowski 1994b:98–100; Murro 1994). Near Cerro Vicús, Matos noted the presence of a style he named Vicús. Larco Hoyle (1965a, 1967) published a corpus of objects, enlarging the concept of Vicús, and some excavations were made around Cerro Vicús in the late 1960s (Amaro 1994; Disselhoff 1971; Lumbreras 1979; Murro 1994). Later fieldwork took place at several sites where both Moche and Vicús material was found (Campana 1999; Guffroy, Kaulicke, and Makowski 1989; Hocquenghem 1995; Kaulicke 1991, 1994, 2000; Makowski et al. 1994; Richardson et al. 1990:420–425; Shimada 1994a:75–77).

Ceramics, as well as ornaments of cut and hammered gold, in Vicús style come from deep shaft and chamber tombs in the Piura Valley. The ceramics, sometimes with negative painting, often feature rather ill-defined animals, people, captives, sacrifice, and sexual scenes. Vicús shares with Early Moche many motifs and ceramic forms—including bridge-spout, stirrup-spout, and double bottles (Figure 2.5). The style, however, is generally cruder and less realistic than that of Moche art, although some Vicús designs can be quite complex. Vicús and Gallinazo seem to be about contemporary in the early phases, during the first and second centuries BC; the Moche style seems to have appeared slightly later. Vicús existed alongside Early Moche and sometimes alongside Gallinazo. Objects of Moche style in Piura seem to be associated with Vicús: many tombs contained ceramics of both cultures, and Moche style ceramics were strewn on the surface of looted Vicús cemeteries (Makowski 1994b:99, 111). Certain bottles have been called Vicús, Moche, or Moche-Vicús; essentially Moche, their subject matter can differ somewhat from mainstream Early Moche.

FIGURE 2.5 Vicús double bottle. *Courtesy Museo Larco, Lima, Peru.*

Quantities of Early Moche art, notably goldwork, came from looted shaft tombs on a low, sandy hill called Loma Negra, one of several cemeteries around Cerro Vicús; the objects date to the third century AD (see Figure 6.3; Jones 1979, 1993, 2001; Kaulicke 1999, 2000:115–141; Lapiner 1976:148–161; Lechtman 1979; Lechtman, Erlij, and Barry 1982; Schaffer 1985). Many Moche ceramics from the upper Piura Valley are extraordinary in the precision and liveliness of their sculptural style; the ware is distinct and well made.

The Moche people may have gone to Piura for prized *Strombus* and *Spondylus* from Ecuador, a trade that may have existed since Cupisnique times (Bruhns 1994:141, 281–284; R. Burger 1992; Cordy-Collins 1992, 2001a; see also Guffroy, Kaulicke, and Makowski 1988:118–119; Hocquenghem 1993; Kato 1993; Onuki 1997; Richardson et al. 1990; *Spondylus* 1999). In the Early Intermediate period, the Vicús area was a port of exchange for shell and probably some gold from Ecuador and Colombia, traded for copper and semi-precious stones from the Central Andes. Gold, copper, and fine clay sources have been found in the region (see Chapter 6).

BEGINNINGS OF MOCHE

No firm evidence yet exists for a place of Moche origin. Early Moche remains are rare south of the Moche Valley. In the north, Early Moche remains survive in the Jequetepeque, Lambayeque, and Piura Valleys. As Cristóbal Campana and Ricardo Morales (1997) have observed, those valleys produced Moche art that shows more traits similar to those of Cupisnique than the Chicama/Moche region does. Matos (1965–66) saw Moche traits in 40 percent of the sherds he examined in the Piura Valley, but although recent archaeology indicates a significant presence of Early Moche style in Piura, and Larco Hoyle (1965a, 1967) saw Vicús as the source of the Moche style, Krzysztof Makowski (1994b:120; see also Castillo and Uceda 2008), who has worked in the region, discounts the possibility of Moche origin there. Examples of Early Moche from Piura and other northern places are probably not all contemporary with ceramics in Phases I/II for the Chicama and Moche Valleys. In the Jequetepeque Valley, tombs with artifacts of Early Moche style have

been found by Alfredo Narváez (1994) at La Mina and by Christopher Donnan (2001) and Guillermo Cock at Dos Cabezas, but the actual dates found for Dos Cabezas are AD 450–550 (Donnan 2007). Conservatism in the north likely caused this style to persist there longer than in the south; there may even have been a later start with the Early Moche style.

Recent archaeology at Huaca Cao Viejo indicates that it contains earlier Moche phases than have yet been found at the Cerro Blanco Complex, which might suggest that the Chicama Valley may have seen the beginning of Moche development. It has many earlier sites: a Cupisnique site lies just to the north of Cao Viejo, and another Cupisnique site is not far away. The Preceramic site of Huaca Prieta is also close by.

The Moche were likely descendants of those who produced the Cupisnique style, who may have been overpowered or ousted for a time, but this was the land of the ancestors, and in the Andes, ancestors are often powerful and usually sacred. Many scholars, beginning with Larco Hoyle (2001, I), have reached the conclusion that the Cupisnique people were considered ancestors of the Moche (Benson 1972:14–15, 22–28; Bourget 2003:266; Campana 1994:15; Campana and Morales 1997; Cordy-Collins 1992, 1998; Franco, Gálvez, and Vásquez 2001a:149; Jiménez Borja 1938:18–19; Kaulicke 1992; J. Rowe 1971; Zevallos 1989). Régulo Franco (1998) points out the similarity of Moche architecture to that of the impressive Huaca de los Reyes; Alan Sawyer (1966:24), who in the 1960s and '70s made many contributions to Moche iconography, noted that Phase I sculptural ceramics continue the Late Cupisnique style; John Rowe (1971) demonstrated Moche archaizing use of Cupisnique style and motifs. Moche concepts and craft are more like Cupisnique than Gallinazo and Salinar; Moche ceramics use Cupisnique forms and frequently display Cupisnique motifs, often as if the motifs were an integral part of Moche tradition. Sometimes, notably in Phase III, they are presented in a deliberate revival of the old style. The Moche clearly considered themselves to be the Cupisnique heirs. Various fine objects recently excavated at Kuntur Huasi display motifs that relate to Moche iconography (Kato 1993; Onuki 1997). Among shared Cupisnique and Moche motifs are: felines (notably, a backward-looking one [see Cordy-Collins 1998]), a man carrying a dead deer on his shoulders, spiders, cacti, and the step-wave motif.

If the Moche were known as descendants and inheritors of Cupisnique authority and craft traditions, there was reason for Gallinazo, Vicús, and peoples in the sierra to accept and defer to them. The Moche would have taken—or retaken—power by means of sacred Cupisnique ancestors. The Moche were in the Piura region as an elite class, with rich burials. This would fit into the multiethnic pattern posited by Makowski (1994b:131–135), who believes that the Vicús people became subordinate to the Moche and eventually faded away.

MOCHE CONTEMPORARIES

The Moche not only had notable predecessors but also interacted with interesting and individual contemporary cultures. Gallinazo was one such group, as were the people of Cajamarca, up the Jequetepeque Valley in the highlands. A Cajamarca presence is found in the Zaña Valley, and Cajamarca kaolin ceramics appear in Moche sites, especially in the late period (Dillehay 2001:264, 268; see also Bourget 2003:266; Castillo 2000b, 2001; Donnan and Castillo 1992; Franco, Gálvez, and Vásquez 2001a:149; Gálvez and Briceño 2001:141–42; Shimada 1994a:92–93; J. Topic and Topic 1983; Uceda and Armas 1998:104–105; Verano 2001c:115–117).

The Recuay culture was centered in the Callejón de Huaylas, a large, high valley between the two main cordilleras of the Andes, between Moche sites and Chavín de Huántar (Grieder 1978; see also Larco Hoyle 1962; Lau 2000, 2002–4, 2004; Makowski and Rucabado 2000; Millaire with Molion 2009; Reichert 1982; Schaedel 1948; J. Topic and Topic 1997). Sawyer (1966:21, 24) believed that Cupisnique, "to-be-Moche people," were in contact with people in the Callejón when they were forced out of their homeland by Salinar and Gallinazo occupations. The headwaters of the long Santa River, which reaches the North Coast, rise in the Callejón. Some motifs associated with the Moche people's ritual chewing of coca leaves appear in Huaylas stone sculpture (see Chapters 3 and 10), and Recuay and Moche have other motifs in common, notably the Crested Animal (Figure 2.6) (see Chapter 7).

FIGURE 2.6 Recuay double bottle with a feline effigy holding a human head in its mouth, and a mirror image of the Crested Animal painted on the body. *Courtesy Museo Larco, Lima, Peru.*

The Trujillo coca variety came originally from the Marañón River region, beyond the Callejón, and might have linked the Moche with both Recuay and Chavín. Terence Grieder (1978), excavating at the Recuay site of Pashash, found a few Moche sherds mixed with Recuay remains. The Moche may have traded with Recuay for metals. There was some Recuay occupation in the Santa Valley, where Moche presence seems somewhat tenuous and fragmentary (Chapdelaine and Pimentel 2003; Donnan 1973a; Wilson 1988). The Moche people shared the Nepeña Valley with a Recuay population (Larco Hoyle 1966:104; Proulx 1982:83–87, 1985; see also Bonavia and Makowski 1999; Daggett 1985; Narváez 1994:78–80). There the Moche built their southernmost imposing site, Pañamarca, a frontier showplace. Unfortunately, it has never been thoroughly excavated, although recent unpublished work by Lisa Trever and Jorge Gamboa documents new discoveries. Moche contacts with Recuay, Gallinazo, and

Cajamarca people surely changed through time. Relations with highland peoples might have been tense as both groups sought to control water sources and trade routes.

The Moche also had contact with the Lima and the later Nievería cultures of the Central Coast, which are little known because their remains are largely buried under the modern city of Lima and its environs. The Moche had some communication with Pachacamac, a very important city on the Central Coast (Bonavia 1985:135–146; Castillo 2001; Lumbreras 1974:119–122). Mural painting and some Lima and Nievería ceramics survive. Many Pachacamac remains endure, and conservation work has been done there. The Moche people seem to have interacted also with the Nasca culture of the South Coast, who used polychrome paint and distinctive vessel shapes for their ceramics, but also shared certain motifs used in Moche art (Silverman and Proulx 2002).

Nasca and earlier Paracas fish monsters with human arms holding a knife and a detached human head suggest a common coastal mythology. Later Nasca art shows the apparent influence of Moche iconography and the freer Moche style. Moche may have felt Nasca influence: the lima bean, a long-prominent South Coast motif, appears in Moche ceramics late in Phase III and increases in importance in later phases (see Chapter 10). The later Moche may have been in touch also with the southern highland sites of Tiahuanaco and Huari, although their influence on Moche art may have come indirectly through Pachacamac and other sources.

CHAPTER THREE

The Reality of the Moche Worlds

AS THE MOCHE BECAME SUCCESSFUL, their worlds changed with acquisition of new agricultural lands, trade routes, and centers of control, as well as the construction of large-scale public projects. Much of the population lived in settlements scattered on the edges of valleys, waterways, and urban areas, with centers for administrative activity often placed at the margin of irrigable land. Near the centers, high-status houses were built of adobe bricks, while simple houses had "walls" of woven cane or wattle and daub (*quincha*). Even today, poorer houses are simple and often virtually roofless. Only privacy, shade, and windbreak are required in a normally rainless, tropical climate, although nights may be cold near the sea or in the upper valleys.

Moche society was stratified. Each city or kingdom surely had a lord or lords under whom it functioned. There may have been dual rulership, a frequent pattern in the Andes, where duality was a common concept in many functions (Bourget 2006; R. Burger and Salazar-Burger 1993; Netherly 1977, 1990, 1993; Netherly and Dillehay 1986). Occupational groups in cities and hinterlands would have had leaders who might have held office through kinship or special talent and were answerable to the principal lord or lords (Chapdelaine 2001; Dillehay 2001:263–264; Ramírez 1995:302; Richardson 1994; Rostworowski 1990:137–159). Those with positions in a hierarchy under the rulers would include figures portrayed in ceramic art, some wearing priestly dress and some military dress, and some wearing a combination of the two (see Chapter 9). There would also have been craft specialists, musicians, and bearers or keepers of ritual objects. Engineers designed and constructed canals; there is archaeological evidence for

the work of architects, surveyors, adobe makers, and masons. Surely the overall social structure included fishermen, raft makers, farmers, traders, and guides for llama trains. As full-time or part-time work, knowledgeable people tended canals and water distribution, twined fishing and hunting nets, cured fish, hunted, and gathered guano for fertilizer.

AGRICULTURE AND IRRIGATION

The Moche channeled water from the mountains into irrigation systems that supported livelihood. Water control presumably began with flood control and developed with population expansion and the need to produce food—and with greater social organization of larger villages in communication with each other (R. Burger 1992; Castillo and Uceda 2008; Chapdelaine 2003; Hocquenghem 1987; Kosok 1965; Morales Gamarra 2003; Netherly 1977, 1984; Salomon and Urioste 1991; Schaedel 1988; Sharon 2000; Urton 1981). The Moche reconstructed some ancient canals and constructed new ones, some intervalley canals as well as small local ones. Water control is difficult in rugged terrain, and water sources had to be maintained and protected. Canals sometimes have apparently defensive walls, perhaps to block an enemy who wanted to reduce the food supply of irrigation users or to give some protection from El Niño flooding. In the past, care of water would have been an important part of political administration and ceremonial life, as it is today (Gose 1994:95–102). In the Virú and Moche Valleys and elsewhere, there have long been festivals in connection with the cleaning of ditches before the waters come in full force in December. The flow of North Coast rivers is seasonal, and most are dry part of the year; normally water is most abundant in March and scarcest in October.

Pre-Conquest irrigation systems were larger than those today because requirements of modern cities reduce water available for cropland. Moreover, two of the North Coast's three major commercial crops, sugarcane and rice, are introduced plants that use more water than major pre-Hispanic crops (maize, for instance, needs relatively little water). Cotton, the third modern commercial crop, is a different species from that grown in early times, but it can be cultivated with little water.

CROPS AND OTHER PLANT MATERIAL

The New World was richer in plant foods than the Old World. The list compiled by ethnobotanist Margaret Towle (1961) of food plants known to have been raised on the coast during the Moche period includes maize, common beans, lima beans, peanuts, sweet potato, manioc, peppers, yacon, achira, crook squash, squash, and pepino. Some gourds were possibly used for food as well as for utensils. Towle also lists fruits that may have been cultivated on the coast or given some horticultural care: chirimoya, pacay, guanábana, tumbo, granadilla, guava, lúcuma, ciruela del fraile, papaya, avocado, and pineapple (or a relative). Since Towle's publication, more plant remains have been found, and more is known about them (see, for example, S. Coe 1994; S. Pozorski and Pozorski 2003; Vásquez and Rosales 2004:366). Many types of plants are depicted on effigy ceramic bottles.

Several plants (including maize) grew both on mountain slopes and in valleys. Maize (*Zea mays*) could be boiled or roasted as a vegetable, the stems could be pressed for a sweet juice, and the kernels were an oil source. *Chicha*, a drink made from a mash of crushed kernels, was probably consumed in rituals and used as an offering. Maize had almost mystical significance in many places in the Americas, where it is regarded as a criterion of the beginning of civilization and as a status food. Maize ears from burials at Pacatnamu had more rows than those in trash middens; maize used for burial offerings was apparently

chosen for this trait (Gumerman 1997; see also S. Pozorski 1976:122). Maize ears are represented in Phase IV ceramics, sometimes with the face of a major supernatural being with a fanged mouth emerging from the plant (Figure 3.1; also see Chapter 7).

A supernatural face appears as well on manioc (*Manihot* spp.), also called "yuca" or "cassava," or it can be shown naturalistically (Figure 3.2). Widespread in tropical lowlands, it was likely planted on the Peruvian coast by 2000 BC, according to Sophie Coe (1994:16–18). A scene celebrating the harvest of the yuca crop appears on a Moche III textile from El Castillo, in the Santa Valley (see Figure 6.7; Chapdelaine and Pimentel 2003).

The potato, that staple of northern European diet, originated ca. 3500 BC in the Andean highlands and was unknown in Europe until the sixteenth century. More than 200 varieties in 5 species were developed in the Central Andes (R. Burger 1997; see also S. Coe 1994:21, 182–183). Potato remains are not common in excavations, but Moche effigy bottles depict the tubers realistically. The eye of the potato may be shown as a human eye, and often the tuber has a human face (or faces) showing symptoms of one of two tropical diseases: tumor-causing verruga or lesion-causing leishmaniasis (*uta*). Most bottles depict the latter. In modern times the valleys in which the diseases are

FIGURE 3.1 A cluster of maize ears sprouting heads. The large head is a supernatural being with a fanged mouth and snake ear ornaments. *Courtesy Staatliche Museen zu Berlin— Preussischer Kulturbesitz, Ethnologisches Museum, VA 4652, Macedo Collection.*

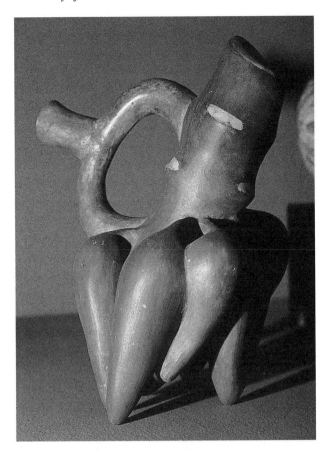

FIGURE 3.2 Bottle in the form of a manioc (yuca) root. *Staatliche Museen zu Berlin—Preussischer Kulturbesitz, Ethnologisches Museum, VA 62141. Photograph by the author.*

its domestication may have contributed to successful settling of the coast. Anne-Marie Hocquenghem (1987:107) sees a parallel between domestication of beans and the progress of people, both going from "wild" to cultivated states. At Pacatnamu, *P. lunatus* and *P. vulgaris* come from different burials, which may imply status differences (Gumerman 1997).

The peanut (*Arachis hypogaea*) developed in the tropical forest, but by 1000 BC it was common on the coast (S. Coe 1994:28, 34–36). An elegant necklace of gold and silver peanut-shaped beads, half of them gold, half silver, from the tomb of the Lord of Sipán, not only demonstrates the status of the high-protein peanut but probably points to the ruler's responsibility for successful agriculture (Alva 1994: Fig. 90; Alva and Donnan 1993:92–94). The resemblance of the peanut shell to a human burial bundle may have had symbolic significance. Some effigy vessels depict a peanut shell containing a human playing a flute or panpipes, instruments that have funereal or liminal connotations (Figure 3.3).

Some cactus fruits were edible, and spines could be made into pins and combs. The San Pedro cactus (*Trichocereus pachanoi*) was likely used as a ritual

endemic, upward of 1,000 m, have produced the best potatoes. The potato cultivation period coincides with the time of maximum infectiousness of the insect-carried diseases. Not long ago, guardians of potato fields were required to suffer from one of these diseases (Weiss 1961). The large *Solanum* (potato) genus also includes pepino (*S. muricatum*), which was grown on the coast; it is now considered a fruit (S. Coe 1994:189–190; Towle 1961:85, 116). Yakon, or llakum (*Polymnia sonchifolia*), is a highland root also seen in Moche ceramic effigies. Bernabé Cobo, in the seventeenth century, noted that the root is edible for a long time, especially when dried (S. Coe 1994:185). Root crops were easily transported and stored. Oca (*Oxalis tuberosa*) and ulluco (*Ullucus tuberosus*) were traded from the highlands.

Lima beans (*Phaseolus lunatus*) are a frequent motif on later Moche ceramics (see Chapter 10). The common bean (*P. vulgaris*) was a staple food, and

FIGURE 3.3 Effigy vessel depicting a figure with a peanut-shell body and human face and hands, playing a flute that is also of peanut shell. *Museo Nacional de Arqueología, Antropología e Historia del Perú. Photograph by the author.*

hallucinogen (see Chapter 10). Coca (*Erythroxylum novogranatense*) for millennia has been a sacred plant whose leaves have been used for ritual and medicinal purposes (see Chapter 10; see Pennington, Reynal, and Daza 2004:336–337; Plowman 1984). It is also the plant from which cocaine is extracted in a procedure invented in the nineteenth century. Coca grew originally in the moist forests of the lower mountain slopes and appeared on the coast in the Late Preceramic period. The so-called Trujillo variety was adapted to drier habitats and cultivated on some slopes on the North Coast.

The algarrobo tree (*Prosopis* spp.) is a critical resource that grows in virtual desert, putting out taproots to underground water and growing to 15 m height. It gives shade and provides wood for house and fence construction. Its gum can be used for many purposes, the pods are fodder for modern domestic animals, its decaying leaves make fertilizer, and its wood has many uses, including charcoal and fires for metalworking. In the past its beans were used as food and medicine, and it is still employed in folk medicine. Other useful trees include huarango, or espino (*Acacia macracantha*), sapote (*Capparis angulata*), and pacay (*Inga* spp.), a shade tree whose seeds are held in a sweet, edible pulp. Lúcuma (*Pouteria lucuma*), which can grow 10 m tall, is found upvalley in cloud forest; it provides useful wood and an edible fruit that is still considered a delicacy (Pennington, Reynal, and Daza 2004).

Ceramic scenes of combat, sacrifice, ritual running, and deer hunts often include cacti, bromeliads (*Tillandsia*), and other plants floating in the air with roots dangling; they are not simply part of the setting but have symbolic value (see Figures 10.1, 10.3, 10.4). The plants may indicate association with agriculture, rites of crop divination, or the conquest of new land for planting. In his novel *Deep Rivers*, the Peruvian writer and anthropologist José María Arguedas speaks of an act of purification in which a plant was pulled up and thrown into water with its roots and the earth that nourished it; the flowers were removed and burned. Ceramic paintings suggest that uprooted plants were used also in a Moche rite.

Various grasses, rushes, reeds, and canes were important to North Coast people (Campana 1999:49–56; Gálvez et al. 2003; Netherly 1977:67–77; Vásquez and Rosales 1998, 2004). Salt grasses grew from brackish underground water near the shore. Large canes—caña brava (*Gynerium sagittatum*) or caña de Guayaquil (*Gradua angustifolia*)—were used for house construction, baskets, utensils, and coffins. Rafts, mats, and probably cordage were made from a rush, totora (*Schoenplectus* [*Scirpas*] *californicus*). The reed enea (*Typha angustifolia*) was also useful. *Tillandsia* spp., a relative of pineapple, was used for fiber and fuel. Some plants provided medicine or dye. Gourd utensils were usually made from *Lagenaria*, and in modest homes in recent times, *chicha* may be offered in a gourd cup, sometimes with an ancient Moche design.

The Moche farmer's principal tools were the foot plow, usually made of algarroba wood (sometimes with a copper point), a spade or shovel, and a hoe, as well as clod-breaking stones attached to wooden handles, and knives or a kind of pruning hook.

ANIMALS

The Moche had few domesticated animals: llamas, dogs, and guinea pigs, or cuyes, are the known examples. Cuyes (*Cavia porcellus*) are extremely prolific and an excellent meat source. Their bones, dated in the southern sierra to as early as 5800–4500 BC and common in Late Preclassic highland middens, are infrequent on the coast but have been excavated in the residential area of the Cerro Blanco Complex (Vásquez and Rosales 1998, 2004, 2008) and in a burial at Pacatnamu (Donnan and McClelland 1997:34; see also R. Burger 1992:43; S. Coe 1994:174–175; Shimada 1994a:184–186). Today, cuy is customarily eaten on special occasions and is also used in folk curing and prognostication.

Like the rest of pre-Hispanic America, the Andes had no draft animals, but the llama (*Lama glama*) was a useful pack animal. Basically highland denizens, llamas were brought to the coast and bred and herded there, as indicated by remains in burials and middens, and by Moche ceramic depictions of llamas mating and mother llamas with young (Berrin 1997: No. 28; S. Pozorski 1979a, 1979b; S. Pozorski and Pozorski 2003:122–123; M. Shimada and Shimada 1981, 1985; Vásquez and Rosales 1998, 2004, 2008; Vásquez et al. 2003). A llama can carry about 50 kg in saddlebags, and laden llamas are a common ceramic motif. They are usually shown singly bearing cloth- or reed-wrapped bundles with fish, jars, or gastropod shells, probably *Strombus galeatus* (Figure 3.4).

Llamas were likely a major source of meat for the Moche, and also provided wool, hide, sinew, and bone for making tools. Llama dung, which archaeologists have found used as fuel for firing ceramics, was critical to the development of potato cultivation in the highlands and may have also been used as fertilizer on the coast. Alpacas (*Lama pacos*), traditionally high-altitude animals, are now bred in the Lambayeque Valley (and in many highland and lowland locations in the United States). They were present on the coast in Moche times (alpaca remains have been found in excavations at Huaca de la Luna [Vásquez and Rosales 2008]), and alpaca wool was used extensively, but some of the wool may have been brought in from the highlands (see Chapter 6).

Dogs, present in the New World about as long as humankind, have been found in some Moche burials (see Chapter 12) and in some middens (Schwartz 1997; Wing 1989:269). Dog images appear as effigy vessels and in ritual and mythic scenes (see Figures 4.3, 8.1). Hairless dogs, described by early Spaniards, are now often pets at archaeological sites. Alana Cordy-Collins (1994) argues that the hairless dog was brought to Peru from Mexico, and that its earliest Peruvian depictions date to Late Moche times. In most earlier Moche portrayals, it is not clear whether the dog has hair or the wrinkled skin usually typical of hairless dogs.

Hunts for white-tailed deer (*Odocoileus virginianus*) by richly and specially dressed men are common in Phase IV ceramic scenes that show various plants (see Chapter 10). Deer surely appeared in riverine and scrub-growth environments during the moist season, but their remains are scarce in middens explored by archaeologists.

The coastal fox (*Pseudalopex sechurae*) is a significant and frequent motif in Moche art (Benson 1995b, 1997a:35–42; Castillo 2003:85; Jones 1979:72–78; Narváez 2001; see also Cárdenas, Rodríguez, and Aguirre 1997:144; Eisenberg and Redford 1999:284–285). Foxes are still common on Cerro Blanco, and their remains have been excavated nearby (Ricardo Morales, personal communication, 2001; Vásquez and Rosales 1998, 2008). In Moche ceramics, humanized foxes appear in warrior, priestly, or runner dress on Phase IV effigy bottles and in painted scenes. Quite realistic fox-

FIGURE 3.4 Bottle in the form of a llama bearing a load. *Courtesy Museo Larco, Lima, Peru.*

faced finials or headdress ornaments, usually of copper, often gilded, are found fairly often. Ceramic scenes show fox-head finials on many objects (see Figure 1.4), and a fox body sometimes appears attached to the belt of a man in warrior garments; a deity in a Huaca de la Luna mural has a "belt" that ends in fox heads.

Lizards (*Dicrodon hombergi*) that eat the seeds or fruit of algarrobo trees were likely trapped for food, as they are today, by being driven to a long roll of matting raised like a fence across a field (S. Coe 1994:213; Gillin 1947:26; Holmberg 1957). Moche ceramics show hunts for large land snails (*Scutalus*), which are still gathered (see Chapter 10). Archaeological remains of anurans are not reported, but ceramic effigy frogs and toads occasionally have a back draped with leaves and fruit, emphasizing association with water and fertility. A *Bufo* toad lives in the region, yet I know of no Moche evidence for a psychoactive drug that has been prepared elsewhere from *Bufo* toxin.

TRADE AND TRIBUTE

Local lords likely received donations from their people and then redistributed these items, which would have been traded between Moche groups, with neighbors, and from group to group over considerable distances up and down the coast, into the highlands, and perhaps over the mountains toward the Amazon Basin (J. Topic and Topic 1983). Marked roads or trails were probably obliterated by later road builders, the Chimu and the Inca. Different valleys and altitudes produced diverse crops and products for exchange. Fish, and probably guano, from coastal villages could be traded for fruits, vegetables, plant products, and cotton for nets and cloth.

Superregional trade of elite goods would likely have been more important than military expansion. Elite goods formed much of the trade: ceramics were obviously traded, as were metal objects and cloth. Ore sources exist on the western slopes of the Andes, but some of the copper, silver, and gold for ornaments and implements could have come from outside. Exotic birds—or their feathers—would have been other trade items; some feathers may have come from parrots in upper-valley pockets of coastal forest. Monkeys, which appear in the art, might have been found in forested valleys; some could have been brought over the mountains, from what is now Ecuador. Felines are prominent in art (see Figure 2.4), but their remains seem to be lacking. Small or young felines, or their hides, may have been transported. Small feline species lived in some valleys, but there is confusion in identification (Alarco 1997; Cordy-Collins 1998; Mackey and Vogel 2003:328–329; Sharon 2000:3; Sunquist and Sunquist 2002). The pampas cat (*Oncifelis colocolo*) was probably present, and possibly the margay (*Leopardus wiedii*); the larger puma (*Puma concolor*) frequented the nearby mountains. Jaguars (*Panthera onca*) prefer moist tropical forests but can survive in various climates and might have roamed through lower passes. Any sighting of this large and powerful cat, associated with rulers and shamans throughout its range in the Americas, surely would have seemed a mythic event. A smaller feline might have substituted for it in rites or images.

The Moche, powerful people in their world, undoubtedly exacted tribute in addition to engaging in trade. Some tribute would have been paid in service or labor for building and various projects (Cobo 1979 [1653]:231–234; S. Ramírez 1995). On the other hand, dependent on water from the highlands, the Moche might have paid tribute for water rights, although María Rostworowski's (1990:452–455) arguments suggest that despite Colonial evidence for highland water control, the thriving Moche may have held highland territory and had some power over highland lords.

MOCHE POLITICAL STRUCTURE

What kind of political structure supported, and was supported by, this framework? Many responses have been made to this question. Some scholars conceive of a Moche state comprising all the regions where measurable Moche remains have been found, with a capital at the Cerro Blanco Complex, long the best-known Moche site. However, recent excavations elsewhere suggest that other sites may have been of equal or close-to-equal importance, at least at certain times. Discovery of murals with similar themes and insignia at Huaca de la Luna and Huaca Cao Viejo might suggest unification of these two sites, at least at one time. Although Cao seems to have earlier levels than Luna, toward the end their iconography is virtually identical. At one time the Moche Valley polity may have attained hegemony over the entire northern area in a brief integration of north and south, but a single state would likely have been short-lived because of its attenuated shape, internal tensions, and the political and religious differences evident in southern and northern archaeology and iconography. Also, cities were thriving at different times. From the Moche Valley south to the Casma, a series of centers was likely under control of the Cerro Blanco Complex, but the valleys generally seem to have been multicultural, with Moche enclaves and power bases. Further examination of sites that have been identified as Gallinazo may shed light on this (see Chapter 2).

Some scholars posit northern and southern Moche states separated by the Pampa de Paiján, the very arid 90 km stretch of desert between the Chicama and Jequetepeque Valleys. Differences in art and customs between north and south may indicate separation: the southern region shows that it needed an active, developing iconography to express changing situations, whereas the northern region was conservative in expression in ceramic art. Variations in deity concepts and the use of inherited motifs suggest separation with different needs and solutions (see Chapter 7), but did the north consist of one state or several polities?

It is possible that "city states" or "valley states" may have operated as small kingdoms, cooperating or competing, and regional polities may have been assembled from them. Classic Maya society, in the same era, had a complex cultural unity but apparently lacked a central government, having instead some 60 kingdoms as fundamental political units (Martin and Grube 2000:7, 18). They arranged marriages and made alliances; they fought, and one kingdom might take another over. Maya cities, with buildings proclaiming military-religious-ancestral themes, were essentially regal-ritual centers from which rulership emanated. The Maya elite achieved and/or expressed much of their power through apparent manipulation of the supernatural. All of this may be generally true of the Moche (Benson 2008; Castillo and Uceda 2008). Jürgen Golte (1994a:17) posits the existence of a network of small political units participating in a larger economic space with trade networks, especially of goods for elite consumption; he also believes that small states created finer art than a larger, more unified polity might have produced.

Bartolomé de las Casas (cited in Means 1931:65–66; see also Ramírez-Horton 1982:126) is quoted as saying, in the sixteenth century, that at one time the North Coast was divided among many independent chieftaincies. Evidence indicates that some chieftains controlled not only coastal areas but areas in their mountain hinterland, and that none was totally dominant over the others; there was exchange and trade between the polities.

Walter Alva and Christopher Donnan (1993:220; see also Castillo and Uceda 2008; Jones 1993, 2001; Narváez 1994) write that tombs at Sipán, Loma Negra, and La Mina demonstrate tremendous wealth concentrated in the hands of a few powerful individuals, and excavations at Huaca Cao Viejo add that site to the list. The Chicama and Moche Valleys can be considered almost a single entity, but extensive work by Régulo Franco, César Gálvez, and Segundo Vásquez at Cao Viejo seems to indicate a powerful dynasty in that Chicama site. Nearby Mocollope is less well known, but it was apparently a major site, probably in Phase III (Gálvez and Briceño 2001:144–145; Reindel 1993:286–292; Russell and Jackson 2001; Russell,

Leonard, and Briceño 1994, 1998:67–70). Each valley perhaps had one or more "courts," connected much as European royalty was at the time. Distinctive headdresses—those like a medieval crown seen in late murals at Cao Viejo (Franco, Gálvez, and Vásquez 2005:17–18; Franco and Vilela 2005) and Huaca de la Luna (2009:30–31), and those of cane covered with cloth and metal plaques found at Dos Cabezas (Donnan 2001, 2003, 2007; Jiménez 2000:77)—might refer to lineages; a distinctive "hat" with danglers recurs in Loma Negra goldwork.

Irrigation is a facet of this consideration (Kosok 1965; Moseley 1992:125–127; Moseley and Deeds 1982; S. Pozorski and Pozorski 1987). A great deal of labor organization would have been required to design, construct, and operate a large canal project. It is undoubtedly true that Moche systems were instituted and run at some official level, or that the ruler required farmers to work land and tend irrigation systems as part of a labor obligation. If there were no large state, construction and maintenance might have been local obligations and, where the system linked or served two or more groups, a cooperative enterprise. Garth Bawden (1996:45–48) points out that civilizations of the Indus Valley, Egypt, and Mesopotamia were each united by a drainage pattern that was part of one great river system centered on a dominant river, whereas Andean rivers are mostly separate, each providing a source only for its own system, a pattern that encourages self-sufficiency and autonomy. Patricia Netherly (1984), studying North Coast post-Moche water control, did not find evidence for state control in Chimu and Inca societies. She discovered close associations between construction, maintenance, and repair of a canal, the land it watered, and the group with rights to land and water. Rostworowski (1990:450–455) argues that information obtained for one North Coast river drainage cannot be transferred to another because the inherent situations and the relationships with highlanders differed from valley to valley.

NORTH AND SOUTH

Political, cultural, and religious differences between the Moche of the north and south are reflected in ceramic forms and iconography. Stirrup-spout bottles existed in the north, especially in early and late ceramic phases, but more common were globular jars with a flaring neck, bottles with "loops" at the neck, and bottles with spouts and handles. All had relatively simple decoration. They show elements of the Moche world, but not the elaborate myths or rites of the narrative tradition that developed in ceramics in the south in Phase IV. In the north, Early Moche continued, succeeded by Phase V, with little or no evidence of III and IV (Castillo 2001:307–308; Castillo and Donnan 1994a:157, 1994b:129–131; Makowski et al. 1994). Conservatism may explain the presence of ceramics of Phase I style in burials with III/IV dates at Dos Cabezas and the fact that Moche ceramics from the Piura region are of I/II style, while the metallurgy has III/IV iconography (Donnan 2001, 2003; Jones 1993; Shimada 1987:133). The metal sample is skewed because of looting, but skillful and inventive gold-work in rich tombs of powerful rulers at Loma Negra,

Sipán, and Huaca el Pueblo demonstrates an emphasis on metallurgy rather than pottery. There was surely trade between regions, but the scarcity of Phase IV in the north seems to imply philosophical and socio-economic differences, as well as a break in political integration.

The Moche seem to have lacked a state in modern terms. Although they had a chain of power places that displayed their general cultural unity, these do not necessarily imply political unity. Control seems to have shifted with changes in power between valleys, and changes in Moche power over other groups, as well as with problems such as drought and El Niño. Whatever the political structure, in the early phases the widely scattered Moche people, apparently without strong political linkage, had an iconography that reflected similar origins and beliefs, sharing myth and ritual from the unifying heritage of the Chavín/Cupisnique past, the uses of which varied through time and space.

CHAPTER FOUR

The Life of Things

"REALISTIC" IS A TERM often used to describe Moche art, but the "other world" is frequently depicted, and even naturalistic images may have pre-ternatural significance. Discussion of the real Moche world and a numinous world that exists beside it is valid because otherworldly depictions often parallel realistic ones. The dichotomy we perceive, however, is surely based largely on our cultural view, where these are separate entities. For the Moche, the parts appear to have been interrelated aspects of a unified reality, as they are for many peoples; the quotidian world was affected by actions in or with the other world. This may be another aspect of the dualism and complementarity inherent in the Moche world. Expression of otherworldliness was exemplified, in part, by "anthropomorphized" animals and "animated" objects. These are not exact words to describe Moche animals and objects with human attributes, but they approximate the intrinsic energy and vitalism implied in this art and in much other art in the Andes.

The Moche world that we see in the art teemed with sacred or otherworldly beings, but only a few were godlike. I use the word *god* to refer to a few prominent supernatural beings in Moche art, but "major mythological personage" might be more accurate, although awkward. Such a being personified a force to be reckoned with, a forefather or a deity of the ancestors, identified with nature or the power to affect nature, and a focus of ritual as a contract for survival. Gods and other supernaturals can be identified by physical traits, clothing, and accessories, and by context and activity. These elements may change through time, place, politico-religious context, and varying encounters in narrative. In general, gods are

esoteric and protean. Just as the Greek gods changed form, and Maya and Aztec gods shared and exchanged attributes, so did Moche deities. A number of scholars have worked to define a Moche pantheon—notably Daniel Arsenault, Yuri Berezkin, Jürgen Golte, Bärbel Lieske, and Krzysztof Makowski—but there is frequent disagreement about the number of beings that can be called gods and the category in which they belong. Some scholars eschew the word *god* completely. I almost do.

THE ANIMATED WORLD: HUACA AND CAMAY

Early Spaniards reported that the Quechua language of the Inca people apparently had no word for *god*, but a word for something that was sacred or supernatural, *huaca* (Arriaga 1968 [1621]:23–32; Classen 1993; Rostworowski 1996:9–10). Bernabé Cobo (1990 [1653]: Bk. 1, Ch. 11) spoke of huacas as having divinity residing in them. Andean peoples saw—and still see—a "landscape alive with the diverse sacred beings called huacas," as Frank Salomon (Salomon and Urioste 1991:16–19) observes, noting that a huaca is "any material thing that manifested the supernatural," and that huacas are "made of energized matter, like everything else, and act within nature, not over and outside it as western supernaturals do." Basing his definition on the early-seventeenth-century writings of Garcilaso de la Vega (1987:76–77, 79–80), Salomon's list of huacas includes mountains, springs, lakes, rock outcrops, ruins, caves, temples, mummies, and manmade things that have power. Huacas, as living bodies, were ritually fed, clothed, and tended in hope that they would favor those dependent on them. Richard Burger (1997:30; see also Bastien 1978, 1987:183) speaks of sacrificing material rich in energy to win supernatural favors.

The Quechua word *camay* connotes the energizing of existing matter. Anthropomorphized objects belong to the camay concept, one of whose meanings is "to animate or to impart specific form and force" (Salomon 1998:7; see also Allen 1988, 1998; Burger 1997:29; Salomon, in Salomon and Urioste 1991:16). Some huacas have constant power or life; others gain life or power at certain times, usually through ritual nourishment.

Concepts of the aliveness of things, which surely predate the Moche era, still exist. When Catherine Allen (1988:36) began her ethnographic studies in a village in the southern highlands of Peru in 1975, she did not realize that the earth resented the hoes that cut into it for planting potatoes, nor was she aware that the surrounding peaks and ridges were watching the planting critically. Eventually, Allen learned that this knowledge was part of potato cultivation.

Such examples abound. In highland Bolivia, where cloth is important in daily life, the mountain spirits are said to value the yarn and the loom (Grace Goodell 1969, cited by Conklin 1996:326). Offering a pre-Moche, Peruvian example, textile expert Mary Frame (2001:88) writes of the animation of objects embroidered in Paracas textile art from the South Coast, first millennium BC: "Crafted objects, made from animal, vegetable, and mineral sources, are animated in the mythic world depicted in the embroideries." The elements that turn into created objects have a liveliness that they impart to the objects. Moche ceramic versions of vegetables had life because the original vegetables did, because the clay that the ceramics were made from did, because the vessel was created, and because it likely had been used in a ritual that enhanced its spirit.

Such thinking is widespread in the Americas. A line from the Huarochirí manuscript (Salomon and Urioste 1991:51) reads: "This world wanted to come to an end." A modern Mexican poet, Francisco Alarcón, has written poems based on the Colonial Mexican manuscript of Hernando Ruíz de Alarcón; many are direct translations. One, entitled "Cutting Wood," is very close to Andean concepts of the life that exists in nature and in things:

> tree
> don't hurt my ax
> enjoy it
> as your mirror
> I offer tobacco
> for your shin.

FEATURES OF THE LANDSCAPE AS HUACAS

Landscape features and attributes of local climates could be powerful beings, and there were surely myths about them, as well as natural reasons for believing in their power. Steve Bourget (1995:87–89, 2001a) has noted a dark arch of andesite embedded in the pale color of Cerro Blanco (see Figure 1.3). The geologic marking was probably one reason why Cerro Blanco was sacred, and may have been viewed as a diagram or duplication of the Milky Way, which was important symbolically throughout Latin America (Urton 1981) and elsewhere. A Milky Way myth might explain the appearance of the andesite. Bourget relates the arch to skybands on Moche vessels. The skyband motif is used so widely that the andesite arch would have had resonance as a natural manifestation of a known symbol.

Huaca de la Luna also was imbued with spiritual power, partly by its proximity to Cerro Blanco and sacred rocks, and partly by ritual that gave numinous life to the structure and the people and things inside it. This huaca and other man-made mountains emulated natural ones.

Mythical ancestors are, or reside in, peaks that dominate and may be thought to control the destinies of the valleys. The Incas and more recent peoples call the peaks *apu*, godlike mountain beings. "Great snowcaps are great creators" (Salomon, in Salomon and Urioste 1991:19); in the Huarochirí manuscript, Pariacaca, who is called a god, became the sacred, snow-capped mountain of the same name. The Moche may have regarded the eastern mountains—or a mountain—as a venerated place of origin or as a progenitor (see Conklin 1990:54–55; Hocquenghem 1987:59; Makowski et al. 2000; Uceda 2004).

In many places in the world, rock formations were linked to creatures of myth or legend. Sometimes stone turned into people. A famous legend relates that stones near Cuzco turned into soldiers to assist the Inca Pachacuti's army in defense of the city. Stones also guarded Inca fields. In Early Colonial times, Antonio de la Calancha (1974–1982 [1638], IV:1242; J. Rowe 1948:51; see also Arriaga 1968 [1621]:118; Salomon and Urioste 1991) learned that certain stones on the coast of Peru were considered divine; they were sons of the Sun, and ancestors of the people on whose land they stood. Rock outcrops were more than natural altars for rites; the stones themselves were huacas.

Outcrops are not common on the sandy North Coast; one exists at La Mina, a cemetery site (Narváez 1994), and some appear in Moche ceremonial centers, around or over which walls have been built. Pañamarca (Bennett 1939:17; Schaedel 1951, 1983:23–28), Mocollope (Russell, Leonard, and Briceño 1998), and Huancaco (Bourget 2003, 2010: Fig. 7) have walled outcrops; a wall bisects an outcrop at Huaca de la Luna Plaza 3A (Bourget 1997c, 1998, 2001a; Bourget and Millaire 2000; Bourget and Newman 1998). The sacrifices that Bourget found within the walls were "intimately associated with" El Niño events (see Figure 10.9; Bourget 2001b:106); they may also have nourished the sacred rocks.

In José María Arguedas's (1978:18–19, 6–11) novel *Deep Rivers*, stones of Inca walls talk, sing, move, flow like water, and swallow children. The snakes carved on the stones slither and follow people. Each stone "was like a beast that moved in the sunlight," and "the lines of the wall frolicked in the sun."

THE HUMAN BODY

As in many cultures, the human body is the core image of Moche art; it is basic to visualizing the Moche supernatural. Joseph Bastien (1978:37, 1987:92–93) reports on a contemporary group in Bolivia that calls places on the mountain on which it lives and plants "head, heart, bowels, and legs" (see also Bergh 1993; Classen 1993; Roe 1982:136; Salomon and Urioste 1991:15). In the Andes the human body is seen as a hydraulic system, circulating fluids and semifluids: water, air, food, blood, urine, and semen. Cosmological diagrams of circulation of water through landscape show it flowing from the Milky Way, a heavenly river, to the mountain streams and then to the sea. Liquids have vital significance for all cultures; water and semen are critical to concepts of fertility. The Andean ritual drink chicha, made from fermented maize, has similar or substitute value as an offering. Some Moche bottles, which might have contained chicha, take the form of a group of mountain peaks—usually three or five—with the central mountain shown as a phallus, symbolizing power, vitality, and liquid (Chapter 12). The bowel is associated with decay, burial, and rich earth. Phallus and bowel together form an earth-nourishing image. Villagers feed the mountain with produce, which it gave to them; by giving something back, the people earn more food.

Ceramic scenes of sacrificial victims in mountains confirm a similar belief for the Moche, who showed themselves nourishing a mountain with blood; the mountain then gave them river water from snowcaps and springs (Chapter 10). Some mountain vessels show sacrificial rites (see Figure 10.8), while others depict a supernatural being, sometimes with maize in one hand, manioc in the other, standing against a mountain as if he were a part of it or it was part of him (Hocquenghem 1987: Figs. 182–191; Sawyer 1966: Fig. 72; Zighelboim 1995:171).

ANTHROPOMORPHIZED ANIMALS OR ZOOMORPHIZED HUMANS

Transformation is a major theme of indigenous people of the Americas. In many ethnographic accounts a shaman ritually takes a psychoactive drug and is transformed into an animal being, most often a jaguar (Saunders 1998). Many a character in South American folk literature is mentioned first as an animal and later, without explanation, as a human being, or vice versa. In ancient Mexico, Olmec stone carvings that seem to show this rite reveal feline features beneath the human face; the jaguar is inside the shaman (Furst 1968). In Moche art a mouth with feline canines surely denotes divinity or sacredness (Benson 1974).

Certain supernatural figures are seen in Early Moche art, but recognizable anthropomorphized animals are rare until Phase III. It is not clear whether animals were given human bodies or human figures were given animal heads and appendages. These otherworldly creatures may refer to a role in myth or rite, or to a quality of life the creature has, or they might represent visions of a ritual participant after consumption of a psychoactive substance. Transformation likely wakened or materialized an aspect inherent in the transformed being. The figures might be described as animal imitators in a rite. It is true that when ritual dancers dress as animals, they may be believed to become those animals, but when Moche craftsmen wanted to depict an imitator, they could do so: some portrayals of an owl-human sacrificer clearly show a mask over a human face (Benson 1972: Figs. 3–9; Bourget 1994a: Fig. 5.24).

Wild animals—felines, foxes, deer, iguanas, fish, and birds—are often anthropomorphized in Moche art, whereas domesticated llamas and dogs appear to never be humanized. Ducks, however, are humanized; although the Muscovy duck (*Cairina moscata*) was domesticated in various places in the Americas, it is a forest creature, and evidence for its domestication by Moche people seems weak. Enrique Angulo (personal communication, 1998) argues that virtually no duck remains are found in middens, and that many Moche depictions should be identified as shovelers (*Anas clypeata*), a wild species whose remains have been found at Moche sites, although such finds are rare (Vásquez and Rosales 2004).

JARS WITH FEET AND WAR CLUBS WITH HUMAN HEADS

Vegetables and fruits are rendered naturally in three-dimensional ceramics, especially early bottles; later bottles can show a fanged supernatural or a human face. Other objects are enlivened in different ways. Reed rafts can have human legs to run them through water. One Moche bottle shows jars, bowls, and gourds with human legs and feet leaning over to pour themselves in a scene with well-dressed human figures and smaller priestly figures (Figure 4.1).

A globular bottle may have a human head portrayed in high relief at the top and details of priestly dress painted on the vessel body. Pedro Weiss (1961:72–73) sees Moche figurative art as an instrument of animism, with each effigy vessel containing the essence of the being it represents.

A "weapons bundle"—a warrior's heraldically arranged gear, usually an upright club, shield, spears, and sometimes a sling—is a common southern Moche motif, appearing as the sole subject on a bottle or carried by a warrior or an anthropomorphic animal in warrior dress, usually a fox or bird (Donnan and McClelland 1999; Kutscher 1983: Abbn. 91–95). It is also a common motif on the spout of many Late Moche stirrup-spout bottles in the north, no matter what the subject on the bottle is. The late Huaca de Mayanga murals show wings added to the animated weapons bundle, which is the sole repeated

FIGURE 4.1 Drawing of a scene on a stirrup-spout bottle showing jars pouring themselves into waiting cups as priests oversee the ritual. *Courtesy Museo Larco Archives, Lima, Peru.*

motif (Bonavia 1985:99–104; Donnan 1972).

At least one Phase III weapons bundle has a war club whose head is human (Donnan and McClelland 1999: Fig. 3.35). The human-headed club becomes common in Phase IV (Donnan 1978: Nos. 239–242; Donnan and McClelland 1999: Figs. 4.71, 6.73; Kutscher 1983: Abb. 119; Larco Hoyle 2001, I: Figs. 235, 255); it is usually stuck upright in the sand near the military man to whom captives are presented, or carried by a priestly figure with a captive (see Figure 9.1). Often someone near the club holds a bag that may have held shamanic materials (Benson 1978). The human-headed club surely had multiple meanings: it represents invigorated Moche military power; it signifies sacrifice of the presented captive; and it may symbolize the victim's severed head. (Decapitation seems to have been the most common means of sacrifice.) Sometimes the whole weapons bundle is enlivened as an entire human-warrior figure, with the shield as its body; it often holds a cup or goblet, and sometimes a captive (Donnan and McClelland 1999: Fig. 6.73; Golte 1994a: Fig. 22; Lieske 2001:199–203).

In one depiction of a ritual (Donnan 1978: Fig. 242), a supernatural warrior holds to the mouth of a club a cup that probably contains blood. The human-headed club is the repeated motif on a ceramic goblet from a San José de Moro tomb (Figure 4.2; Castillo 1996). Another goblet, in the Ethnologisches Museum, Berlin, tested positively for traces of blood, and a plain wooden club unearthed at Huaca de la Luna was tested and found to be coated with remains of human blood (Bourget and Newman 1998). The bloodying of the actual war club and the sacrificial feeding of the pictured human-headed club undoubtedly awakened inherent life and gave the objects power. It would not be surprising to learn that all weapons were fed with ritual offerings. (A few of the clubs in drawings have animal heads and may refer to animal sacrifice.)

As far as I know, a club carved with a human head has never been found archaeologically or by looters. Thus the image of a human-headed club likely expresses a concept, not a concrete object.

FIGURE 4.2 Goblet found in a priestess burial at San José de Moro. Marching around the goblet are anthropomorphic weapons bundles with shields for bodies and human-headed clubs, each lifting a goblet. *Courtesy Luis Jaime Castillo and Proyecto Arqueológico San José de Moro.*

THE "REVOLT" OF OBJECTS

A 1928 article by Walter Krickeberg on Mexican-Peruvian parallels compared a "revolt of objects" in the Huarochirí manuscript (Salomon, in Salomon and Urioste 1991:53, n.81) with one in the Popol Vuh (a roughly contemporaneous Maya manuscript from Guatemala; see Tedlock 1996:72) and mentioned that a mural showing animated weapons attacking warriors seen by Eduard Seler (1923:369–371) in Huaca de la Luna in 1910 might represent the same theme.

The Popol Vuh myth describes the destruction of an early, unsatisfactory creation of wooden people, who were "crushed by things of wood and stone" (their water jars, tortilla griddles, cooking pots, and grinding stones); dogs and turkeys talked back to the wooden people and threatened them. In the Huarochirí version, mortars, grinding stones, and llamas began to eat people, and rocks banged against each other; this occurred at the time of a five-day "death" of the Sun. (The Maya had five "dead" days in their calendar.) These accounts reflect a widespread creation myth concept, likely tied to a major natural event—possibly an earthquake—and based on belief in the potential life of objects.

A complex Moche ceramic scene that might seem to depict a "revolt" is crowded on a late Phase IV globular stirrup-spout bottle in the Staatliches

FIGURE 4.3 Drawing of a complex scene on a late Phase IV globular stirrup-spout bottle. The scene has been variously interpreted as a "revolt," a mythical event, or an astronomical/calendrical occasion. *Staatliches Museum für Völkerkunde, Munich. Drawing by Donna McClelland.*

Museum für Völkerkunde in Munich. Gerdt Kutscher (1950:44–45) described it in a long caption, interpreting the scene in terms of deities, not rebelling objects (Figure 4.3). Patricia Lyon (1989; see also Bonavia 1985:82–84), after examining this and other so-called "revolt" depictions, concluded that there is virtually no correspondence between the manuscript myths and Moche bottles, and that the Munich scenes must relate to another mythical event. I agree, but a number of other authors have accepted or argued for the revolt interpretation (Makowski 1996:20; Quilter 1990, 1996, 1997). Allen (1998) does not compare the subjects but uses them as examples of the premise that matter is animate, and all action between people and things is interactive. Hocquenghem (1987:142–156)—who interprets the Figure 4.3 scene as an astronomical/calendrical occasion—is interested in the subject of chaos and the restitution of order, and she sees the revolt in terms of chaos.

The scene is so far unique, although it portrays characters familiar from other contexts. A supernatural warrior dominates one side of the bottle. He stands in the upper register, holding a club and shield; he has a fanged mouth, and radiances emanate from his body. Before him a small, sacerdotal figure, with clasped hands raised, is either seated under a tree or turning into a tree. Between warrior and priest stands a dog with vegetation attached to or growing from it. On the other side of the bottle, on a lower level, the major figure is an owl warrior standing on a stepped platform, holding a large club; in front of him is another dog. Dogs are widely known, both in ethnographic accounts and in archaeological finds, as companions and guides of the newly dead on the way to the underworld (Benson 1991; Schwartz 1997), where both warriors may be heading during an astronomical event. These figures surely had astronomical identity, as important supernatural beings did in Inca, Aztec, Maya, and other New World mythologies. The relative positions of these figures could indicate different moments in time. A supernatural female, recognizable from other portrayals (Chapter 8), appears twice. With her back to the owl and a display of objects that might be offerings, she bridges the middle and lower tiers; in a smaller version, she faces the radiant warrior.

The rayed warrior and the tree/priest are framed by figures, and other figures are scattered over the vessel in a chaotic manner uncommon in Moche art. Most figures relate to one or the other of the big warriors. Three anthropomorphic animals hold or pull an animated helmet, a belt, and a nose ornament. A large human-raptor bashes the face of an animated shield, which has a priestly cloth headdress and a club. A duck warrior grasps the hair of a small, animated warrior garment.

The objects shown are not household utensils, as in the ethnohistorical accounts, but significant prestige goods, and if they revolted, they have now been taken captive by anthropomorphic wild animals. There are anomalies. A huge, metal warrior's backflap, with a face, is not a captive but the captor of a small human. An apparent spindle floats in the air, and there are other probable spinning and weaving tools; these are not animated, and although they are domestic objects, they are not the food preparation utensils named in the myths. Behind the owl warrior, floating in air, are two ear ornaments that appear to be shining, a bottle, a possible box, and a dancing spindle, the only one of these objects that is animated.

The vase scene was painted when the Moche world was beginning to fall apart. Something extraordinary is being depicted; the scene does not conform to the usual iconographic program of the known sample, but it also does not fit the "revolt" pattern, and it is more complex than the description in the myth. The animation of objects is a consistent facet of Middle and Late Moche art; in many scenes, objects seem to be alive, not in revolt but in the Moche cause (Donnan and McClelland 1999: Fig. 5.74). Like the stones outside Cuzco, the weapons become warriors to defend the Moche or to fight on their behalf.

In a modern shaman's rite on the North Coast of Peru, "the artifacts of daily life take on their supernatural aspects" as the shaman's staffs and swords used in "spirit battles" (Sharon and Donnan 1974). In the Maya region of Mesoamerica, the lowland Lacandon Maya still think of their offering pots as living beings that transfer sustenance to the gods (Freidel, Schele, and Parker 1993:214), and the Maya of Zinacantan, in highland Chiapas, believe that domesticated plants, salt, household fires, wooden crosses erected in sacred locations, musical instruments, and other objects of value possess a soul (Vogt 1969:37).

The Munich scene may show mythic reenactment of a striking event, perhaps something like astronomical positions at a time of earthquake. It may also depict a vision, invoked ritually by the seated priest, possibly with hallucinogens. A description from Mexico of a shaman's journey to the edge of social order may fit this scene: He "enters the underlying chaos of the unconceptualized domain which has not yet been made a part of the cosmos by the cultural activity of naming and defining" (Barbara Myerhoff 1976, cited by Sharon in Joralemon and Sharon 1993:166).

Vegetation on the seated man and the dog suggests agriculture as well as the underworld, from which plants grow; Hocquenghem (1987:171) identifies

the man as *mallqui*, meaning "ancestor," "tree," or "seed"—something put into or coming from the earth (see also Arriaga 1968 [1621]:27, 119; Classen 1993:21–24; Kaulicke 2000:26). Mallqui relates to ancestors as fertilizing agents (Chapter 12). The man-tree motif appears again: a Huaca Rajada Sipán silver and gold nose ornament features two matching horizontal figures, each in front of a tree (Alva 2001: Fig. 23); a priestly figure in Complex Theme murals at Huaca Cao Viejo and Huaca de la Luna is in a tree or part of a tree (Franco and Vilela 2005: Figs. 51, 52); a Loma Negra gold nose ornament takes the form of a supernatural being standing as the trunk of a tree (Schaffer 1981: Fig. 18); bottles depicting a supernatural male copulating with a woman seem to show an ulluchu tree growing from the woman's loins, or from the copulation (see Chapter 10; Bourget 2006:167–169).

The Huaca de la Luna mural, parts of which were found separately by Seler and by Alfred Kroeber (1930; see also Bonavia 1985:73–84) was in the late Platform III (Figure 4.4). The warriors attacked and captured by animated Moche gear appear foreign, like warriors in certain ceramic scenes related to a coca-chewing rite who wear Recuay-style garments (see Chapter 10). In one part of the mural a small priestly figure holds a goblet; a plain cup or bowl floats near his feet. This ritualistic, probably shamanic, aspect and the animation of a Moche warrior's paraphernalia are shared with the Munich bottle, which does not, however, have the "foreign" figures; the mural was late, and its themes are mixed.

An island scene on a Phase V bottle presents a priestly figure in a house and two captives sitting with ropes around their necks amid animated warriors' gear. That the setting is probably an island is indicated by a line of fish and sea lions swimming around the lower border (Donnan and McClelland 1999: Fig. 5.74). Rites on offshore guano islands are indicated by objects symbolizing militarism, sacrifice, and offering (Chapter 11; see also Benson 1995a; Bourget 1994b; Kubler 1948). In Moche iconography, houses usually signify sacred space for ritual. It would seem that the warriors' gear is being energized, sacralized, or empowered by sacrifice.

The scene depicting vessels with human legs (see Figure 4.1) likely shows preparation for a funerary rite or some other significant occasion. The orderly,

FIGURE 4.4 Drawing of mural remains found in Huaca de la Luna Platform III depicting animated Moche warrior gear and foreign-looking captives. *From Kroeber 1930.*

FIGURE 4.5 "Collage" vessel of a head incorporating attributes of the Snake-belt God, an owl, and a sea lion. *Kate S. Buckingham Endowment, 1955.2321, The Art Institute of Chicago. Photograph © The Art Institute of Chicago.*

animated urns seem to be obedient to the priestly master of the rite and his assistants.

"COLLAGE" BOTTLES

One way of visualizing another world is exemplified by "collage" bottles with distorted, overlapping images. I have called these "fantasy" bottles, but Donnan's use of "collage" expresses better their appearance and separates them from other nonrealistic art. Some examples may represent a guano island with marine motifs and supernatural, animal, and priestly forms wholly or partly represented (Figure 4.5; see also Chapter 11). Other examples depict a potato with supernatural, dead, diseased, or distorted faces and

symbolic animals merged into the potato form. This kind of iconography may relate to basic belief in the aliveness of objects; it might represent a world seen in ritually drugged distortion; or it may describe a visually distorted underwater trip to the underworld.

THE DEAD

The worldview that included the concepts of huaca and camay may explain why animated dead people are portrayed on many Moche bottles (Chapter 12). For the Moche, inanimate things were not really inanimate, and the dead were not really dead. Reflecting this belief, a volume on Andean mortuary practice edited by Thomas Dillehay is titled *Tombs for the Living.*

FIGURE 1.5 Phase III bottle depicting a coca ritualist holding a stick and a container for lime. He has around his neck the string of a bag for coca leaves. His face has inlays of turquoise or chrysacolla. *Courtesy Museo Larco, Lima, Peru, XSC-007-004.*

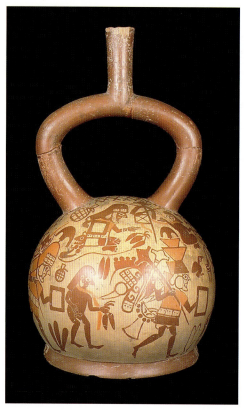

FIGURE 1.6 Phase IV bottle depicting warriors, captives, and weapons. *Museo Nacional de Arqueología, Antropología e Historia del Perú. Photograph by Christopher B. Donnan.*

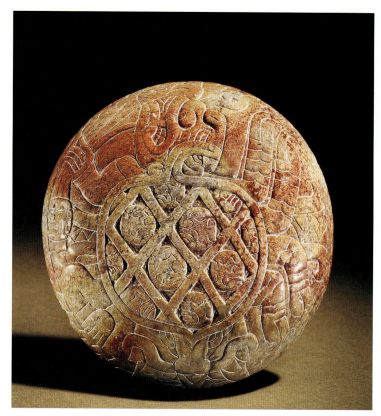

FIGURE 2.1 The underside of a Cupisnique shallow steatite bowl showing a spider anthropomorph with trophy heads in the web. *Courtesy Dumbarton Oaks Research Library and Collection, Washington, DC, B-580.*

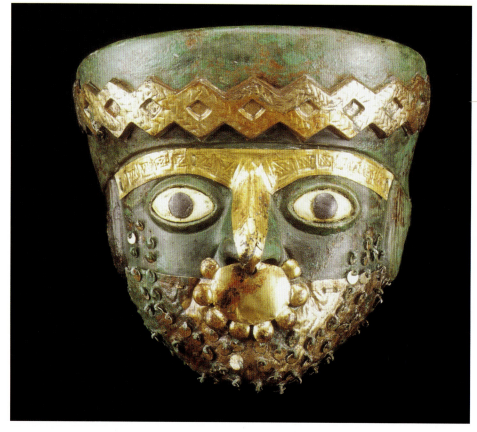

FIGURE 6.2 Burial mask with gilded copper and inlaid shell and stone, excavated from a tomb at Dos Cabezas. *Proyecto Arqueológico Dos Cabezas. Photograph by Christopher B. Donnan.*

FIGURE 6.4 Large gilded copper and silver figure with shell and stone inlay from the tomb of the Old Lord of Sipán (Tomb 3). 56.5 cm high. *Courtesy Museo Tumbas Reales de Sipán, Lambayeque.*

FIGURE 6.5 Gold and turquoise ear ornament from the tomb of the Lord of Sipán (Tomb 1). *Courtesy Museo Tumbas Reales de Sipán, Lambayeque.*

FIGURE 6.6 A garment with gold elements to be worn on the back. Found in the burial of the Lady of Huaca Cao Viejo. *Courtesy of Régulo Franco Jordán and the Proyecto Arqueológico Complejo El Brujo.*

FIGURE 7.5 Gold backflap from a looted Sipán burial, 45.5 cm high. Above the blade shape, an X Sacrificer holds a knife and a trophy head. *Courtesy Museo Tumbas Reales de Sipán, Lambayeque.*

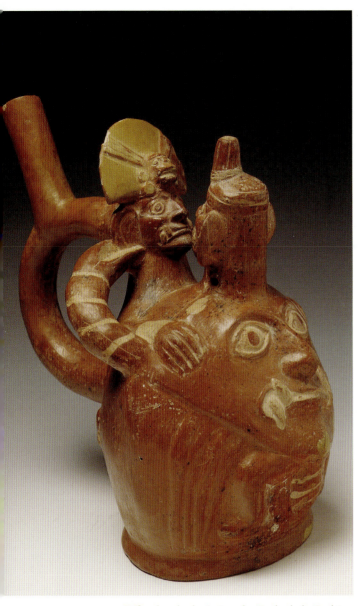

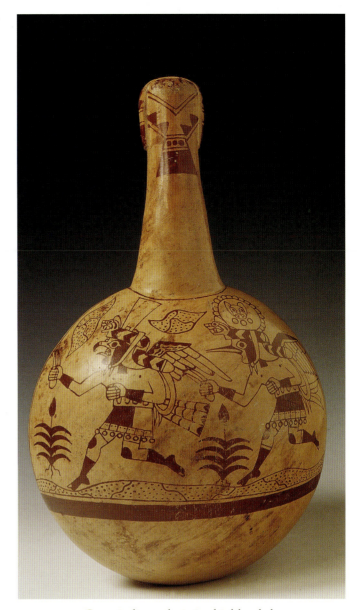

FIGURE 7.10 Effigy bottle depicting the Snake-belt God in the grip of a supernatural crab. *Courtesy Museo Larco, Lima, Peru, 079-005-003.*

FIGURE 10.3 Ceramic dipper depicting bird-headed runners holding bags. At the end of the handle is the headdress for a face on the other side, where there is a round hole for dipping in the body of the vessel. *Courtesy Museo Larco, Lima, Peru, 066-005-008.*

FIGURE 12.3 The richly painted space where the Lady of Huaca Cao Viejo was found buried under the floor. *Photograph by the author.*

FIGURE 13.2 Huaca de la Luna. A pavilion wall showing the Complex Theme, in front of the North Facade. *Photograph by the author.*

CHAPTER FIVE Ceremonial Architecture
and Murals

UNEXCAVATED MOCHE RUINS look like sand-colored hills in the desert. Some mounds are so immense that it is hard to believe that such a mass can be constructed of adobes. It is also hard to imagine what they looked like in their splendor, placed to echo the shapes of mountains or dominate the seaward skyline, because El Niño rains have eroded the adobes, and windblown sand has blurred their shapes. When archaeologists excavate these "hills," they find rooms, courtyards, and tombs—remains of generations of use and rebuilding. Excavations often reveal walls of colorful painting and/or reliefs of life-sized and abstract designs that sacralized the space and proclaimed its builders' worldly, and otherworldly, power. The massive architecture displayed the grandeur and sacredness of Moche rulers and cities, forming the cores of Moche society and the image presented to the world (Bawden 2001:288–289; Dillehay 1995:17; Uceda 2000a, 2000b). Until recently, Moche architecture and its significance had been little studied, but that has changed (see, for example, Campana 2000; Canziani 2010; Franco 1998:100; Gálvez et al. 2003; Moore 1996; Reindel 1993; Uceda and Mujica 1997:11; see also Larco Hoyle 2001, II:198–225). Ricardo Morales (2003), in particular, has examined the architecture for symbolic and ritual meaning, and has analyzed a pattern of measurement used in construction at Huaca de la Luna and some other sites (see also Donnan 2009b).

Important southern Moche sites usually share similarities: a principal structure with an asymmetrical platform, facing north across a plaza; painted facades and precincts; and ramps, windows, niches with lintels, and adobe pillars (Franco 1998; Franco, Gálvez, and Vásquez 2001b:166, 2003:171; Uceda 2000a, 2000b; see

also Bonavia and Makowski 1999; Kaulicke 1994:329). Sacred structures are often placed near or against a hill.

Duality in the placement and use of Moche buildings has been noted by many authors (Bourget 2001:114–115; Campana 1994:17; Franco 1998:107–109; Makowski 1994a; Moseley 1990). Morales Gamarra (2003) observes the relationship of Huaca del Sol to the river, and of Huaca de la Luna to Cerro Blanco, the most important features at the sites, and Michael Moseley (1992:166–167) deduces that the two structures may indicate dual kingship. Patricia Netherly and Thomas Dillehay (1986) have examined architecture in the Zaña Valley for evidence of duality, which is depicted also in fine-line ceramic scenes that show two structures.

THE CERRO BLANCO COMPLEX

The Cerro Blanco Complex, in the Moche Valley, lies about 6 km inland on the southeast side of the Moche River. The pale, isolated hill, Cerro Blanco, against which Huaca de la Luna is built, rises to a conical summit 500 m above sea level (see Figure 1.3). Cerro Blanco can be seen from afar, looming over—and dwarfing—the immense structures of Huaca del Sol and Huaca de la Luna. Surely a huaca itself, the hill must have been a major reason why the city evolved in that place and undoubtedly added religious force to the secular power and prestige of the city and its rulers. Isolated hills have strong significance in coastal myth, and the Moche urban and ceremonial center belongs to a long tradition related to Cerro Blanco. Gallinazo and Salinar remains are found there, and it was a place of pilgrimage in the later Chimu epoch

(Bourget 1997b; Morales Gamarra 2003; Morales, Solórzano, and Asmat 1998; Uceda 1997b; Uceda and Mujica 1997:14). Max Uhle investigated a shrine on the summit (Menzel 1977:40–41, 110; Morales Gamarra 2000b), where murals and other remains were mostly Chimu, although Moche material was present.

Huaca del Sol and Huaca de la Luna were the manmade foci of a city covering at least 10 km² in a valley that measures approximately 15 km at the mouth and includes the nearby Colonial, and modern, city of Trujillo. The Chan Chan–Moche Valley Project excavated there and elsewhere in the valley. Theresa Topic (1977) investigated Huaca del Sol and habitation sites between the huacas. Christopher Donnan and Carol Mackey (1978) produced a volume on burial patterns, and Shelia Pozorski (1976) studied subsistence patterns. Since 1992 an intensive, long-term excavation, Proyecto Arqueológico Huacas de Moche, has been carried out by the Universidad Nacional de Trujillo under the direction of Santiago Uceda and Ricardo Morales (Uceda, Mujica, and Morales, 1997, 1998, 2000, 2004, 2006, 2008a, 2008b). Its investigation of Huaca de la Luna and the urban area nearby revealed Luna's long architectural sequence of six building stages (Uceda and Canziani 1993; Huaca de la Luna 2009), exposed many murals, and yielded a set of 31 carbon 14 dates for Luna and the urban area (Uceda, Chapdelaine, and Verano 2008) that have produced information on stratigraphy, burials, and ritual sacrifice.

HUACA DEL SOL

The massive mound of Huaca del Sol was possibly the largest solid-brick platform erected in the Americas (see Figure 1.3). The huaca, most of which was built in Phase III, now measures about 340 × 160 × 40 m at the highest point, but it was once much larger. Michael Moseley (1982:16) estimates that about two-thirds of it was washed away in 1602 when a Spanish landowner changed the course of the river to facilitate his search for gold in the structure (Calancha, cited in Bonavia 1985:72; Shimada 1994a:14; T. Topic 1982:263). Some 2,800 kg of precious metals were reportedly retrieved, suggesting the presence of high-status tombs within the huaca, which was apparently the center of community life (Franco 1998:107–108;

Hastings and Moseley 1975; Menzel 1977:37–39; Moseley 1992:166–168; S. Pozorski 1976; T. Topic 1977, 1982; Uceda and Mujica 1997:13–14). Although it has not yet been thoroughly excavated, there is some evidence of habitation, and food remains in large middens associated with a platform suggest ceremonial banquets related to a system of reciprocity and redistribution. The huaca may also have contained a series of administrative quarters associated with rulers.

Constructed of more than 140 million adobe bricks, Huaca del Sol rose in four steplike sections, built over centuries in a widespread North Coast method of construction first described by Alfred Kroeber (1925, 1930). Separate groups of workmen on Moche structures raised standard columns, or towers, of blocks of adobes, with spaces left between to be filled with columns made by later teams (Figure 5.1; see also Campana 2000; Hastings and Moseley 1975; Meneses and Chero 1994:249; Moseley 1975b; Shimada 1997). Teams—some probably fulfilling labortribute obligations—could have worked at the same time on different parts of a structure. A similar technique appears in Gallinazo buildings, with differently formed bricks: the adobes have mortar at top and bottom, but the sides are mortarless. Such segmented construction makes the structure relatively earthquake resistant, although Moche huacas have been damaged severely by El Niño rains and flooding.

ADOBES

At Pacatnamu, Donald McClelland observed that Moche period bricks seemed to be made of river silts of different colors. At Huaca del Sol, Carlos Ramírez-Gamonal and Bertha Herrera, working in 1991, identified adobe compositions from different geologic deposits in the valley. Theresa Topic (1977:339) has noted that in 1977 clay for adobes was still being quarried downriver from Cerro Blanco, a possible source in the past. A thorough study of adobes at Huaca Cao Viejo by César Gálvez et al. (2003) revealed, among other things, variations in size of adobes at different building stages, and reuse of adobes (see also Bonavia 1985:43; Campana 2000; Hastings and Moseley 1975). Early adobes had been handmade, but cane molds were developed in Late Gallinazo times, and adobes

FIGURE 5.1 Wall in Huaca Cao Viejo showing column construction technique. *Photograph by the author.*

with cane-mold markings reflect Gallinazo techniques. Some adobes in Huaca de la Luna were also made with wooden or cane molds, indicating that the Moche sometimes used Gallinazo methods, or Gallinazo masons were working for the Moche.

Some Moche adobes bear marks, presumably designating the maker, or perhaps associated with a social group. A high proportion of marked adobes have been observed in apparently later sections of Huaca del Sol (Moseley 1975b, 1975c). Platform III of Huaca de la Luna, a late structure, has adobes of different manufacture than elsewhere in the huaca (Uceda and Tufinio 2003); most of them are marked. At Huaca Cao Viejo, excavators also find relatively late marked adobes (Figure 5.2) (Franco, Gálvez, and Vásquez 1994; Gálvez et al. 2003). Some bricks at Pacatnamu (Donald McClelland 1989) and Pampa Grande (Shimada 1994a:162–166, 1997) are marked. Various arguments have been made concerning the marks. Ramírez-Gamonal and Herrera (1994) see them as indicants of labor specialization and control of adobe making. Other researchers have postulated that the adobes were used to fulfill tax obligations, and that outside labor was used. Given that Early Moche adobes seem to lack marks, the system may have developed as populations and projects increased.

FIGURE 5.2 Adobe bricks showing marking, Huaca Cao Viejo. *Photograph by the author.*

The dearth of marks in some structures and the fact that adobes with the same marks are not always laid together suggest complicated practical reasons for the presence or absence of marks, perhaps having more to do with where adobes were made than with who laid them. There might be even more esoteric reasons.

HUACA DE LA LUNA

The religious heart of the Cerro Blanco Complex was Huaca de la Luna (Morales Gamarra 2003; Tufinio 2004a; Uceda 2000a, 2000b, 2001a, 2004, 2006; Uceda and Mujica 1997:11; Uceda and Tufinio 2003; Uceda et al. 1994). Not only is it located in a sacred place, on the rocky western flank of Cerro Blanco, but its spaces are exalted with numinous images; sacrifices were carried out there, and religious officials were buried within its walls. No evidence of domestic use has come to light. A structure of three platforms and four plazas on different levels, surrounded by walls, Huaca de la Luna measures 290 × 210 m (north-south) and rises 32 m above the plain that now separates the huacas. Each platform and plaza was built over an older, smaller one and was supported by new construction and by adobes and other fill packed into former rooms. The present structure is the result of successive "burials"—as the excavators call them—of older buildings, which provided structural stability as well as a metaphor of regeneration. Thick

sediment, including sand—often deposited between building stages—indicates that some rebuilding was associated with intense El Niño events.

The immense Platform I of Huaca de la Luna measures 100 m on each side and 25 m high. The last, upper construction stage was almost completely destroyed, mostly by looters; only the perimeter remains. The earliest phases are also little known. The later structures seem to be Phase IV. Platform I had two principal levels with enclosures and terraces with corridors, patios, and covered galleries. Some walls had niches or windows. Some enclosures were roofed, and roofs of larger enclosures were supported by columns and pilasters.

Plaza 1 (Armas et al. 2004), a huge north-south-oriented ceremonial space measuring 175 m long × 75 m at its widest, could have held as many as 10,000 people. The principal entrance to the plaza and the entire complex lies at the far end, where a kind of baffle controlled access; the public would not have had easy entry to the sacred precinct. The access to Platform I from Plaza 1 was a long ramp that begins on the east side of the plaza and ascends the platform's north facade (Figure 5.3). Ramps seemingly had special significance and characterized Moche monumental architecture. They are also depicted on ceramic vases, and it is thought that the upward-spiraling dances shown in ceramic scenes likely took place on ramps.

High in the northeast corner of Platform I, near the climax of the ramp system, a space encloses an

FIGURE 5.3 Part of the restored ramp at Huaca de la Luna going from Plaza I to Platform I, with a North Façade mural to the left, and Huaca del Sol in the right background. *Photograph by the author.*

FIGURE 5.4 Space in Huaca de la Luna Platform I overlooking Plaza I, with paintings and a throne or altar. *Photograph by the author.*

altar or throne with an opening, possibly for offerings (Figure 5.4; Armas et al. 2002; Morales Gamarra 2003; Tufinio 2001b; Uceda 2001b, 2006; Uceda and Tufinio 2003:198, 200). Postholes in the floor indicate roofing with a separate covering. The enclosure, which looks across Plaza 1 to the valley beyond, had three building stages, with three sets of superimposed paintings.

A rock outcrop at the southeast corner of the complex is surrounded by a wall that encloses Plaza 3A and Platform II. Rocks are numinous in the literature of many regions, and there may have been Moche myths about the Plaza 3A rocks that enhanced the power of the hill. Steve Bourget (1998) unearthed an extraordinary series of sacrifices at the outcrop, and other sacrifices have since been excavated in nearby Plaza 3C by Chlorinda Orbegoso and Moisés Tufinio (see Chapter 10).

Platform III and Plaza 4, just outside the northeast corner of the main structures, are of later date and of

intermediate size. These have recently been excavated, chiefly by Tufinio, who has done most of the recent excavation on Huaca de la Luna.

THE URBAN AREA AT THE CERRO BLANCO COMPLEX

Between the two massive huacas lies a 500 m wide area that before excavation looked like a huge, fairly flat plaza, but is actually crowded with buried remains of residential and related structures of a city that probably had a population of 10,000 at its peak. The site is windy, and aeolian sand and debris fill spaces quickly, sometimes to a depth of 7 m. Moreover, the surface has been water-scoured; runoff from Cerro Blanco, caused by heavy El Niño rains, has leveled the surface and affected subsurface preservation. Extensive looting over time has added to the problems for scientific excavators.

Theresa Topic (1977, 1982:268–270; see also Larco Hoyle 2001, II:200–225) described three types of domestic architecture near Huaca del Sol: structures with walls of perishable material and unplastered floors, well-built architecture with no elaboration, and complex buildings with storage facilities. Some low-status dwellings had walls of worn adobes or cobbles set in mud; any roofing was probably perishable. A residential area near a pottery workshop, investigated by Shelia and Thomas Pozorski (2003), had a paved patio, a wall with an adobe frieze, and a cultivation zone with canals. Two residential groups nearby were solidly built, with level, plastered floors. Adobe walls could be sealed with clay plaster and built to considerable heights. Storerooms, bins, and niches were found, as well as an adobe platform with a headrest.

In the present project at the Cerro Blanco site, more than 30 elite residences and other structures in the urban network of hundreds of architectural units have been examined by Claude Chapdelaine, Ricardo Tello, and others (articles in Uceda, Mujica, and Morales 2000, 2004; see also Chapdelaine 1997, 2001, 2003; Chapdelaine, Kennedy, and Uceda 1995; Chapdelaine et al. 1998; R. Tello, Armas, and Chapdelaine 2003; Uceda and Armas 1998; Uceda and Mujica 1996:14, 1997, 1998:10). The city was planned, with streets, plazas, and canals that brought water to houses and workshops. Residential units were built along a grid of narrow streets that converged on a public plaza. Filling the area were large courtyards and adobe residences with niched walls, low platforms, and gable or shed roofs supported by pilasters, pillars, or columns. Windows could be set low or high, doorways had high thresholds, and some walls had relief or painted designs.

A 16.5 m wide street, excavated under the direction of Ricardo Tello (1998), can be interpreted as an avenue separating the urban zone from the ritual zone associated with Huaca de la Luna. Streets led through a kind of maze to the huaca. Well-built dwellings (with murals) and workshops near Luna were apparently related to religious, and perhaps funerary, activity. Houses of fine masonry with storage rooms and patios with benches, excavated nearer Huaca del Sol, apparently had functions related to other activities.

The city, probably begun in the fourth century AD (Phase III), became a major ritual center and was occupied well into the eighth century. Excavation shows successive occupations. Chapdelaine (2001) defines the Cerro Blanco Complex as a city because it had a dense population, monumental architecture, and diversity of functions, and lacked agricultural tools. He sees a stratified population supporting a powerful elite, and he believes that at least some members of the upper echelon lived at the foot of Huaca de la Luna. He found most residential complexes to be multifunctional, with domestic areas (a hearth, grinding stones, and benches for sleeping) and storage areas greater than necessary for domestic activities only. Some compounds may have been organized by occupational specialty: chicha making, pottery making, weaving, and so on. He found no lower-class housing in this sector, and few lower-middle-class houses. Most of those in the lower class lived outside the urban area, where they performed jobs like adobe making and road and canal maintenance.

HUACA CAO VIEJO, CHICAMA VALLEY

The important ceremonial structure called Huaca Cao Viejo (or Huaca Blanca) is part of a Moche site known as the El Brujo Complex because witches, curers, or shamans were (and are) said to hold rites there. The Proyecto Arqueológico Complejo "El Brujo" is being carried out by Régulo Franco (Fundación Augusto H. Wiese), César Gálvez (Instituto Nacional de Cultura, La Libertad), and Segundo Vásquez (Universidad Nacional de Trujillo).

The complex lies at the northern margin of the Chicama Valley, near the littoral, with the early Huaca Prieta about 1 km away, on the sea, and a Cupisnique structure between them. Huaca Cao Viejo is southwest of Huaca El Brujo (a Moche structure known also as Huaca Partida or Huaca Cortada), in relatively the same position as that of Huaca de la Luna to Huaca del Sol, again with 500 m between the structures. Cao Viejo, a truncated, stepped pyramid with four building stages, rises 28 m and measures 120 X 100 m at the base (Franco, Gálvez, and Vásquez 2001b, 2003). Its north facade faces a rectangular, walled plaza, 140 X 75 m. Ramps led from the plaza to the summit of the huaca. Prominent in the southeast corner of the plaza is a pavilion with murals; similar and similarly placed painted pavilions were found in earlier building stages of the huaca, and a pavilion with paintings very similar to a pair at Cao Viejo was recently excavated at Huaca de la Luna (see Chapter 13). Huaca Cao Viejo includes high structures similar to the high place on the northeast corner of Huaca de la Luna Platform I; they resemble the simplified stepped platforms in ritual scenes depicted on ceramics. Clay war clubs probably ornamented the roofs of these structures; clubs also adorned the roof of a pavilion with murals in the plaza at each site (Franco 1998; Franco, Gálvez, and Vásquez 1999a, 2001b, 2003; see also Bourget 2003; Morales Gamarra, Solórzano, and Asmat 1998; R. Tello 1998).

Remnant small structures at the El Brujo Complex include residential areas and cemeteries, and a well reached by a shaft with a spiral staircase has been explored. There are also Lambayeque and Chimu remains at the site and the ruin of a colonial church. This is a small piece of land with a very long history of occupation.

JEQUETEPEQUE VALLEY

Pacatnamu, dramatically situated on cliffs above the sea at the mouth of the Jequetepeque River, may have been a significant port and trade center and also a sacred place. In addition to its maritime resources (middens indicate heavy use of fish and shellfish), it had the advantages of nearby agricultural fields.

Although most buildings are adobe, some walls are made of cobbles in mud mortar. Heinrich Ubbelohde-Doering (1967, 1983) excavated there in the 1930s and 1960s; Richard Keatinge did a surface survey in 1974; Gisela and Wolfgang Hecker (1985, 1992) worked there and also published many of Ubbelohde-Doering's findings; and Donnan and Guillermo Cock led the Pacatnamu Project, 1983–1987, for the Instituto Nacional de Cultura and the Fowler Museum of Cultural History at the University of California, Los Angeles. Donnan and Cock put the beginning of Moche occupation of Pacatnamu in Phase I; the Phase II/III occupation was most intense; there is evidence for Phase IV; and the Phase V occupation lasted until AD 900 or later, longer than at most other sites (Chapter 13).

Just to the south, within sight of Pacatnamu and the sea, stands Dos Cabezas, recently explored for the first time by Donnan along with Cock, Alana Cordy-Collins, and others (Cordy-Collins 2001b; Donnan 2001, 2003, 2007; Jiménez 2000; Moseley, Donnan, and Keefer 2008). They cleared most of the base and a long facade, and excavated a ramp and several remarkable burials. Bourget is working there at the time of this writing.

North of Pacatnamu, on the Pan-American Highway, lies San José de Moro, which had a Phase III occupation, some evidence of Phase IV, and an impressive Phase V (see Chapters 12, 13). The extant ruins in the southern part of the site are hard to decipher because of later usage and heavy looting over many years. Massive platforms with plazas were constructed for rituals, especially funerary rites. Artificial mounds likely contain remains of residences for those involved in ritual. San José de Moro was explored by Hans Dietrich Disselhoff in 1955 and 1956. In 1979 Donnan and Luis Jaime Castillo did preliminary work there, and in 1991–1992 they began the Proyecto Arqueológico San José de Moro, which has continued since then under Castillo for the Pontificia Universidad Católica del Perú, at times with the help of Carol Mackey, Andrew Nelson, Julio Rucabado, and others.

LAMBAYEQUE VALLEY

Sipán, near the Reque River, became famous when burials in the Huaca Rajada there were being looted in 1987, and Walter Alva, of the Museo Arqueológico Nacional Brüning de Lambayeque, quickly organized official excavations, which have yielded remarkably rich and informative finds (Alva 1988, 1994, 2001; Alva and Donnan 1993; *El Comercio*, 2 September 2007; Millaire 2002:45–51). Huaca Rajada is a burial platform 230 m long, 165 m wide, and 33 m high. Within it is a complex of tombs—12 known so far—and Alva believes that a sanctuary like those at Huaca del Sol and Cao Viejo existed on the summit. The mound stands near two enormous pyramids that have not yet been seriously explored.

At Pampa Grande, a Late Moche site about 20 km upvalley from Sipán, two immense platforms stand dramatically where the valley emerges from the Andes foothills, a sacred place and a natural point for control of water from the sierra (Shimada 1994a). A broad irrigation ditch runs from Pampa Grande to Sipán (Chapter 13).

THE SOUTHERNMOST VALLEYS

The Virú Valley contains Gallinazo sites and mixed sites along with some Moche burials, notably the Tomb of the Warrior Priest, which was not placed in impressive architecture (Strong and Evans 1952; see also Reindel 1991:247–250). The large, *cerro*-based Castillo at Huancaco has some Moche features, but Bourget (2003, 2010), working there recently, did not find fully characteristic Moche architecture (see also Millaire 2010). Sites in the Santa Valley were surveyed, but little had been done there until Claude Chapdelaine's recent work (2008, 2010; see also Donnan 1973a; Larco Hoyle 1962; Wilson 1988).

Pañamarca is the southernmost prominent Moche site. The main structure was a stepped pyramid, 650 m x 300 m, and once about 50 m high, built on a rock outcrop near an earlier structure of fine-cut stone. Facing the pyramid, across a plaza, was a temple with polychrome murals. Donald Proulx (1982:83), who conducted surface surveys in the Nepeña Valley in 1968 and the 1970s, observed that Moche ceremonial centers were often built atop remains of respected earlier structures. This would have been useful to the Moche, who occupied only parts of the valley, for it gave local people a sense of ritual continuity in a time of political change. There are Moche cemeteries, but evidence of Moche habitation is rare in the Nepeña Valley; it may lie beneath modern agriculture, or its absence may reflect brief and superficial Moche control.

ARCHITECTURAL MODELS

In many cultures a house can be a four-sided cosmic diagram and a symbol of civilization, with walls enclosing what may be sacred space. In Peru, temples and special houses were huacas, sacrosanct places. Moche ceramic bottles with effigy and/or two-dimensional structures may present a concept of the cosmos as a house. The house representations seem to be a kind of shorthand for the presentation of cosmological, political, and religious ideas; they may show status and record events (see Figure 12.5). Many effigy bottles picture a single structure; two or more buildings may represent a ceremonial center. Both elaborate adobe and simple wood structures can be depicted, and both types are mounted on a status-signifying platform; sometimes the building is raised on a pyramid. A roof comb with a double-step motif appears to indicate power or sacredness; roofs can also display war clubs, snakes, foxes, or *Strombus*-shell monsters.

A house can tell much about the nature of a scene. Closed houses may depict funerary chambers; figures in priestly dress sometimes stand outside. A figure on a rack is painted below one house; another house-bottle displays a sacrificial victim, suggesting that the cosmic house was sustained by sacrifice. Open structures often show, inside, a chieftain or one or more supernaturals, sometimes enthroned (see Figure 4.2). Steps are usually indicated below. Symbolic designs can be added: rows of knives on a stepped platform, or painted foxes or felines ascending a ramp.

Some examples of house representations may have been models for sacred structures (Benson 1997b:94–95; Campana 1983; Morales Gamarra 2003: Fig. 14.1). House models are not always clay bottles. A carved stone found at Huaca Cao Viejo may have been a model for architecture at the site (Franco and Murga 1998, 2001); clay models were placed in niches in late burials at San José de Moro (Castillo 2001: Fig. 8; Castillo and Donnan 1994b:125–133; Castillo, Nelson, and Nelson 1997); and a Sipán burial yielded an elaborate copper scepter in the form of a temple with war clubs

on the roof (Alva 1994: Láms. 19–22; Alva and Donnan 1993: Figs. 47, 48).

THE MURALS

Moche sacred structures were probably all enriched, inside and out, with painted relief designs, mural paintings, or plain paint. The paintings sometimes have a sculptural third dimension formed by a depth of worked clay; features of a face could be attached or built up on reed dowels. Surely hundreds are lost. Preservation is due largely to the fact that murals were usually embedded in later construction, protected behind walls of adobes and fill. Some painting lies almost directly on top of earlier painting, but in other cases a thick (2 m) wall separates them. Duccio Bonavia's 1985 book presents a wealth of information on then-known murals, but extraordinary new discoveries have been made in recent years. Extensive mural art is now known at three sites.

Pañamarca once had the largest number of known Moche murals. Ephraim George Squier noted paintings there in 1877; Wendell Bennett described in 1939 remains of plastered walls with traces of design and red and yellow paint; important figurative murals were later reported by Richard Schaedel (1951) and Bonavia (1961); and a few other paintings there have been published more recently (Bonavia and Makowski 1999). The best-known painting there is the only recorded mural depiction of a rite originally published as "the Presentation Theme" (see Chapter 8; also Bonavia 1985; Donnan 1978), but little is now left of most of the first-known paintings because of vandalism, site clearing, the severe 1970 earthquake, and El Niño damage. Nevertheless, in current excavations by Lisa Trever and Jorge Gamboa, more paintings are being discovered.

Eduard Seler, visiting Huaca de la Luna in 1910 (see Seler 1915, 1923:368), discovered traces of painting in Platform III; these and other fragments, found later by Kroeber (1930), showed animated warrior's gear attacking humans (see Figure 4.4). The Seler portion had disappeared by 1919, and the Kroeber sections have also virtually vanished, but drawings exist of both. A Phase V mural recently excavated in Platform III shows fox warriors on a ramp (Morales Gamarra 2003:467). A mural inside Platform I was exposed briefly in 1955

(Bonavia 1985:84–97, Pl. 14–18; Mackey and Hastings 1982; Uceda 2000a:212, 2001a:60). This mural, cleared again in 1972 by the Chan Chan–Moche Valley Project, is in the "throne" room in Platform I, superimposed on two other murals with thin layers of plaster between them. In the earliest, textile-like painting, a standing frontal figure holds a two-headed serpent. Painted over it is a pattern of squares with a supernatural head from which long-necked birds emerge. The top layer presents profile figures with staffs.

Since 1990 archaeologists have revealed many murals at Huaca de la Luna and Huaca Cao Viejo. Common elements include northern facades with murals in horizontal tiers, repeated, with variations, through successive building stages. The main facade of Cao Viejo shows warriors facing each other, a procession of warriors and captives, and what is likely to be a ritual war dance. A more complete and complex painted facade has been revealed at Huaca de la Luna (see Chapter 13). Frontal sacrificers, holding a knife and a human head, appear inside Cao Viejo (Figure 5.5) and in early phases at Luna (Gálvez and Briceño 2001: Fig. 24; Uceda 2001b:59, Fig. 9). A Cao Viejo sacrificer has apparent spider attributes, a likely northern influence; the belt of one sacrificer ends in condor heads, while that of another has fox heads.

An early patio excavated at Huaca Cao Viejo has a design of *life* (a North Coast catfish, *Trichomycterus* sp.) on the long wall (Figure 5.6), and an adjacent wall is covered with a pattern of Crested Animals (see Chapter 7). A wall perpendicular to that shows splayed figures, rare in Moche art, which might have spider attributes; each of these figures wears a different garment, although the basic figure is the same, and each figure has a condor on either shoulder. It was in this section of the huaca that the burial of an important woman, the Lady of Huaca Cao Viejo, was found in 2005 (see Chapter 12).

Murals on interior walls at both Huaca Cao Viejo and Huaca de la Luna repeat supernatural or geometric motifs. A deity face framed in a rhomboid is a shared motif (Morales Gamarra and Torres 2000). Morales Gamarra (2003) observes that some paintings in both huacas feature a watery ambiance of designs based on catfish, rays, serpents, seabirds, and/or waves, often in diagonal bands. Color was significant. Some deity faces in Luna were repainted; one was originally red, with a yellow nose, but the face was later painted blue

FIGURE 5.5 Huaca Cao Viejo relief mural showing a sacrificer with an abraded face, holding a trophy head. *Photograph by the author.*

FIGURE 5.6 Huaca Cao Viejo mural with catfish. *Photograph by the author.*

(in a special rite?), then red and yellow again, with the colors reversed. The paint in the center of one of the marine walls at Cao Viejo is iridescent.

In the last paintings at both sites, a different kind of mural appears (Chapter 13). Remains of earlier murals are found in many spaces, and fallen bits of painted clay give evidence of painted ceilings in several spaces in Huaca Cao Viejo and Huaca de la Luna. Interior columns might be of algarrobo wood covered with braided fiber, plastered, and painted with designs; there are some remains of these.

Murals are known also at Mocollope, as well as

at Huancaco, where Steve Bourget's (2003; see also Reindel 1993: Abb. 106) excavation revealed paintings of vivid color in a style somewhat different from that of other known murals. A rich tomb, found by looters in 1989, at La Mina, near Pacatnamu and Dos Cabezas, was excavated by Alfredo Narváez (1994). The burial chamber, at a hill above a valley, was partly in bedrock. On its walls murals repeated, in squares, a double-crenellated wave with snake and ray heads; below were step motifs. Murals in a tomb at Huaca Cao Viejo repeat a standing figure holding a club (Franco and Gálvez 2010: Fig. 2). Mural remains reported in the Lambayeque region include those at Huaca la Ventana (La Leche Valley), described in 1937 by Julio Tello (cited by Bonavia 1985:97) as "fragments of adobes . . . with polychrome relief figures like arabesques." Some mural fragments recovered from Huaca Rajada Sipán are exhibited in the Museo Tumbas Reales de Sipán in Lambayeque.

At Pampa Grande four fragmentary murals were recorded, and traces of paint remain on many walls (Bonavia 1985:97–99, Pl. 19, Fig. 72; Shimada 1994a:235–238). A mural found there by Martha Anders (1981) depicts the legs of a frontal figure with fan-shaped plumage, flanked by stafflike objects; a small figure with a club and shield stands in a corner. Clubs and shields are common motifs. Murals at La Mayanga (Huaca Facho), Moche Valley—found by James Ford in 1958 and later published by Donnan (1972; see also Bonavia 1985:99–104; Mackey and Hastings 1982; Reindel 1993:94, 95; Wilson 1988: Fig. 107)—were located in a plaza with perhaps 30 wall niches, each showing a running, winged, human-headed war club with a round-shield body and a human foot; the style is late. At El Castillo, in the Santa Valley, a polychrome club and shield mural was partially revealed on the outside of a structure.

MURAL MATERIALS

Kroeber noted techniques of a small sample of murals in Huaca de la Luna in 1926. The Proyecto Arqueológico Huacas de Moche has worked with a much larger sample and made a more refined study. The project's first objective was to examine painted reliefs that Morales Gamarra (1994, 1995) had found on

adobes from the collapsed south face of the huaca. He and his colleagues set out to determine the architectural space and construction phase in which the paintings belonged. The project's objectives became more complex as more murals were found. Conservation is now synchronous with excavation in an ever-widening body of material (Morales Gamarra 2003; Campana and Morales 1997; Uceda and Mujica 1997:10–11; conservation articles in Uceda, Mujica, and Morales, eds., 1997, 1998, 2000, 2004).

For Huaca de la Luna murals in relief, the wall was plastered with a mortar rich with whitish clay, 1 to 2 cm thick, and spaces were marked off with cotton string. While the mortar was fresh, motifs were outlined with firm, freehand incisions, and a white clay ground was applied, either while the mortar was damp or after it had dried. Color was then added.

Analysis by Morales Gamarra (1994:478–481; see also Franco, Gálvez, and Vásquez 2001b:137) of the colors at Huaca de la Luna and Huaca Cao Viejo indicates that the reds and pinks are generally hematite, and the yellows limonite; black can be ferric oxide at Luna and vegetal carbon at Cao Viejo. White comes from carbonated calcium (from shell) at Cao Viejo, and from talc at Huaca de la Luna. At both sites blue was made from a mixture of colors. The pigments at Luna are all inorganic. The medium used to apply these colors has been identified as juice of a cactus, apparently either San Pedro (*Trichocereus pachnoi*) or the related *Cereus macrostibus*.

La Mayanga murals were yellow and red with blue-black and white. The motifs were drawn freehand with light incision; then color was applied, and later a line of blue-black outlined the color areas. Red or yellow pigment was generally applied before white and blue-black. The murals of La Mayanga, Pañamarca, and Huaca de le Luna are similar in pigment and technique, with the palate varying from place to place (Bonavia 1985; Bonavia and Makowski 1999).

Today murals emerge from the rubble with color, clarity, and strength. How striking the paintings must have been in the sacred inner sancta, and how spectacular the facades of these buildings must have looked to the outside world! At Huaca de la Luna and Huaca Cao Viejo, and surely other sites, the outer murals would have been a striking sight from a kilometer or more away.

CHAPTER SIX

Art and Craft

EXCEPTIONAL CREATIVITY CHARACTERIZES Moche civilization. Artists surely worked in a prescribed symbolic language, but they had some freedom within its limitations and could produce remarkably fine work. Moche art is more naturalistic and spatially open than other pre-Hispanic Andean art, in which designs are generally more geometric, and figures more confined.

The art informs us about religion, social organization, and kingly power. Extraordinary metalwork implies the presence of patrons—lords of the cities—who also supported weavers, lapidaries, and ceramists. Jürgen Golte (1994a:14–15) notes that Moche artistic development was combined with the exercise of power and the use of craftsmanship and art to solve political-religious problems. Christopher Donnan and Donna McClelland (1999:15) have argued that local lords received from their subjects food, raw materials, and goods for redistribution, and that the surplus supported artisans whose work demonstrated the ruler's puissance. Political-ceremonial centers flourished largely because of their display of creative power and their ability to participate in trade networks of sumptuary goods (Chapdelaine 2003; Lechtman 1993; Morales Gamarra 2003; Quilter 2001; Russell and Jackson 2001: Uceda and Tufinio 2003).

CERAMICS

Of all the arts and crafts that exemplify Moche achievement, ceramics—especially those from the south—are the most plentiful and rich in information. Pottery lasts (or its sherds do), and more of it is preserved than of any other type of Moche art. Because the Moche produced little from stone or wood, materials that were scarce in the desert, pottery was also their primary art medium. Moche sculpture was usually ceramic, and the fine ceramics were most often vessels. The question of whether or not they were used or made especially for funerary purposes has been debated (Bourget 2006:48–49; R. Tello, Armas, and Chapdelaine 2003:175–176). Some scholars feel that pottery of such high quality must be primarily funerary, but much of it shows signs of wear. Elaborate examples would likely have been used in funerary and other rites; everyday use seems unlikely.

Northern and southern Moche ceramic vessels differ. Early northern examples often resemble southern stirrup-spout bottles but are distinct in proportion, color, and finish, and the subject matter differs somewhat from that of the south. These appear with more typical northern bottles with spout and bridge, and long-necked globular bottles with a loop at either side. Middle Moche northern stirrup-spout bottles might be in the shape of a feline or a fruit, for example, or they might be globular with a bird or geometric design drawn on the side or a face on the neck, but the people in the north did not develop the elaborate scenes of southern ceramics. The painting of scenes is usually described as "fine-line," and often the line is fine, but it can also be thick. Fine-line painting is mostly a southern phenomenon until Phase V, when, especially at San José de Moro, it appeared in quantity (see Chapter 13).

MAKING POTTERY

Moche ceramists coiled clay and formed and treated it in many ways (Bankes 1980; Castillo and Donnan 1994b; Chapdelaine, Kennedy, and Uceda 1995; Donnan 1978; Donnan and McClelland 1979, 1999; Hocquenghem 1980a; 1981; Jackson 2008; Kroeber 1925, 1926; Larco Hoyle 1948, 1963, 2001,II:107–121; Makowski et al. 1994; Donna McClelland 1997; McClelland, McClelland, and Donnan 2007; Russell and Jackson 2001; Russell, Leonard, and Briceño 1994, 1998; Sawyer 1966; Shimada 1994a, 1994b; Shimada and Maguiña 1994). In early phases, ceramics were frequently modeled, often elaborately. In Phase III potters began to use two-piece press molds. Molding and modeling could be combined, and even after the introduction of molds, vessels might still have been shaped by hand. A special stone or plate was sometimes used as a kind of potter's wheel, which the Moche did not use. Designs could be stamped, or appliqué or inlay added to the basic form.

Most of the finest Moche ceramics in all phases are bottles with a stirrup spout, a form used by Cupisnique and other ancient predecessors in several nearby regions, surely associated with revered ancestors and considered sacred. Handles and spouts of stirrup-spout bottles were made separately and attached to the body. Sometimes the bottle had a form rather like a vinegar cruet, and the upper part might be made to look like a club head. In Phase III, in the south, old forms continued as new forms came in, continuing into Phase IV. Some vessels have a wide, open neck; others have a spout with a strap or tube handle (see Figure 7.8). There are also dipper-shaped bowls, often called "corn-poppers" (see Figure 10.3), which are painted on one side, have a hole on the other, and usually show a full-round human head in a soft headdress on the handle end. Floreros, flanged-rim bowls, often on a pedestal base, show scenes or motifs on the wide rim (Figure 6.1). Goblets, or pedestal cups (see Figure 4.2), uncommon among recovered Moche artifacts, are depicted in certain scenes, often with a bowl or gourd, which might be a lid. Double vessels are usually "whistling" vessels, with a whistle inside, a small sphere of clay with an opening (McEwan 1997); some of these vessels are designed to

FIGURE 6.1 *Florero* depicting a sequence of events from the saga of the Snake-belt God. *Courtesy Museo Larco, Lima, Peru, XXC-000-210.*

sound when liquid moves in them, and some are activated by blowing into a spout or tube.

Form and decoration of Moche stirrup-spout bottles from the southern region vary from globular forms with linear designs to effigies shaped as supernatural beings, humans, animals, vegetables, and other objects. In between are bottles with high or low relief, created by cutting away clay. Often methods were combined, such as low relief painted or bordered with a painted design, or an effigy—a "deck" figure—sitting atop a painted scene (see Figure 11.5). Designs were often incised before paint was applied. Some bottles have a post-fire application of "fugitive" organic, carbon pigment, indicating face paint or patterns on clothing, but it quickly wears off with handling or burial in moist soil. Some vessels, most often from Phase III, have inlays of turquoise, shell, or a black, tarry substance, and some ceramic figures are adorned with copper bracelets or ear or nose ornaments.

Fine ceramics were usually painted, excepting black ware and sometimes a rare white ware of kaolinlike clay from the highlands. Some pieces were fired in a reducing atmosphere, which impedes air circulation and prevents oxidation, giving vessels a gray to black appearance. Potters fired, usually in open ovens, a fine-textured paste, normally tempered with fine-grained sand, to produce a well-fired oxidized ware with reddish-brown and cream colors. Vessels could be slip-painted with cream or red slips. Colors are usually limited to two or three on a vessel, although four may appear, especially in Phase III, when colors included ochers, pinks, purples, and grays.

A number of bottles might be made in the same mold but colored variously or given different spouts or ornaments. Objects were often, if not always, made in pairs or multiples, but it is clear that the Moche felt strongly that no two objects should be identical. Bourget (2006:55) sees these similar but different vessels as another expression of the Moche concept of duality.

Certain artistic conventions are associated with different meanings in Moche art. For example, humans and animals depicted as part of larger scenes are usually in profile; important or supernatural personages are larger than lesser beings, but rarely full-face; and owls and certain sacred beings are presented frontally.

Plants and other elements floating in space refer to the setting or the nature of the scene, and drawings of stirrup-spout bottles appear to be a kind of gloss to mark significant or sacred space (see Figure 4.1). Some scenes are set inside structures. A wave motif defines an island or shore. Irregular, curving forms with interior dots seem to indicate a sandy place. Small, dark circles suggest a night sky. A three-dimensional deck figure atop a globular bottle may repeat a personage painted in the fine-line scene below or may represent an upper or other world. Some subjects appear almost always in fine line, whereas others are usually in relief. Still others occur only three-dimensionally, yet many figures from fine-line scenes can be presented singly and full-round.

Non-effigy bottles are usually globular. Because of the intrusion and alignment of the spout, the globe has two major spaces, parallel with the stirrup. Scenes or motifs placed centrally in those spaces have emphasis. A figure may be repeated on both sides, or two figures can stand in relation or opposition, each dominating a side of the bottle. Bottles can also be decorated with a continuous scene, sequential scenes, or pairs of scenes. A horizontal division is apt to indicate one world over the other, with the supernatural scene above (see Figure 8.1). Other divisions seem to indicate time and space, as well as order of importance. Roll-outs of complex scenes, especially those created by Donna McClelland, are of great value to researchers, who must, however, remember that the figures and objects have a different spatial relationship on flat paper than on a globular vessel.

In addition to changes in form and technique in Phases I through V, there is a progressive development of subject matter, which becomes increasingly complex (Benson 1983, 2003; Larco 1948, 2001). Phase I globular vessels often display a painted step motif; some bottles bear relief or painted birds or sea life. Other Early Moche subjects include effigy animals, seated humans, and monsters holding a human head and a knife; multiple-figure scenes are rare. In Phase III, compositions with two or more figures are more common, and new motifs appear, used in ways that may appear random compared to the formalized themes of Phase IV. Phase IV shows new characters and elaborations, and motifs appear in thematic clusters associated with the Moche belief system and its rites (see Chapter 10). A theoretical circle enclosing motifs for one Phase IV complex may overlap circles of other complexes. The complexes belong to the same system, and general rules apply, but the rules are not hard and fast.

The ceramics do not inform us entirely about the Moche worlds: they show beliefs, myths, and rites performed by certain people at certain times. At a glance, the array of themes—especially in the south—seems vast, but with study it becomes clear that subject matter is limited to a few themes.

CERAMIC WORKSHOPS

Some vessels were obviously painted by the same artist or in the same workshop. Donnan and McClelland (1999) identified 48 painters and schools in a sample of some 1,800 fine-line pots, and archaeologists have located several workshops: scattered small ones, household workshops, and specialized shops or complexes that produced for the local lord or for wider distribution.

In the far north, at Pampa Juárez, Yécala, near Piura, Krzysztof Makowski (1994b:108–109, 124–126), who has identified different Moche schools and painters, excavated part of a large field of ceramic ovens grouped in workshop clusters between a residential area and a cemetery. The ovens were of different sizes and forms to suit the firing of various products. Four Moche workshop areas have been found in the upper Piura Valley, two of which produced elite ceramics, probably including those at Loma Negra. A likely workshop at Pampa Grande, Lambayeque, investigated by Izumi Shimada (1994a:195–200, 2001; see also Shimada and Maguiña 1994:48–52), had Late Gallinazo and Moche III remains. At Pampa de los Incas, in the south, fragments of molds suggest a Phase IV workshop near the center (Wilson 1988).

A deep litter of ceramic remains indicated a workshop for large-scale production, mostly Phase IV, at Cerro Mayal, adjacent to Mocollope (Chicama Valley). Projects at Cerro Mayal from 1989 to 1997, directed by Glenn Russell and others (Jackson 2008; Russell and Jackson 2001; Russell, Leonard, and Briceño 1994, 1998), yielded finished pieces, molds (one- or two-piece and possibly multiple-piece),

polishing stones and other tools, production trash, unfired ceramics, and raw clay, as well as open pit and subterranean kilns. A burned floor was lined with ash from a shore plant (known today as "horse's tail"), probably as cover for firing; remains of algarrobo wood were also found. Ground-penetrating radar and a magnetometer were used to locate at least seven probable kilns. Modeling, molding, and decoration with painting, polishing, and incision were carried out. Cerro Mayal appears to have been a site of craft specialization, organized at a communal level with households near workshops, but with elite patronage. A variety of pottery was produced, including stirrup-spout bottles, floreros, and other bowl, urn, and bottle shapes. Musical instruments and figurines, both solid and hollow, were common. Mold production was found also at Pampa de Jaguey, up in the valley neck, where pottery of Phase III and IV was reported by César Gálvez and Jesús Briceño (2001).

At the Cerro Blanco Complex, a number of workshops have been found in the urban area (Chapdelaine, Bernier, and Pimentel 2004; Chapdelaine, Kennedy, and Uceda 1995; T. Topic 1982:265, 275–276; Uceda and Mujica 1997:12, 1998:10). A workshop near Huaca de la Luna, with three Phase IV occupation periods, was subject to depredation by huaqueros in the 1970s and 1980s, but was excavated in 1992 by Santiago Uceda and José Armas (1998). Excavating as thoroughly as the site's condition allowed, they found ovens, water storage facilities, jars, tools, molds, matrices, pieces of crude and fired clay, and objects—figurines, whistles, ocarinas, rattles, pendants, beads, and spindle whorls—presumably destined for religious and funerary activity at Huaca de la Luna. The complex contained both habitation and storage areas. A group of workshops southwest of Luna produced ceramics for ritual funerary offerings (Uceda and Mujica 2004:15).

A Phase V workshop for utilitarian wares at Galindo, near the neck of the Moche Valley, was a modest, stone-walled compound with an open pit to produce a partial reduced-firing atmosphere. The excavator, Garth Bawden (1996:98–101), suggests that it served both the community and long-distance trade. It was smaller than Cerro Mayal, and fine ceramics were scarce, but stirrup-spout vessels, floreros, plates, urns, bowls, and figurines were found. Associated with the workshop was a corral for llamas, probably used to transport raw materials and finished products, in addition to providing dung for fuel. A Phase V workshop found by Izumi Shimada (1994a:195–201, 2001:190–191) at Pampa Grande, in the Lambayeque drainage, consisted of a cluster of rooms with ash, mold fragments, and stone burnishers, as well as urns, bowls, floreros, figurine fragments, and remains of fine-line stirrup-spout bottles.

THE SOCIAL STATUS OF POTTERS AND PAINTERS

In 1949, after a survey of the Virú Valley, James Ford and Gordon Willey concluded that the ceramics there were made by a small group of priestly craftsmen, and that there seemed to be a connection between political domination and the use of ceramics as cult objects. In 1998 Uceda and Armas (1998:107–108; see also Chapdelaine 2001) deduced that a man and a woman buried in a workshop area in the Cerro Blanco Complex with impressive grave goods—her body was covered with fine ceramics—were involved in making ceramics for rituals at Huaca de la Luna, and that they had elite status for that reason. Two tombs excavated during the 2002 season in the heart of the urban area also are thought to be burials of a man and a woman who were ceramists. The burial has been described by Uceda, Armas, and Mario Millones (2008), who think it probable that pottery making was an inherited family occupation.

A number of Phase IV bottles depict a man wearing high-status, probably priestly garments and a headdress similar to one worn by a certain kind of distinguished male figure in Early Moche ceramics (Bankes 1980:19; Benson 2010: Fig. 22; Lapiner 1976: Figs. 255–258; Makowski 1994b: Fig. 142A; Sawyer 1966: Fig. 52). The Phase IV man holds a figural vessel in his left hand and a clay-working tool in his right. He is a potter and a man of relatively high rank. In Classic Maya art, where some polychrome vases and sculpture bear the glyphic name of the carver, royal personages are occasionally identified as the artists (M. Coe and Kerr 1997; Reents-Budet 1994:36–71). Maya art can also show gods and high-ranking humans as artists. In later Mesoamerica, artists were either

members of the nobility or had special status because of their ability. In the Inca world, a master artisan's title meant "possessing creation" or "creation holder" (Allen 1998:21; Helms 1993:52–61). In the Americas generally, pottery—made with earth, water, and fire—was precious, even sacred. For the Moche, the material was significant, the forms were symbolic, and a vessel not only recorded vital information, it was, in a sense, what it depicted. Pottery had life; therefore, its creator had the ability to create life. Given the numinous energy of ceramics and ritual objects, Moche craft specialists may have had shamanic status, especially painters of murals (Morales Gamarra 2003).

Moche ceramic traditions continue today. Contemporary potters of Mórrope, in the lower Lambayeque Valley, have been using the techniques of the ancient Moche (Shimada 1994a:197–201), as did Eduardo Calderón, in the Moche Valley, a shaman as well as a ceramist (Sharon 1972, 1978; Sharon and Donnan 1974).

METALLURGY

The Andes developed one of the great metallurgy traditions of the ancient world. Heather Lechtman (1993:262) points out that in the Old World metalworking was developed primarily for warfare, transport, and agriculture, but in the Andes, "metals performed . . . in the realm of the symbolic" (see also Carcedo 1998, 2000; Larco Hoyle 2001,II:128–165; Lavalle 1989; Lechtman 1979, 1980, 1984a, 1996). In the rugged mountains, without riding or draft animals, cavalry weapons and wheels were of no use, and the wooden foot plow was adequate for cultivation. Shields of wood or hide, slings, and wooden clubs sufficed as weapons, and most tools were of stone or bone. The Moche did have metal weapons and tools—*tumis* (an Inca word for knife), spears, shields, clubs, and spindle whorls—but these were used ritually and would have had symbolic significance even if used practically.

The Moche used metal to make ear, nose, and headdress ornaments, backflaps, belts, bracelets, anklets, necklace beads, and collars (or pectorals). They attached gilded-copper danglers with wires, and sewed platelets onto garments and banners. They

FIGURE 6.2 Burial mask with gilded copper and inlaid shell and stone, excavated from a tomb at Dos Cabezas. *Proyecto Arqueológico Dos Cabezas. Photograph by Christopher B. Donnan.*

also produced hollow figures, cups, bowls, tweezers, rattles, and bells. Lost-wax casting was rare in the Central Andes, but the Moche used it to create objects of varying shape and size called chisels, spatulas, and scepters. The "handles" or finials of one of these tools usually presents one or more figures, and the blades vary in width and thickness (Benson 1984a; Donnan 1978:18–19). Pre-Hispanic ritual objects commonly include a blade form.

The North Coast was a center for metallurgy, which had been established there by Cupisnique and possibly Chavín smiths (R. Burger 1992:55–56, 98–99, 1996; Castillo 2000a:27; Lothrop 1941, 1951 Shimada and Merkel 1991:81). Sheet gold and gold-plated copper objects are found in Cupisnique burials; some silver was worked, and at least a few objects were made of gold and silver. Moche smiths, however, produced some of the most spectacular and sophisticated work known in the pre-Hispanic Americas. They greatly advanced gold- and copper-based technology, but knowledge of Andean goldwork is limited, largely

because the Spaniards did a thorough job of "mining" gold objects in huacas and melting them down. Fray Reginaldo Lizarraga wrote, ca. AD 1600, that in the "famous big *huaca* made of little adobes" (Huaca del Sol) there was a great quantity of treasures of gold and silver: jars and other vessels and cups for drinking. An offering cache discovered by Max Uhle in Huaca del Sol included three gold figurines and a gold lizard pendant with turquoise inlay (Jones 1979; Kroeber 1944:133; Menzel 1977:39). At a cemetery near Huaca de la Luna, Uhle found copper objects in 15 graves, and gold objects in 3. In Dos Cabezas Tomb 2, Donnan recently excavated an almost life-sized metal burial mask with gilt-copper additions and shell and stone inlay (Figure 6.2).

In 1969 looters began to target hundreds of cemeteries around the northern end of Cerro Vicús, in the Piura Valley, and objects from the Loma Negra cemetery made of gold, silver, copper, and their combinations went into various collections (Figure 6.3). The Metropolitan Museum of Art set up a project, supervised by Julie Jones and Heather Lechtman, to locate, describe, study, and conserve Loma Negra objects (Jones 1979, 1993, 2001; Lapiner 1976:112–115, 148–161; Lechtman 1984b; Lechtman, Erlij, and Barry 1982; Schaffer 1985). The next exciting discovery, at Huaca Rajada Sipán, was the richness of the tombs excavated by Walter Alva. He initially found three intact tombs within the burial platform, with quantities of remarkable gilded-copper ornaments; other rich burials there have been excavated since (Alva 1994; Alva and Donnan 1993). Metalwork was found also in burials at La Mina (Narváez 1994), San José de Moro (Castillo 1996; Castillo and Donnan 1994b; Castillo et al. 2008), Huaca Cao Viejo (Franco 2009), and, recently, by Steve Bourget at Úcupe (Atwood 2010; *El Comercio*, 5 July 2008, 26 July 2008). Intensive looting may account for scarcity in the south, yet there does seem to be a stronger focus on metallurgy in the north.

Half-gold, half-silver objects appear at Huaca Cao Viejo, Loma Negra, and Huaca Rajada Sipán (see Figure 6.3); the gold-silver combination is thought to have male-female, sun-moon, right-left symbolism, as well as dualistic significance (Alva 1994: Fig. 90; Alva and Donnan 1993:221–223; *El Comercio*, 18 May 2006; see also Classen 1993:22–23; Cordy-Collins 2001a:45–46; Diez-Canseco 1994: Figs. 119, 120; Lechtman

FIGURE 6.3 Loma Negra silver nose ornament with gold fox-snake heads and danglers. *The Metropolitan Museum of Art, New York, 1979.206.1225.*

1996:38–39). Most of the nose ornaments buried with the very important Lady of Huaca Cao Viejo are half-silver, half-gold and often, like many nose ornaments, show two figures (Franco 2009). There were also pairings of gold and silver objects. The Lord of Sipán was buried with a gold ingot in his right hand, a silver one in his left, and a necklace with peanut-shaped beads, half of them gold, half silver (Alva and Donnan 1993:63).

METAL RESOURCES AND TECHNOLOGY

In modern times Peru has been the largest producer of gold in Latin America and one of the largest in the world. Most Andean rivers contain some gold: the well-known placer gold sources are on the eastern slopes, but western slopes also have gold and silver (Bawden 1996:96; Guffroy, Kaulicke, and Makowski 1989; Hocquenghem 1993; Lechtman 1976, 1980; Netherly 1977:37–38; Shimada 1994a:43–44). Most North Coast placer gold contains silver; silver could also be extracted from sulfite ores. The Moche panned

gold from most of the rivers in the Piura Valley, and possibly also from the Lambayeque and Zaña valleys. Gold sources exist near Kuntur Wasi, a Cupisnique site up the Jequetepeque River, and also on the way across the mountains; these could have been Moche sources—and possible reasons for contact with Cajamarca.

Copper was mined with stone picks from shallow deposits along the margins of foothill valleys, and almost every North Coast valley has abundant deposits of copper-bearing minerals. Abandoned copper mines near Pampa Grande (Lambayeque) have pre-Hispanic associations, and other ancient mines and smelting sites have been identified. Ingots produced by smelting would have been taken to workshops near (or at) urban complexes, processed into sheet metal, and worked. Copper was smelted in a simple furnace with a forced draft of air provided by wind and men with blowtubes, which were probably cane shafts with ceramic tips (Donnan 1973b; Shimada 1994a:200–206, 1995; Shimada and Merkel 1991). Llama dung and charcoal from algarrobo wood were burned for smelting.

Metal was usually beaten with faceted stone hammers into a thin sheet and then worked by cutting, annealing, hammering over a mold, forming a *repoussé* or embossed design, crimping, or incising, and by combinations of these techniques (Carcedo 1998, 2000; Diez-Canseco 1994; King 2000; Lechtman 1996; Netherly 1977:37–38, 247–249; Shimada and Merkel 1991:81; Uceda, Mujica, and Morales 1996:13, 15). Three-dimensional forms were built from sheet metal using soldering and various welding techniques, and joining the sheets with metal wires, tab-and-slot fastenings, or solder.

Moche metal workshops have proved difficult to locate. Five ovens have only recently been discovered at Sipán (*El Comercio*, 2 September 2007b); remains of three ovens have been excavated at the Cerro Blanco Complex (Chapdelaine 2001:71; Uceda and Mujica 1997:13). A copper workshop existed at Pampa Grande, near the ceramic shops (Shimada 1994a:200–206, 2001:187–190); a Galindo workshop apparently produced mostly copper objects (Bawden 1996:96–97). Shops at those places were located in settings with restricted access in important parts of the sites. A metal workshop was found near ceramic shops at Pampa Juaréz, Piura Valley; gold and copper sources were not far away (Makowski 1994b:109, Figs. 481, 484).

Copper was the backbone of Moche metalworking (Lechtman 1996; see also Carcedo 1998; Lechtman 1979, 1980; Shimada and Merkel 1991). Smiths experimented with copper-arsenic alloys to create a copper-arsenic solder, possibly the earliest Andean use of this bronze alloy, which was produced in considerable quantity by the start of the Middle Horizon, the period that followed the Moche era. Arsenic-bearing ores were available in the lower Lambayeque Valley and elsewhere. Color was significant, and copper was the medium of color change; alloys allowed color variation and richness. Lechtman (1996) points out that depletion metallurgy is a reflection of cultural attitudes: it was meaningful that surface color manifested the innate gold or silver, the essential ingredient within the body of the object. Surface copper could be removed by hammering, annealing, and oxidation.

Few Moche objects are of pure gold. Instead smiths developed what the Spaniards called *tumbaga*, an alloy of about one part copper to four parts gold. Gold with copper and/or silver was malleable and also stronger,

tougher, and more fracture-resistant than gold alone. Tumbaga has a low melting point and is harder than copper but just as flexible. The surface is almost like that of pure gold. Lechtman (1984a) states that electrochemical replacement plating and depletion gilding—the most sophisticated Andean gilding procedures—can be credited to Moche smiths who used mixtures of corrosive minerals available on the desert coast. She found that most Loma Negra metal objects were of hammered sheet copper, cut and joined to produce three-dimensional forms, and covered with very thin coatings of gold or silver. Working in a lab at the Massachusetts Institute of Technology, she ascertained that the thin coatings were relatively uniform, that heat had been applied in the coating process, and that gilding had not been accomplished by any usual modern technique. Lechtman and a team then used heat and anciently available materials in an attempt to re-create the Moche technique (see Carcedo 1998; Lechtman 1984b, 1993:264–267; Lechtman, Erlij, and Barry 1982).

Maiken Fecht (in Alva 1994:238), the conservator of the Sipán objects at the Römisch-Germanisches Zentralmuseum, Mainz, observes that Sipán smiths succeeded not only in preparing refined alloys of tumbaga and finishing surfaces by abrasion, they apparently achieved an electromechanical process for making small objects with exact details, and they joined parts by soldering small, delicate pieces. They also engraved and chiseled designs. Of the objects restored, 70 were of tumbaga, 40 with gold and 30 with silver. Although Sipán silver objects, and many Loma Negra pieces, were covered with a dull green coating when found, after cleaning, they gleam. Almost half of the Sipán objects were gilded, with some of the gilded-copper pieces as thin as a sheet of paper, like those at Loma Negra.

Given their ability to transform raw ore into gleaming crowns, scepters, masks, and pectorals that were beautiful, almost magical symbols of power, Moche metalsmiths must have had particularly high, perhaps shamanic, status. Nicholas Saunders (1999:246) has observed that in pre-Columbian cultures, "Making shining objects was an act of making transformative creation." In a high-status burial at Dos Cabezas, Donnan (2001, 2007) found metalworking chisels in the hands of a richly accoutered corpse.

LAPIDARY, CARVING, AND FEATHER WORK

One of the extraordinary metal objects found in the tomb of the Old Lord of Sipán is a figure 60 cm high displaying complicated metalwork and intricate inlays of shell (Figure 6.4). Although related to other frontal figures with owl necklaces from Sipán, it is larger and more complex in both craftsmanship and iconography, with its skyband headdress, brow mask, and clawed hands and feet.

Metal objects were often inlaid with shell or semi-precious stones that usually came from mountain sources: turquoise, chrysocolla, sodalite, malachite, pyrite, and quartz. Inlay was usually attached with tree resin (perhaps algarrobo gum) to a wooden base, often in intricate mosaic. Round ear ornaments, an elite but nonspecific type, may be the most common inlaid objects; they were often framed with gold beads and sometimes had gold backing. Elaborate examples—with turquoise inlay and particularly intricate gold-work portraying a ruler with weapons, an owl neck-lace, and two accompanying warriors—come from Burial 1 at Huaca Rajada Sipán (Figure 6.5), where there were also inlaid gold nose ornaments (Alva 1994; Alva and Donnan 1993: cover, 83–87). Small figures and objects of stone, bone, antler, or shell had inlaid details. Pectorals and bracelets were made of hundreds of tiny shell (often *Spondylus*), turquoise, and/or cop-per beads, and some metal and lapidary objects were made with movable parts or built up from separate parts. Rock crystal was carved, and various stones and shells were worked for pendants and other objects. White *Conus* shell and pink *Spondylus* came from Ecuador, and mother-of-pearl (*Pteria peruviana*) was present on the North Coast.

A workshop for bead carving was found at the Cerro Blanco Complex urban site (Chapdelaine, Bernier, and Pimentel 2004:168), and traces of a *Conus* workshop were found on top of Cerro Blanco (Bourget 1997b). Remains of a shell workshop were located near metal shops at Pampa Juárez (Makowski 1994b:109), and there is evidence of *Spondylus* at Pampa Grande where metal was worked (Shimada 1994a:213–216, 2001:183). Shimada, in reference to Moche objects that combine materials, has raised questions about craftsmen and workshops: Were

FIGURE 6.4 Large gilded copper and silver figure with shell and stone inlay from the tomb of the Old Lord of Sipán (Tomb 3). 56.5 cm high. *Courtesy Museo Tumbas Reales de Sipán, Lambayeque.*

shops combined? Did one artisan perform many tasks? Did specialized artisans move about? A series of rooms that he excavated at Pampa Grande suggests close relationships between weaving, lapidary, and copper working.

Inlay appears sometimes on wooden objects, including carved staffs of office. One staff and/or dig-ging stick from the tomb of the Warrior Priest was made with complex iconographic carving and inlay (Strong and Evans 1952:156–159, Plates XXIII–XXV; Kubler 1948). Because of the importance of agricul-ture, a digging stick can be an official staff, and staffs are also associated with war clubs. The most impres-sive staffs yet found come from the very large and rich funerary bundle of the Lady of Huaca Cao Viejo: a pair, 2 m high, made of wood encased in gilded copper (Franco 2009).

Plain wooden figures, many of which were preserved in guano on offshore islands, often depict warriors or captives (see Chapter 11). The largest wooden object now known, excavated on an upper level of Huaca Cao Viejo, is an over-life-sized figure of a man standing on a base; its carved headdress takes the form of two large crested animals facing each other (see Chapter 7; also Franco 2001:18–20, 2009; Franco and Gálvez 2003; Franco, Gálvez, and Sánchez 2001b:161, Foto 23, 2003: Lám. 19.5; Gálvez and Briceño 2001:155, Fig. 26). Carved from a single, 2.5 m slab of *lúcumo* wood, it was painted and had several sections covered with metal; garments may have been added on occasion. It was found sealed in adobes, high in the huaca, where it may have been installed as an idol, or brought from another setting for ritual burial during rebuilding.

Many tropical birds have vivid plumage of symbolic colors: sun yellow, sky blue, leaf green, blood red, black and white—all of which probably had various associations. Feathered objects are rarely preserved, but the Warrior Priest's offerings included

a bird headdress sewn into gauzelike cloth, a green parrot-feather fan, and other feathered objects (Strong and Evans 1952:159, 166). The tomb of the Lord of Sipán produced copper headdress ornaments with remains of flamingo and other feathers attached (Alva and Donnan 1993:106–109), and many metal objects from Loma Negra show feather impressions (Schaffer 1985). There may also have been garments like those from Nasca, Huari, and Chimu sites, with brilliant feathers sewn into cloth (Conklin et al. 1996; A. Rowe 1984). Some tunic designs on ceramics may represent feathers, and feather ornaments are shown on headdresses of many prominent figures.

The status of Moche featherworkers is unknown, but a sixteenth-century Spanish account of Naymlap, a post-Moche royal (perhaps mythic) personage, recounts that he settled sites in the Lambayeque Valley (J. Rowe 1948:37, 47; Donnan 1990). One of his courtiers was the Purveyor of Feather-Cloth Garments, and one town was settled by Naymlap's feather-cloth maker, suggesting high status for feather craftsmen.

In 1999 a spectacular mixed-media confection was excavated from a burial offering in Huaca de la Luna. It has a gold-encased, wooden feline head and a long body of hide and cotton cloth with gilded silver, gilded copper, sea shells (*Conus*), feathers, cinnabar, and resin (Asmat and Fernández 2002; Asmat, Morales, and Fernández 2004; Morales Gamarra 2004; Morales, Asmat, and Fernández 2000; Tufinio 2004b). A similar object, with a human face, has recently been found in the tomb of the Lady of Huaca Cao Viejo (Figure 6.6) (Franco and Gálvez 2010: Fig. 31).

CLOTH

The high value that cloth had in the Andes is hard to imagine (Conklin 1979, 1996; Larco 2001, II:182–194; Lavalle and Gónzalez 1991; Lechtman 1984a, 1993, 1996; Millaire 2008; Murra 1962; A. Rowe 1984). On the south coast, Paracas mummy bundles were dressed and redressed, over time, in new, elaborately embroidered garments. On the North Coast, later Chimu burials were rich in fine garments. Later still, the Inca rulers gave cloth as gifts and important offerings, paid soldiers in cloth, and controlled the use of camelid wool. Weaving was not only a major art, but a symbolic process,

FIGURE 6.5 Gold and turquoise ear ornament from the tomb of the Lord of Sipán (Tomb 1). *Courtesy Museo Tumbas Reales de Sipán, Lambayeque.*

FIGURE 6.6 A garment with gold elements to be worn on the back. Found in the burial of the Lady of Huaca Cao Viejo. *Courtesy of Régulo Franco Jordán and the Proyecto Arqueológico Complejo El Brujo.*

Morales, Solórzano and Asmat 1998). Sadly, because of salts in the sands and occasional serious flooding, Moche cloth is rare, although some is turning up in recent excavations (Fernández 2001; Franco 2009; Jiménez 2000), and impressions left in clay and other materials are providing information about the textiles that once lay next to them.

Fabric art would have begun with manipulation of bromeliads, cane, and sedges or rushes in cordage and nonfabric confections, with twining and weaving to follow. Fiber for cloth was usually spun on a handheld spindle with a whorl of ceramic, stone, wood, or, rarely, metal; the whorl usually had symbolic form or carving.

Cotton, widely used in Moche textiles, occurs naturally in colors from white to grayish mauve to dark brown; it does not take dyes as easily as does animal fiber. Vegetable dyes and a few mineral dyes were used in the Andes (Jiménez 2000:I, 79; A. Rowe 1984; Vreeland 1992b). The common blue color was indigo, from the plant *Indigofera tinctoria*, and could be varied from pale blue to nearly black. Various plants produce yellows, oranges, and browns. Some reds come from the root of a madder. Cochineal red, from the scales of a cactus-feeding insect, is found in the Americas, but its use in ancient Peru has been questioned. Nevertheless, some red dyes have been analyzed as cochineal-derived, and it is present in Peru today. Threads could also be colored red with cinnabar (mercuric sulfide). Camelid and human urine and various acids were used as mordants in dying (and in depletion gilding); ferrous mordants were used for black.

Alpaca wool is second to cotton as a fiber in Moche textiles (Uceda, Mujica, and Morales 1996:13; V. Vásquez et al. 2003; see also Alva 1994; Alva and Donnan 1993:22; Bruhns 1994:157; Conklin 1979:168–169; Donnan and Donnan 1997; Jiménez 2000:78; Prümers 2000; A. Rowe 1984:25; Schaffer 1985:96–101). Although llamas and alpacas were present on the coast, Moche wool may have come from the highlands as yarn, for most of it was spun in a counterclockwise (Z) direction, a highland trait, whereas Moche cotton was spun clockwise (S). Spindles found on the coast usually hold cotton yarn. Needles and spindle whorls indicate a textile production compound at the Cerro Blanco Complex (Chapdelaine 2000:70–71; T. Topic 1982:276), and Shimada (1994a:206–210, 2001:184–187,

and everything about cloth was significant, so woven garments and bags could indicate rank and activity. William Conklin tells us that in the Andean world, meaning was conveyed by textile structure as well as by images, not only in the types of woven cloth but sometimes in variations in the weaving. Cloth surely decorated temples and shrines, and many textiles were placed in Moche burials (see Chapter 12). Conklin suggests that some large Moche textiles might have been cosmological charts used to denote sacred space (Conklin 2008). Paintings on the walls of huacas often seem to imitate woven cloth (Morales Gamarra 2003;

194) found evidence for cotton processing and a possible weaving workshop at Pampa Grande.

Backstrap looms were common in the Andes and are still in use there. One end is attached to the weaver's waist, the other to a post or tree, and the weaver's movements provide the necessary tensions. With this simple equipment, Andean weavers produced some of the most complex textiles of the preindustrial world. One Moche florero shows weavers, usually identified as women, at work in the presence of supervisors (Donnan and McClelland 1999: Fig. 4.94; Millaire 2008), but both men and women can be spinners or weavers in the Andes. Moche weaving seems to have been a female activity; implements for spinning and weaving are found in female graves and inside houses (women's space). On the north coast today, women not only spin and weave the cloth, but also cultivate the cotton (Bruhns 1994:159; Conklin 1996:324; Donnan 1995:150; A. Rowe 1984:19; Vreeland 1992b).

Moche cloth is found in plain weave, twill, gauze, tapestry, and double cloth; when there are designs, they are usually woven into the fabric. Woven rectangles of cloth were used to make garments, including short and long shirts, or tunics, sewn at the sides, with neck slits usually created during weaving. A sleeved shirt was found at Pacatnamu; the Moche may have invented the sleeve, which is a later North Coast trait. In some cases, a sleeveless shirt is wide enough to provide a sleevelike drape over the upper arm. Capes and loincloths are also found. Figures depicted on ceramics appear to be wearing something like a kilt. Donnan and Donnan (1997) call the soft headdresses of priestly figures "headcloths"; known examples are made from gauze and a decorative tapestry band. Some of the most elaborate weaving is found on bands and bags of tapestry and cloth with supplemental weft designs.

Pacatnamu, with moderate preservation conditions, has yielded a fairly large collection of Moche textiles, predominantly cotton. Heinrich Ubbelohde-Doering (1967:28–29, Plates 72–73; see also Conklin 1979) excavated a grave containing Phase V ceramics and many textiles, notably fragments of a large, elaborate, slit tapestry with wool weft and cotton warp, and a primary design of an animated *Strombus* shell. One textile fragment depicts a supernatural figure in a temple. Donnan and Donnan published 181 textiles, all but two from burials. Many are plain weave, and most are

incomplete and in poor condition. Widths of rectangular panels average 40 to 50 cm, a convenient size for a backstrap loom. Garments are identified as shirts, loincloths, headcloths, long capes, and bags. At nearby Dos Cabezas, textile fragments with vivid colors have been recently excavated in burials (Jiménez 2000). A rare large textile excavated at El Castillo de Santa, in the Santa Valley, shows a rite related to the harvesting of yuca (Figure 6.7; Chapdelaine and Pimentel 2003).

Remains of textiles from Huaca Rajada Sipán have been examined and treated in the Römisch-Germanisches Zentralmuseum (Alva 2001; Alva and Donnan 2003:214, Figs. 17, 243, 244). The conservator, Heiko Prümers (2000), noting disintegration of wool fiber in some 60 textiles from the unfavorable conditions of Tomb I, estimates that a third of the cloth there was lost. In Tomb III, fragments of eight tapestry-weave textiles were bunched near the left leg of the wrapped major burial; three had elaborate tapestry-weave designs. Capes beneath the corpse included gauzes. Another textile from the same context combines two kinds of warp-faced twill with two

FIGURE 6.7 Phase III textile showing a yuca (manioc) harvest, from an excavation at El Castillo de Santa, in the Santa Valley. *Courtesy of Claude Chapdelaine.*

kinds of weft-faced twill in a design of fish; this may be unique for ancient Andean weaving technique. All decorated textiles in the tomb were lined, mostly with cotton plain weave with double warps and wefts; lining was previously unknown in Moche garments.

Few textiles have been found in the Moche Valley. María Montoya (2004; see also Conklin and Versteylen 1978) reported the discovery of seven textile fragments in a tomb at Huaca de la Luna. At Galindo, textile remains had cotton wefts and warp for the ground weave, and bands formed by supplemental wefts of wool (Conklin 1979).

PERFORMING ARTS

A chapter on art should include the performing art of ritual. For preliterate people, communication through movement, gesture, dance, and sound is particularly significant and symbolic. The presence of Moche music is attested to not only by depictions on the ceramics, but by fragments of musical instruments that Uhle (Menzel 1977:38–39, 60, 64) encountered in offering caches in Huaca de la Luna and a platform of Huaca del Sol. They have also been found in urban area house remains (Chapdelaine 1998) and in burials, offerings, and workshops in other valleys (Donnan 1973a; Russell and Jackson 2001:166). Ceramic vessels sometimes show a sea lion or a sea bird holding or playing an instrument, and deer are sometimes depicted dancing on their hind legs (which they do naturally when they stand on their hind legs to browse high foliage).

The Moche played panpipes of clay or cane; flutes of cane, ceramic, bone, or stone; trumpets of clay; whistles or ocarinas, as well as whistling vessels, of ceramic; and various bells, rattles, and drums (Bourget 2001a:107–109; Donnan 1973a:95–97, 1982:99; Hocquenghem 1980a; Jiménez Borja 1950–1951; Larco 2001, II:166–181; Olsen 1992). Many objects are jewelry, accessories, vessels, or figurines, but they are also rattles, whistles, or bells, adding sound to events in which they were worn or used. Metal rattles or bells could be sewn onto garments; rattles attached to the legs of dancers in ceramic scenes are thought to be dried endocarps of seeds or perhaps metal or ceramic pieces or shells (see Figure 9.6; Jiménez Borja 1955; Donnan 1982[1983]:89–90; Hocquenghem 1987:122; Muelle

1935:77). (Twentieth-century dancers in Cajamarca used seed rattles.) Knife-shaped gold or copper warrior's backflaps, found in Sipán burials, can include a rattle, and some copper spatulas, or scepters, also produce sounds. Rattles are usually in pairs but can be used separately and are often depicted held by ceramic figures. Paired rattles were found in the grave of the Señor de Úcupe (Steve Bourget, personal communication, 2010).

Instruments had rank, with panpipes at the top of the Moche hierarchy. They are played by a major supernatural, held by the largest human figures in a scene (Figure 6.8), and played by the dead (the ancestors). They can also be shown floating in the air above an important figure. In scenes with several musicians, pipers are usually the largest and most elaborately dressed. Some appear in pairs with a tie between the panpipes. Dale Olsen (1992) suggests that the instruments had supplementary scales, allowing two pipers to alternate and interlock notes to form melodies that one player could not achieve. Trumpets, straight or recurved, have next-highest status. Actual trumpets are found with the bell taking the form of a snake head or a well-dressed human warrior, who may hold panpipes; a human figure can be appliquéd on the side of a trumpet, and similar figures appear as whistles (Benson 1982b). A pair of flutes and a drum are often played together, as if a fife and drum corps served special occasions. Sometimes an effigy or deck figure holds a drum or, more rarely, a vertical flute (*quena*). Vertical and horizontal drums are played by a man, a skeletal figure, or an animal-headed being. Rattle poles, or staffs, hung with what look like shells or metal disks, are carried by figures in procession (Benson 1972: Fig. 5–16); these objects appear with other instruments and appear capable of producing sounds. Arturo Jiménez Borja (1950–1951:48) suggests that the staff was pounded on the ground to sound the rattles. In the seventeenth century, Pablo José de Arriaga (1968 [1621]: 89–90) saw people dancing in a harvest rite with maize stalks tied to torn-off branches; the stalks were then burned. Some dancing skeletal figures on low-relief vessels hold objects that look like corn stalks (Donnan 1982:99; Kutscher 1950: Fig. 34, 1983: Abb. 153).

Trumpets of gastropod shell, often *Strombus*, are still widely used in the Andes to announce or punctuate a rite or event. Phase IV ceramic scenes commonly

FIGURE 6.8 Scene showing large, elaborately dressed figures playing panpipes, and smaller figures playing trumpets. A conch trumpet floats to the left. *Fowler Museum of Cultural History, University of California, Los Angeles. Drawing by Donna McClelland.*

FIGURE 6.9 Priestly dancers holding hands as they approach a richly dressed man wearing a *tumi* and disk headdress. *Museo Nacional de Arqueología, Antropología e Historia del Perú. Drawing by Donna McClelland.*

show a conch trumpet (*pututo*) in the context of the coca rite (see Chapter 10). It is rarely seen with the instruments described above and seems to have a different kind of role, although one does appear floating at the side of Figure 6.8.

Early Spaniards described Inca dances that used a rope or cord (Zuidema 1992:21, 23; see also Betanzos 1996 [1551]: Chap. 31; Hocquenghem [citing Molina] 1987:122–123). Some dancers on Moche bottles hold a long strip of cloth; in processions without the cloth, participants may hold hands (Figure 6.9; see also Chapter 9). Murals at Huaca de la Luna and Huaca

Cao Viejo show hand-holding figures, and figures in a Pañamarca mural may be dancing with a ribbon (Franco, Gálvez, and Vásquez 1994: Fig. 4.12, 2001b: Foto 5; Schaedel 1951:154, 1967:114; see also Bonavia 1985:53–59; Classen 1993:77–78; Muelle 1936). Donnan (1982) points out that the ribbon can be held either in front or behind, and that it allows more body movement than hand-holding. Like other artists and artisans, musicians and dancers surely had special status. Music and dance were significant elements in rites of power; even a supernatural being can be seen dancing (Donnan 1982: Fig. 8).

CHAPTER SEVEN

The Snake-Belt God and the Monsters

A PAN-ANDEAN CONCEPT of a cosmic god or primary supernatural had long continuity, even though descriptions varied somewhat from one culture to another, and even within a culture. Despite my reluctance to use the word *god*, it seems that a few of the supernatural beings depicted by the Moche can be considered deities. One is a figure with two snakelike projections that appears on Huaca Prieta fabrics (Bird, Hyslop, and Skinner 1985); also frontal images at Chavín de Huantar (see Figure 2.3), Tiahuanaco, and Huari are generally similar to a major Moche supernatural image (Benson 1972, 1975:105; Burger 1992:150; Campana 1994:143–145, Fig. 52; Campana and Morales 1997; Makowski 1996, 2000; Moore 1996:131–133; Rostworowski 1996:21–60; J. Tello 1923). The Cupisnique/Chavín supernatural beings seem to have evolved into Moche supernaturals with varying aspects in early and late, northern and southern forms, notably two that I will call "the Snake-belt God," primarily a southern deity, and the generally northern Decapitator, or X Sacrificer, who, I believe, became the owl-related, war-and-sacrifice god in the south, the Plate-shirt God (see Chapter 8).

I first called the Snake-belt God the "fanged" god, following Strong and Evans (1952). Fangs often identify supernatural or sacralized beings, but other beings also have fangs or feline canines, and so I later called this being "the Snake-belt God," as have a number of other authors; however, other supernaturals occasionally have a similar belt, the belt does not always have a snake head, and it is not exactly a belt. Thus it is not a perfect name, but it seems to me the most appropriate one available, and after a period of calling him "the major god," I went back to it. Rafael Larco

Hoyle called him "Ai-Apaec," a name known in the region in later times. The Moche god was ancestral to Ai-apaec and may have been called by that name, but I do not use it because it refers primarily to a later being. "Wrinkle Face," the name proposed by Christopher Donnan and Donna McClelland, is currently favored, but I find it inappropriate because in early effigy versions his face rarely has wrinkles; middleperiod versions, on fine-line bottles, can be wrinkled on one side of the bottle and plain or painted on the other; and sometimes the face is half and half. Only in Phase V does the face seem to be consistently wrinkled. Jürgen Golte (1993:50, 1994b), who calls the god "Quismique" (old one) (Salas 2002:32), describes him as looking sometimes old, sometimes young. He may be older and more wrinkled in one scene, and younger, or regenerated, in another. Wrinkles might emphasize his ancestral aspect, or might have been caused by immersion in the sea; they are not a consistent attribute of the Snake-belt God (although total consistency is, of course, not to be expected).

THE CRESTED ANIMAL

Also present in the mythic scenes are several so-called monsters that presumably had roles in Moche origin myths. Virtually all monsters can be seen holding a sacrificial knife and a trophy head. The monsters behead only human beings, whereas the Snake-belt God grips a monster head and rarely beheads humans. Most monsters appear in confrontation with the Snake-belt God, but they can also share some of his attributes.

The best-known monster is a quadruped variously called Moon Animal, Moon Monster, Moon-Eater, Lunar Dog, or Crested Animal (Mackey and Vogel 2003; see also Bankes 1980:24; Benson 1985, 1997b, 2008; Donnan 1978:No. 138; Donnan and McClelland 1999; Isbell 1997:233, Fig. 7.6B; Kutscher 1983; Lieske 2001:171–177; Menzel 1977:62–63; Narváez 2001:131–133; Schaedel 1948). The Crested Animal, as I will call it, normally stands or crouches on a long, curving element and has a matching crest stretching back from its head (Figure 7.1; see also Figure 2.6). In different depictions it resembles different animals, but it most often seems to derive from a feline, fox, or dog, although it can be rather serpentine, and its tongue can be bifid. Anne-Louise Schaffer (1981) notes that it often has bird claws, a trait of some non-avian creatures in Cupisnique/Chavín art. The variable head is usually of the type that serves as a finial on many Moche objects in numinous scenes—on rafts, litters, the god belt, and the cord end of a sacrificial knife—to indicate aliveness. Most often the head looks mammalian and foxlike. Some Loma Negra metal heads (finials or headdress ornaments) are clearly foxes, although many snouts resemble those of certain dogs. The head sometimes looks like that of a constrictor that lives on the North Coast (Bourget 1994a:134, 136–137; Jesús Briceño Rosario, personal communication, 2000; Pimentel and Álvarez 2000; Sharon 2003). I will call heads with snake tongues and canine ears "fox-snake" heads.

The Crested Animal does not confront the Snake-belt God as other monsters do, and the god never beheads it. It rarely interacts with other creatures, as do most Moche monsters; occasionally, it holds a human trophy head. Prominent in Early Moche contexts, it seems to have non-Moche origins, and its composition is outside the usual Moche artistic canon. The animal does not appear in Cupisnique art, but similar creatures exist on Salinar and Gallinazo ceramics (Donnan and McClelland 1999: Fig. 2.1; Mackey and Vogel 2003). Very common in Recuay art (see Figure 7.2), it is usually thought to have originated in the highlands, where it is normally an accessory figure or it appears on a vessel in multiples. The creature had high status in Early Moche, when it was made into an effigy bottle (in one example, with elaborate shell inlay) and used as the single motif on painted vases.

In later, fine-line images it often stands on a crescent, surrounded by star shapes, hence its designation as a moon animal. In Recuay, however, it lacks moon associations, according to Raphael Reichert (1979 and personal communication; see also Bruhns 1976; Grieder 1978; Kutscher 1983: Abbn. 309A-311), as it does in Moche Phase I. It had not been found with sky symbols on objects dating before Phase III until Carol Mackey and Melissa Vogel (2003) discovered a moon-associated example in a Phase II context; they believe the creature had coastal origins. It may be a supernatural from a very early creation myth, or an adopted god or ancestor spirit of a group conquered by the Moche.

Crested animals often occur in pairs. The large wooden figure discovered in Huaca Cao Viejo was topped by a pair facing each other (Franco 2001:18–20, 2009; Gálvez and Briceño 2001:154, Fig. 26; Ídolo Moche 2001). The Crested Animal—or pair—may have been emblematic of the valley, the site, or its ruler. Among a number of representations, it is repeated in paintings on a wall in an important space in Huaca Cao Viejo. A Phase I effigy vessel, probably also from the Chicama Valley, presents a seated man with a tunic drawn over his knees; the tunic designs comprise facing versions of the Crested Animal (see Figure 1.4).

Recent excavation revealed these creatures painted in squares on a wall near the elaborate burial of the Lady of Huaca Cao Viejo (see Figure 12.3). Among the many nose ornaments found in her grave, some had a pair of crested animals as the major motif (*El Comercio* 18 May 2006; Franco 2009; Williams 2006). Crested animals are also paired on some Loma Negra pieces and in ceramics from Dos Cabezas (see Figure 7.1).

OTHER MOCHE MONSTERS

Other monsters depicted by the Moche include a dragonlike creature with claws, a longish (probably reptilian) body, a textured or serrated back, and an animal head at the end of its snaky tail (Figure 7.2) (Donnan and McClelland 1999: Figs. 4.52, 6.16; Kutscher 1983: Abbn. 10, 13–17, 226, 258; Lavalle 1989: Fig. 7; Lieske 2001:163–166; Makowski et al. 1994: Fig.

FIGURE 7.1 Early Moche style bottle from Dos Cabezas, one of two slightly different ones depicting the Crested Animal. *Proyecto Arqueológico Dos Cabezas. Photograph by Christopher B. Donnan.*

291). A creature with a head on its tail is common in Cupisnique/Chavín teratology (R. Burger 1992: Fig. 142). The Moche Dragon rarely has a bifid tongue, but the tail head does. A dragon with a headless tail is repeated in reliefs of the last construction phase of Platform I at Huaca de la Luna, where it holds a trophy head (see Figures 5.3 and 13.1; Huaca de la Luna–Moche, Perú, 2009).

The Conch (or *Strombus*) Monster resembles the Dragon with a gastropod shell added; it may have a forked tongue (Bourget 1990; Kutscher 1983: Abbn. 29–45, 257; Lieske 2001:145–149). Often mostly a shell with head, foot, and tail, it can be a mammal or a scaly reptile with a shell attached. This monster, which likely first appeared in Phase IV, was pictured in a Pañamarca mural (Bonavia 1985:53; Bonavia and Makowski 1999: Fig. 26). Usually portrayed alone, not holding a trophy head, in one image it hovers threateningly over a small human with clasped hands and traits related to the coca rite (Donnan and McClelland 1999:4.25); in another case an elaborately dressed Snake-belt God is about to behead the monster's tail (Figure 7.3). Cactus and tillandsia plants appear with the Dragon and the Conch Monster. It is possible that gastropods—sea conchs and land snails, particularly—had significance, in part, because they demonstrate animism: the hard, houselike shell has a creature inside, which Moche art expands into a large being. Conch shells were modified for use as ritual trumpets

FIGURE 7.2 The Snake-belt God, in different dress, appears with the Moche Dragon (*right*) and Split Crest (*left*). *Staatliche Museen zu Berlin—Preussischer Kulturbesitz, Ethnologisches Museum, VA 18395, Baessler Collection. Drawing by Donna McClelland, after Kutscher 1983: Abb. 258.*

FIGURE 7.3 A splendidly dressed Snake-belt God preparing to cut off the Conch Monster's snake-head tail. *Staatliche Museen zu Berlin—Preussischer Kulturbesitz, Ethnologisches Museum. Drawing by Donnan McClelland.*

and also imitated as ceramic bottles. The Moche people would not often have seen *Strombus* in the sea because it came from the warm waters of Ecuador; it was probably acquired by trade or possibly brought south naturally by El Niño events. Representations of it might have been based largely on land snails.

The Snake-belt God also appears in conflict with two creatures that have human bodies and monster heads; both can have traits of the Snake-belt God. There are variants for both, and sometimes it is hard to tell which monster is which, or if one is a variation on the Crested Animal. I have come to no conclusions about these creatures. "Split Crest Beast" is the name given to one of them by Alana Cordy-Collins (1992: Fig. 9; Nicholson and Cordy-Collins 1979:234); Donnan and McClelland (1999) have called it "Split Top"; I will use "Split Crest." Often in conflict with the Snake-belt God, it never wins; in many scenes the god grasps it by one or both crest extensions (Figure 7.2) or holds up its severed head. The beast is common in fine-line ceramics and appears also in Loma Negra metallurgy (Donnan 1978: Nos. 151, 152; Donnan and McClelland 1999: Figs. 2.21, 3.22, 6.9, 6.14; Kutscher 1983: Abbn. 213, 214, 217–219, 232, 258; Lapiner 1976: Figs. 360, 365; Larco Hoyle 1945b:21, lower left; Lavalle 1989: Fig. 26; Lieske 2001:158–161). It has been identified as a fish demon because it often has apparent fins, but Schaffer (1981) points out a scene with this creature that shows tillandsia, and I have noticed another with cacti and a fox in an apparent upvalley

location. No Split Crest scene that I know of is obviously set in the sea, so either the "fins" are not fins, or this is a sea demon that came ashore, possibly for human victims.

The Snake-belt God's other human-bodied opponent is called "Curly Top" by Donnan and McClelland (1999: Fig. 2.24), *personaje pez* (fish person) by Luis Jaime Castillo (1989:99–124), and *pez borracho* (drunken fish) by Steve Bourget (1994b; see also Kutscher 1983: Abbn. 215, 216; Larco Hoyle 1945b:21, upper right; Makowski et al. 1994:142; Schaffer 1981). Curly Top often has fins as well as protrusions and/or step motifs; scrolls (which Bourget sees as barbels) can be painted or modeled on the head (Figure 7.4). In some cases the creature has a snake belt, which can slip down to become a tail. Holding a knife, Curly Top may be seen with a human victim or holding a human head. He is the most serious opponent of the Snake-belt God. In one scene they grasp the same trophy head; in another, Curly Top has the god down on his back as they fight over an object that looks more like a staff than a knife; and on the effigy bottle shown in Figure 7.4, Curly Top seems to hold a knife at the god's neck. Eventually, the Snake-belt God is shown decapitating Curly Top.

Curly Top may be a humanoid version of the Fish Monster (see Figure 11.1), a common antagonist of the Snake-belt God who is often seen holding it on a line. The fish-bodied demon has a human leg and arm with a hand that holds a knife; another hand may hold a severed head or even a whole human body (Alva 2001: Fig. 19; Bourget 1994b; Castillo 1989:99–125; Donnan and McClelland 1999: Figs. 4.20, 4.68; Kutscher 1983: Abbn. 234–240, 249, 256; Lieske 2001:151–155). The Fish Monster might personify the sea, which takes human lives as well as providing food (see Chapter 11).

Two other antagonists of the Snake-belt God appear in later Moche times: the Circular Creature and the Wave. The deity himself had changed by then (see Chapter 13).

The serpent with the fox-snake head is not an actor but a definer of a situation or site, an indicator of power or sacredness, or something like a guardian. Serpents form motifs or frames in mural art at Huaca de la Luna and Huaca Cao Viejo. A two-headed serpent is a belt for supernaturals and a skyband presentation. A remarkable figure from the tomb of the Old Lord of Sipán has a two-headed serpent/skyband headdress (see Figure 6.4; Alva 1994:Cover, 178–179; Alva and Donnan 1993: Fig. 204), and Schaffer (1981) has noted that an arching serpent is a common headdress in Loma Negra metalwork. In some scenes, skybands, setting off the upper world from the earth, can

FIGURE 7.4 Curly Top engaged in a struggle with the Snake-belt God. He seems to be holding a knife to the god's neck. *Courtesy Museo Larco, Lima, Peru, 078-004-003.*

have markings like those of a boa constrictor as well as snakelike heads. Various authors believe that some of these represent the Milky Way.

THE OWL, THE SPIDER, AND THE MILKY WAY

Early Moche effigy vessels realistically depict several owl species, particularly in the north. Most common is probably the great horned owl (*Bubo virginianus*). Another Early Moche subject is a warrior wearing a shirt or tunic of metal platelets and a helmet with a *tumi* (knife) flanked by step motifs, or a headdress with two frontal up-and-outward projections. These motifs merge in the owl warrior-sacrificer of Phase IV, an important being in the southern region and a major player in the Presentation Theme (see Chapter 8).

One Early Moche supernatural—variously called Decapitator, Spider Decapitator, Sacrificer, or X Sacrificer—appears frequently in metalwork and in a few ceramics and murals. Spider and Sacrificer were associated in Cupisnique/Chavín times, when spider figures held trophy heads (see Figure 2.3; Salazar-Burger and Burger 1982; Cordy-Collins 1992, 2001b; Salazar and Burger 2000:37–42). Early Moche bottles show a symmetrical, frontal human figure—with a Cupisnicoid head—holding a knife in one hand and a severed human head in the other (Donnan and McClelland 1999: Figs. 2.15, 2.20; Kutscher 1983: Abbn. 221, 222). The figure lacks obvious arachnid attributes but is called a spider because of straight, diagonal projections from the body (suggesting spider legs or a web), doubled ones from the waist and humerus, or paired single bands from shoulder, humerus, underarm, and/or waist (Figure 7.5). The X Sacrificer has a large, usually fanged mouth, like that of the Snake-belt God, but he consistently lacks the belt, and he has traits that the Snake-belt God lacks—notably, owl connotations and the major sacrificial role. Both deities appear to have evolved from Cupisnique/Chavín antecedents but developed differently.

Gold and silver (or gilded or silvered copper) versions of the frontal sacrificer from Loma Negra (Jones 1979, 1993, 2001; Lapiner 1976: Figs. 350, 363, 382; Schaffer 1981: Fig. 64) and Sipán (Alva 1994; Alva and Donnan 1993) appear on blade-shaped backflaps (see

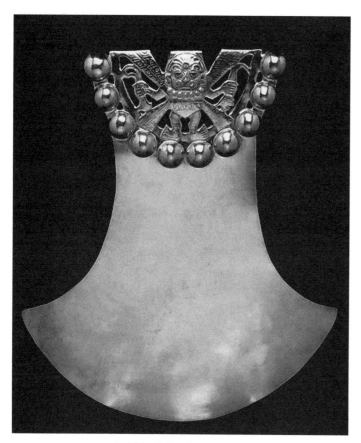

FIGURE 7.5 Gold backflap from a looted Sipán burial, 45.5 cm high. Above the blade shape, an X Sacrificer holds a knife and a trophy head. *Courtesy Museo Tumbas Reales de Sipán, Lambayeque.*

associations. They are used in various kinds of divination, including prediction of rainfall and other agricultural matters (Arriaga 1968 [1621]:34–35; Bourget 1994a:142; Salazar-Burger and Burger 1982:241; Cobo 1990 [1653]:162; Salomon and Urioste 1991:131, 146). Because spiders can be fatally toxic, and are clever predators of insects in their webs, they are associated with death, and Andean folk medicine used spiders to ascertain why someone died. Spiders also kill plant-destroying insects, including those that attack cotton plants, which grow in the north, where spider images are prominent. The web-making connection with weaving would have been particularly significant in a world in which cloth was valuable and venerated.

Large, frontal human figures, usually of gilded copper and often placed on gilded copper banners, were excavated at Huaca Rajada Sipán (Alva 1994). None of them has a knife, trophy head, or god mouth, but the pose is that of the X Sacrificer, and they wear an owl-head necklace and platelets on their tunics (Figure 7.6). The figures may be a royal symbol of Sipán, relating the ruling family to the god. Painted reliefs at Huaca Cao Viejo depict a frontal decapitator, holding a knife and human head, with possible

Figure 7.5), rattles, and other objects. Most have a headdress with an owl head or a necklace of owl-head beads, and all have a perfect X behind them. With the more geometrical Xs, the depiction looks like the god at the center of a cosmic diagram rather than an arachnid, although some spiders can assume a position that forms a perfect X (Preston-Mafham 1991:21, 96, 97). The Moche frequently zoomorphized objects, but if the X is a spider, it is a unique expression of Moche zoomorphizing.

Recognizable spiders are frequent in Moche art in the north. Among the grave goods of the Old Lord of Sipán were gold spiders, beads with a web design, and veristic spider legs on a body with a human face (Alva 1994: Láms. 159–161; Alva and Donnan 1993: Figs. 181, 187). More realistic spiders in gilded copper, as well as spider-decorated nose and ear ornaments, were found at Loma Negra (Jones 1993, 2001:206; Lapiner 1976: Figs. 376, 380). Spiders have had, and still have, many

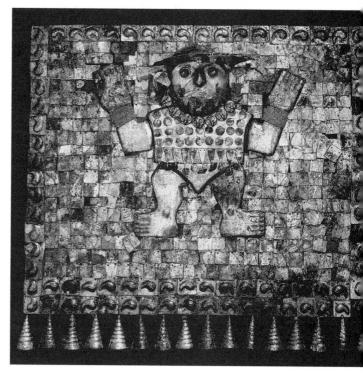

FIGURE 7.6 Gilded copper banner from Sipán. The figure has an owl-head necklace and turquoise bracelets. *Museo Tumbas Reales de Sipán, Lambayeque.*

spider appendages: three straight, parallel projections go out from each humerus, and three down-curving projections emerge from either side of the torso—although the latter look rather like spider appendages, the number is wrong for an arachnid, and they bend oddly (Franco, Gálvez, and Vázquez 2005:28; Gwin 2004:105). The "figure-8" ears are seen on a Cupisnique supernatural and on some versions of the Snake-belt God, but this image is essentially the X Sacrificer.

On an early version of the Huaca de la Luna Platform I facade was a god without spider appendages, wearing a belt that ends in a condor head and holding a severed human head (Uceda 2000b: Fig. 1). The so-called Decapitators, which appear in profusion on the walls inside Platform I, show only the head and so do not show the god as a decapitator; instead they may represent him as decapitated (Huaca de la Luna, Moche, Perú 2009; Morales Gamarra and Torres 2000). Their circular form, surrounded by a repeated raylike motif, may present a solar aspect. Similar heads appear also at Huaca Cao Viejo.

THE SNAKE-BELT GOD

Like an ancestral Cupisnique/Chavín supernatural, Moche gods and some other supernaturals have a fanged mouth with arrow-shaped ends. Early Moche deity depictions have the figure-8 ear ornaments or the stylized ears of the older supernatural, who also often has snake attributes. Traits of the older being include wide-open, staring eyes that are usually round but in earlier phases were sometimes square, with the pupil at the top. In Phase III, when new themes were developing in the repertory, social roles were apparently changing, and supernatural roles were developing, the Cupisnique/Chavín roots were sometimes emphasized by deliberate archaizing (J. Rowe 1971).

The Snake-belt God, like Cupisnique/Chavín supernaturals, is normally accompanied by snakes—the snake belt or fox-headed snaky belt, snake-head ear ornaments, and/or snake heads near his head or shoulder. Many of the early beings have these or other versions of snakes; a Chavín supernatural may have something like a snake eyebrow (see Figure 2.3). The Huaca de la Luna murals depicting a figure with a

condor-headed belt suggest, however, that the basic trait of the "belt" may not be the heads, which could act as a modifier, or the snake body, but its function as a skyband—a part of the deity. The condor, which flies from high peaks to the sea, might emphasize the sky character of the deity or express his symbolic journey.

The Snake-belt God can be depicted frontally and full-bodied or as a head only, but in fine-line scenes, head and legs are usually in profile, with bent knees expressing action. His attire can change within a sequence of scenes on a vessel. In Moche art, headdresses generally seem to be associated with specific rites, activities, and situations, and the Snake-belt God's several headdresses probably reveal the activities he is engaged in. His headdress usually has a feline (probably jaguar) head and paws, and a feather fan at the back; the headdress may be caplike or may take the form of an erect semicircle. He wears a loincloth and a sleeveless shirt, usually with a swirl or step design; he may also have a short platelet garment with serration at the waist. The cluster of repeated costume traits suggests the same being in different contexts, and the general consistency of the snake-belt, the fanged mouth, and the snake earrings seems to confirm the sameness of the identity. The Snake-belt God appears in various aspects and activities, but he is generally accepted as the same basic being. Interpreting variations in appearance as implying different beings seems to go against both the appearances and the tendency to have only a few major mythic characters, even when you are granting animism and numen to many kinds of beings.

In general, in folk literature there is a character who was the founder of the tribe or the "people"—however the group is defined—and he or perhaps another being is the culture hero, undergoing the adventures of the origin story. He might have taught the ancestors to fish and hunt (the Snake-belt God appears as a fisherman and a deer hunter), and some portrayals show him holding plants and tools, implying involvement with crops and farming instruction. His attacks on threatening monsters, who may be his mythic enemies, could be interpreted as efforts to defend the Moche people. Some contexts suggest a longer narrative. The god often has one hand on the neck of a monster, a sea bird, or a fox, and the other around a sacrificial knife, but he rarely holds a human head, and only occasionally does he bear weapons.

Supernatural beings may be associated with one place but are able to be in many places and obviously have adventures going between them; they act out myths. Astronomical identity gives gods one reason for travel.

BIOGRAPHY OF THE SNAKE-BELT GOD

Castillo's (1989) meticulous study of scenes painted on a florero in the Museo Larco Herrera examines a probable journey of the Snake-belt God (see Figure 6.1). Some of the scenes appear separately, or together, on other vessels. The images suggest that the god dies in the sea, which would fit a sun aspect, which he likely has. On the florero and elsewhere he is supported by two vultures or some combination of vulture, woman, iguana, or cormorant. Anne Marie Hocquenghem (1987:130) sees an annual calendrical event in this; I see a daily occurrence (Benson 1987b), with the god revived the next morning. At least two bottles display a scene in which the central deck figure is an owl wearing a cape, and lying next to it is a small, supine version of the god (see Figure 10.5). Dressed owls can be read as masculine or feminine, according to garments; I see this one as feminine. I had thought of this as a curing rite—owls *can* be portrayed as curers—but Krzysztof Makowski (1994a:65; see also Benson 1987b:79; Bourget 2006:88–89; Donnan 1978: Fig. 200; Quilter 2010:130–131) interprets the scene as a preparation for burial, and he has a good case. A dog at the god's feet might be his guide to the underworld (see Chapter 4). On one bottle, a human figure in priestly dress is painted below the deck figures with a llama, a likely funerary offering (see Chapter 12).

An anthropozoomorph, probably based on *Iguana iguana*, accompanies the Snake-belt God on many occasions and rarely appears without him (Figure 7.7). In early and late phase scenes, the iguana carries weapons and other objects (Donnan and McClelland 1999: Fig. 3.22; Lieske 2001:101–107); in Middle Moche, he looks up with raised hands clasped as if it is praying to or applauding the god. He wears a condor headdress and usually has the carrying cloth of a priest or shaman (see Chapter 9). He was surely a mythical

FIGURE 7.7 Detail from a bottle showing the Snake-belt God and Iguana. *The Metropolitan Museum of Art. Drawing by Alan Sawyer.*

character with a proper name and a role, but I call him "Iguana." Golte (1993:52) calls him "Murrup," from a Mochica word for "iguana" (Salas 2002:23). He might have been the conquered hero of a mythic people, an earlier god, or simply a being who is useful to the Snake-belt God, perhaps because he can live on both land and water. I have suggested that he may be the deity's psychopomp (Benson 1975:138); a dog often appears at his feet. One of the contexts in which Iguana appears is that in which the enthroned god is shown facing seated Iguana with a spear point at the elbow of his raised arm (Donnan 1996:129–131).

What seems to be a sequence of scenes—on separate bottles, but presumably linked—shows the god with a woman; the order of the actions is uncertain. Complex scenes in relief focus on the god making love to a woman in a house; on some there is a wave motif around the bottom (Figure 7.8) (Bourget 2006:157–177; Chapdelaine 2001:80–81; Hocquenghem 1987:62–78; Larco Hoyle 1965b:109, 113, 140; Vergara 1990:410). Human figures outside the house have the two-pronged headgear usually worn in marine activities (see Chapter 11), as does a bird-man who seems to be sprinkling on the god's back a substance from a bag or bowl, possibly chicha. Chicha is still used in offerings and curing sessions where liquid is sprinkled over a patient and a rod is sprayed with cane alcohol (Joralemon and Sharon 1993:32, 34). In the Moche scene, Iguana and a small animal stand together outside the house, and two women watch from another house, as they do in some sacrifice depictions; all are making a gesture that looks like applause. As do the sacrifice scenes, the mating scenes often include floating, cut-off human body parts, but there is no evident sacrifice.

The mating of an ancestral god and a more-or-less human woman is a common theme in Latin American origin myths, so this scene may depict the origin of the Moche people. This woman and the other women may relate to existing origin myths about sisters, one of whom mates with a supernatural

FIGURE 7.9 The Snake-belt God in a fish/raft with one woman in front of him, bound to the fish's tail, and another woman, whose throat has been cut, behind him. *Museo del Banco Central de Reserva del Perú, Lima, ACE-2975. Photograph by Steve Bourget.*

jaguar and is killed (Benson 1998:70–71; Roe 1998:3; J. Tello 1923:108–131). The Snake-belt God has jaguar associations, including a jaguar head and paws on his headdress. The Moche women who watch may be there to accompany the third woman to the other world, a pattern of burial found in many places (see Chapter 12). The woman with the god could refer to a woman accompanying an important man in his tomb, another pattern seen in burials. Mythic and ritual narratives are compressed in these scenes. An example of this ceramic subject was found in the relatively rich tomb of a woman that was intrusive into a corner of Plaza I at Huaca de la Luna (Chapdelaine 2001:80–81).

Possibly belonging to this narrative are representations of the god in a supernatural fish-raft facing a woman who is lashed to the tail; behind him is another woman whose neck is slit (Figure 7.9) (Inca–Peru 1990: Plate 109; Larco Hoyle 1966: Fig. 49; Berrin 1998: Fig. 89). Elsewhere the god is shown holding a woman by the hair; she has a jug tied at her waist and carries, in a *manta*, or shawl, a child or small person (Donnan 1978: Fig. 153; Kutscher 1950: Fig. 55).

FIGURE 7.8 Spout-and-handle bottle with relief design showing the Snake-belt God on top of a woman in a house. There are other figures in attendance. *Courtesy Museo Larco, Lima, Peru, XSE-023-003.*

ASPECTS AND TRANSFORMATIONS
OF THE SNAKE-BELT GOD

A recurring image in Moche art is a frontal, effigy figure with attributes of the Snake-belt God who wears a long garment and sits like a sculpture, facing out from a throne or seat in the mountains. Some portrayals suggest that he might have been lithified at that ritual place. Another frontal version portrays him standing against mountains as part of the range, his head one of the peaks, making him an ancestral sacred mountain, *apu*. Origin myths in the Americas describe the emergence of ancestors from a mountain cave (Sawyer 1966: Fig. 71; Zighelboim 1995). In these Moche scenes the active god may stand at one side of the mountain, watching the statuesque version of the god with Iguana on the other side. The active version has the snake belt, and the old frontal god is flanked by serpent heads, suggesting that these may be different aspects of the same being. Sometimes a sacrificial victim is shown falling down the central peak (see Chapter 10). The frontal god may represent a retired creator, a *deus otiosus*, detached from human problems, in contrast to the active god who was closely tied to the Moche people as their nearer progenitor and protector. Seventeenth-century sources name two North Coast deities: a creator and a doer (Rostworowski 1996:59–60).

Chavín, Tiahuanaco, and Huari deities were highland gods. Although I have described the Snake-belt God as the "god who came down from the mountains" (Benson 1972; see also Campana and Morales 1997; Uceda 2004), there is no firm evidence of a mountain origin in the chronology of subject matter. Nevertheless, the ancestral god may well have been thought of as a mountain god, at least in part: the mountains are very close and very impressive, and the sky, uplands, and sources of fresh water were important in the lives of the Moche people. The Snake-belt God seems not to have been exactly a sun god (such a god was later introduced [see Chapter 8]), but he moves as the sun does, from the mountains to the coast and into the sea. He is neither a mountain god nor a sea god predominantly, but a god expressing the duality of a coastal people. On the north coast of Peru, sea and mountains are parts of one complex

whole, an environment that is both supporting and threatening.

An image repeated many times in the murals of Huaca de la Luna and Huaca Cao Viejo is a Cupisnicoid frontal face from which emanate arcs like radiances; the face is framed by snakelike forms (Huaca de la Luna–Moche, Perú 2009). The arcs might signify sun rays, water, waves, vegetation, or sacredness. Cristóbal Campana and Ricardo Morales (1997) argue that it is an image of the primordial god, among whose attributes are a fanged mouth and serpents. Bourget (1994b:433–435), seeing marine imagery, proposes that octopus tentacles project from the head, and that the netlike, woven frames around the head area are made up of rays and catfish (see also Narváez 2001). He sees the images as portraits of the god entering the watery underworld, symbolizing sacrifice, death, and regeneration.

On ceramics, however, the god's most consistent animal attributes are terrestrial: feline (headdress ornament and probably teeth) and serpentine (belt and ear ornaments). He goes to sea in a raft, a land god behaving as mariners do. On the other hand, he can walk among large fishes, attack the Fish Monster, and decapitate a sea bird. He can also turn into a sea being to function in the watery environment. The ability of a supernatural being to change form is common in folklore throughout the world. In Middle Moche ceramic portrayals, the active Snake-belt God always has a godly head and usually a snake belt—his basic symbolic attributes are fairly consistent—but with these he can display the hide of a jaguar, wings of a dragonfly, legs of a crayfish, or spines of a sea urchin. He can also appear in, or as, a conch shell. He surely takes these forms temporarily to achieve some special mythic task, as culture heroes in much Latin American folklore do. An octopus is one of the god's transformations; in this case, however, the sucker pads on the arms are usually indicated, as they are not (as far as I can tell) in the Huaca de la Luna murals. Also, the mural heads are dominant, repeated motifs in sacred architectural space, where temporary transformation is less likely to be represented than in ceramic scenes.

An instance of greater complication is a crab with a human or godly head seen in various contexts— sometimes fishing alone (as the Snake-belt God does), sometimes attacking the god or being caught

FIGURE 7.10 Effigy bottle depicting the Snake-belt God in the grip of a supernatural crab. *Courtesy Museo Larco, Lima, Peru, 079-005-003.*

by him, sometimes standing facing the god (Donnan and McClelland 1999: Figs. 4.67, 6.4, 6.5; Kutscher 1983: Abbn. 241–266; Sawyer 1966: Fig. 74; Schmidt 1929:162, 163; see Conklin 1979:182). Crab and god, facing and gripping each other, do not always seem to be in combat (Figure 7.10). The crab sometimes seems to be supporting the god, as if rescuing or protecting him. This crab often has on its shell a large, well-modeled, almost-human face with a god mouth.

Brothers or twins are frequent in New World origin myths, and María Rostworowski (1996:21–22; see also J. Tello 1923), citing Claude Lévi-Strauss, observes that every Andean male deity has a brother or a double called "brother." In some scenes the Snake-belt God confronts, in almost mirror image, a humanoid who generally shares his traits, and they appear to face each other like argumentative siblings. A Pañamarca mural showed apparently supernatural twins holding each other by the hair and fighting (Bonavia 1985: Figs. 31, 32; Bonavia and Makowski 1999:50, Fig. 23; Schaedel 1951). The same theme has been discovered in relief murals on the facade of Huaca de la Luna, and several ceramic vessels show two facing figures, each with a snake ear ornament and a single snake-belt extension, one of whom wears sea-going headgear and holds a fishing line with a hook. I believe that Hocquenghem (1987:126, 184), seeing the god in the raft (on Phase V bottles) as the twin of the terrestrial Snake-belt God, was the first to use Mellizo Terrestre (Earth Twin) and Mellizo Marino (Marine Twin), terms used also by Castillo (1989) and Makowski (1996:65, 78–90, 2000). The crab does, at times, seem to be a twin of the god, possibly his animal transformation. In Moche mountain scenes with two deities, a father and son relationship can be proposed, or otiose and active versions of the god.

SUPERNATURAL CONCEPTS FROM INCA TIMES

The Spaniards wrote of the last-known pre-Hispanic supernaturals in the Andes—Con, Cuniraya, Pachacamac, Pariacaca, Viracocha, and others—as huacas belonging to different groups but with recurring traits and stories (Rostworowski 1992, 1996; Salomon and Urioste 1991). These provide some possible associations for the Snake-belt God. The supernaturals traveled and changed forms, and became part of the natural world; a supernatural could metamorphose into a mountain, rain, wind, lightning, or a burning fire. Pariacaca became a huge (El Niño?) rainstorm that washed away a village, created a valley, and made a lake in the highlands. Cuniraya, a primarily coastal being also associated with hydraulic transformation of land, created rivers, springs, and irrigation. The Snake-belt God may have performed similarly.

Cuniraya's magic-trick seductions caused fertility that upset normal productive patterns, as water does when out of control. Frank Salomon (1998; see also Rostworowski 1989:167–174) notes that in the arid Andean world, water has positive and negative significance: fertility through irrigation, and devastation from flash floods and rushing storm water that can cut chasms or start earthslides in warlike violence. He observes that green, irrigable valleys have female symbolism, while mountains and water, especially storm water, are male. In one Andean myth, "a water-*huaca* from the heights" weds a "beautiful land-*huaca* daughter" (Salomon, in Salomon and Urioste 1991:9–10, 14–18; see also Bergh 1993; Hocquenghem 1987:59; Sharon 2000:12). The embrace of earth and rushing water was sexual.

Cuniraya changed himself into a bird to seduce a woman weaver and put his semen into a lúcuma fruit for her to swallow (Salomon and Urioste 1991:46–49; see also Salomon 1998:15). She and her child fled into the sea near Pachacamac and turned into two small, stony islands. The Huarochirí manuscript mentions other women transformed after seduction by trickster heroes. Cuniraya himself is said to have lithified at a specific canal, yet he is present in all ages and places. His name is sometimes combined with that of the creator god Viracocha, and he may have been an aspect or son of Viracocha.

Early chroniclers described Con as an old creator god who could take the form of a feline (Rostworowski 1992:21–47; J. Tello 1923:94–98). He personified rain, thunder, lightning, earthquake, volcano, fertility, and sterility: he was the Andes. In some sources he was the son of Sun and Moon; in others he created them. He also created the sky, stars, and earth, as well as human beings, to whom he gave a life of abundance. But when his creations disappointed him, he turned the world into a desert. Later the more powerful Pachacamac arrived, a son of Sun and Moon, and god of sky and earthquake. He and Con were brothers of a sort. Pachacamac had two wives to nourish humankind: Earth and the being who dispensed the "fruits" of the sea. He changed the people created by Con into monkeys and foxes, and after repeopling the earth, Pachacamac returned to the sky or disappeared into the sea. Pachacamac was described as "the greatest maritime *huaca*," and Pariacaca as "the great embodiment of the stormy heights" (Salomon and Urioste 1991:102 n. 472). These later concepts can rarely be related directly to Moche beliefs, but they describe some thoughts of the Andean world, to which the Moche belonged.

Our best means of understanding Andean supernaturals is to observe the worlds that they created—and that created them. As Sabine MacCormack (1991:146) has written: "Everywhere in the Andes, the plains and the mountains, the sky and the waters were both the theatre and the dramatis personae of divine action."

CHAPTER EIGHT

The Later Gods

AN IMPORTANT SUBJECT in Moche iconography was defined by Christopher Donnan (1978:159–173; see also *La Ceremonia del Sacrificio* 2000), who first called it "the Presentation Theme" and, later, "the Sacrifice Ceremony" (Figure 8.1). He describes the scene as an elite religious event involving humans—a sacrificial rite with priestly figures. I believe, however, that the art is more likely to depict a supernatural event than the rite based on it, and that the major figures are more likely to be supernatural than human. I will retain the term *Presentation Theme* because there seems to be more than one Moche sacrifice complex, and if the major characters are supernatural, it is more than a ceremony. The theme appears on ceramics (seemingly late in Phase IV), on a few metal objects, and in a mural at Pañamarca, where it made a

political-religious statement at that southern frontier. The scene can have two levels, with a skyband separating the gods above from the sacrificers and human victims below, although victims sometimes appear on the upper level. What seem to be the beginnings of the theme appear earlier, and traces of it remain in Phase V, often mixed with other themes.

THE PRESENTATION THEME

The three major participants in the Presentation Theme are a helmeted warrior in a military tunic who usually emanates what appear to be rays of brilliance, a woman in a distinctive headdress with two projections, and a warrior in an armorlike garment of

FIGURE 8.1 A depiction of the Presentation Theme. The Rayed God (*left*) faces the Plate-shirt God, with a dog and a floating ulluchu fruit between them. Next is the Moon Goddess, then a human version or imitator of the Plate-shirt God. Below the snake-headed skybar, two bound figures are being sacrificed beside the Rayed God's litter. *Museo Larco, Lima, Peru. Drawing by Donna McClelland.*

metal platelets, who most often has an owl head. The woman is not always present; when she is, she offers a goblet to one or the other of the male gods. In two very similar versions of the scene, there is a fourth figure with a human head, fanged mouth, and dress like that of the owl warrior; he rarely appears, but when he does, he is outside the primary action (see Figure 8.1; Donnan 1978: Fig. 239b). He may represent a ruler sacralized by his presence in this divine world.

The blood of humans sacrificed in the Presentation Theme is presumably collected in a goblet to nourish the gods, who hold or pass it, with a cover—a gourd or a metal or ceramic bowl—in the other hand. (Ceramic and metal goblets, or cups, and shallow metal bowls of appropriate shape have been found at Moche sites.) A human-headed club usually appears in the scene (see Chapter 4), and sometimes the cup is offered to it, or the club holds the cup (see Donnan 1978: Fig. 242; Kutscher 1983: Abb. 303). A human-headed club can also appear as the repeated motif on a goblet (see Figure 4.2).

The Presentation Theme likely illustrates, as one of its meanings, an astronomical event or a series of events involving gods with sky identities whose relationships change as they pass the goblet and bowl. People in early developments of civilization were usually good astronomers, and astronomic events were important to their knowledge of when to plant and fish, and when to celebrate rites. A dog, who accompanies different gods and faces in different directions, may be escorting a waning astral body to the underworld. These variations, and those in the actions of the deities, suggest sky movement: appearances, conjunctions, and disappearances. The three personages are seen in other contexts, notably the complex animated objects scene (see Figure 4.3). If I am right in seeing the rayed warrior as a sun god, then the sun is high in the sky in that scene. The woman, presumably the moon, is once near the sun and once near the plate-shirted owl warrior, whose sky identity is not obvious.

THE PLATE-SHIRT GOD

The Plate-shirt God, who is often a supernatural owl, evolved in the south, apparently in the Phase III/IV transition, from the X Sacrificer or early elements

that combined to form that god. He remained important throughout Phase IV. Until the late period, the X Sacrificer was the most significant deity of the north, and the Plate-shirt God was perhaps second in importance in the southern valleys, where he was the supernatural leader in warfare that led to the capture of prisoners for sacrifice. He wears a tunic of metal plates sewn onto cloth, with a scarf-like extension trailing behind. He has either a helmet with a central knife-shaped ornament flanked by step motifs, or headgear with two diagonal projections, usually with an owl or owl head at the base (or a feline or human head). He often wears a crescent nose ornament. Human leaders in processions are often dressed more or less as he is. Remains of plate-shirt garments have been found in excavations in Sipán (Alva 1994:64, Lám. 127; Alva and Donnan 1993: Figs. 57, 245), Dos Cabezas (Jiménez 2000:80, 87), and Huaca Cao Viejo (*El Comercio* 21 May 2006; Franco 2010).

As taker of captives, the Plate-shirt God was the most significant sacrificer. He may sit enthroned or stand atop a high platform, one of the few beings in Moche art to be so honored (Figure 8.2). He is depicted at one of two moments: holding a knife to a victim's throat or, after the decapitation, with knife in one hand, human head in the other (Benson 1987b; Donnan 1978:Fig. 205; Hocquenghem 1987:Figs. 104, 105; Makowski 1996; Pimentel and Álvarez 2000).

FIGURE 8.2 Owl sacrificer on a platform. *Courtesy Staatliche Museen zu Berlin—Preussischer Kulturbesitz, Ethnologisches Museum, VA 18096, Baessler Collection.*

FIGURE 8.3 Two images of the Plate-shirt God holding a weapons bundle and carrying on his back a small human warrior. *Museo Nacional de Arqueología, Antropología e Historia del Perú. Drawing by Donna McClelland.*

The Plate-shirt God is oversized, as many supernaturals are, and, gripping the hair of a tiny human victim, he wields the knife. The owl warrior and the sacrificer may be one deity or two. Since there is a close connection between war and sacrifice, between warrior and decapitator, the same god may perform both roles. The sacrificer does not always wear the platelet shirt, but he seems always to have owl attributes, while the warrior can have a human face with a godly mouth.

A generally veristic effigy owl of supernatural size, sometimes caped or masked, acts as transporter to the other world (Chapter 4): tied to his back or side is a small person, probably a sacrifice victim (Bourget 1994a: Figs. 5.23–5.28; Schmidt 1929:173). In some scenes the military anthropomorphic owl has tied on its back a three-step throne, in which is seated a small warrior in similar garments (Figure 8.3; see also Donnan and McClelland 1999:6.40, 6.41; Kutscher 1983:Abb. 191). Steve Bourget (1994a:121) argues convincingly that this owl is conveying a high-ranking warrior to the world of the dead, an interpretation that fits with portrayals of an anthropomorphic, nonmilitary owl as priest, shaman, or curer, and with a role as psychopomp. Bourget notes that when the military owl carries the dead, he has raptor claws, as if to hold prey, but when shown as a warrior, he has human feet. Bourget observes also that spears in one of these scenes have harpoons on the ends, and that a sea bird head

forms the holding device on a spearthrower, motifs appropriate for a trip to the watery underworld.

Some apparent sacrificial victims wear the Plate-shirt God's typical headdress and a tunic of metal platelets (Benson 1982b, 1984a, 1987b). In Mexico, Aztec ethnohistorical reports refer to sacrificial victims clad as the god to whom they were offered. Moche captives, wearing some of the most elaborate dress in the art, are portrayed alone, with their broken wrists tied behind their backs. The warriors on thrones carried by the Plate-shirt God may have been these well-dressed captives.

Clear instances of a human imitating a supernatural are owl sacrificers who appear as masked humans; they hold the trophy head but not the knife (Bankes 1980:43; Benson 1972: Fig. 3–9). The Moche, who seem to have been reluctant to show themselves in this role, did not depict human sacrificers. In complex scenes that include sacrifice, an anthropomorphic bat, fox, or jaguar always does the deed, sometimes under the aegis or supervision of the owl warrior. When the owl is shown as the sacrificer, he appears isolated, in the form of a three-dimensional bottle.

Occasionally, a figure like the owl has the beak of a hawk or falcon. These seem to be interchangeable, but the owl dominates, possibly because it is a nocturnal predator. Substitution of one creature for another is common in South American folk narratives.

An anthropomorphic bat with snarling, arrow-ended mouth is the other creature often depicted as a sacrificer (Donnan 2001:71; see also Donnan and McClelland 1999: Figs. 6.40, 6.41). Like owls, bats are nocturnal, shamanic, and associated with death; anthropomorphic bats can be preparers or guardians of funerary ceramics, and objects depicting bats were excavated by Donnan (2007) in the rich Tomb 2 at Dos Cabezas. The vampire bat (*Desmodus rotundus*), which is present on the north coast of Peru, draws blood from its victim and is a natural symbol of sacrifice. Certain other bat species are seed dispersers and pollinators, and thus associated with agriculture. The bat sacrificer gained importance as sacrifice iconography became more complex. Although prominent in some Presentation Theme scenes, it is secondary to the Plate-shirt God and seems to lack godly status.

ANOTHER ROLE OF THE PLATE-SHIRT GOD

The supernatural being who dominates the large coca rite scenes (see Chapter 10) is the Plate-shirt God (Berrin 1997: No. 79; Donnan and McClelland 1999: Fig. 4.64b-c; Hocquenghem 1987:Figs.68–70, 125; Kutscher 1983: Abbn. 125, 126; Morales 2004). His face is human, and he wears pendant-disk ear ornaments and often a headdress with two fruits (ulluchu), traits specific to the Coca Rite, but he has the platelet shirt and sometimes the owl-god's headdress. The battle and sacrifice related to the Coca Rite would justify the god's role in it, although he is not shown here as sacrificer, but as a priest or shaman.

The Coca Rite was apparently held at night, and a skyband arc stretches over the large scenes. The owl is nocturnal; the god's garments of glittering platelets may relate to the brilliance of his night appearance as an astronomical entity lighting darkness, or to a transformation concept. Anne Marie Hocquenghem (1987:184) cites the early Spaniard Juan Polo de Onde-gardo's late-sixteenth-century description of an Inca supernatural as a warrior who could be seen in the night sky holding a club and wearing a suit of light that shines when he moves. The Plate-shirt God could be the Milky Way; in owl form he sometimes stands under a skyband in non–coca rite scenes. He might also be Venus, the Southern Cross, or the Pleiades. In Early Colonial times, Antonio de la Calancha

(1974–1982 [1638], III:835; see also Urton 1981) stressed the significance of the Pleiades in the North Coast region, and Tom Zuidema (1992:181) thinks that Venus was more important in the Andes than we now perceive; in Mesoamerica, Venus was associated with ritual warfare (Carlson 1993).

The Plate-shirt God can be pictured alone or with warriors, appears in large scenes, and has various interactions with the Snake-belt God. Sometimes they meet in confrontation (Castillo 1989). While the Snake-belt God appears to be the protector of the Moche people, the Plate-shirt God sacrifices humans, presumably in the interests of the Moche people. When the Rayed God arrives, the Plate-shirt God meets him in the Presentation Theme to share the goblet featured in that rite or supernatural event.

THE RAYED GOD

The Rayed God began to appear in fine-line scenes, especially in the Presentation Theme, in Phase IV (see Figure 8.1; see also Figure 4.3). Usually a helmeted warrior from whose head and/or body rays project, sometimes ending in "snake" heads, he stands in profile, implying impending action. He may carry a club and shield, but more often he holds the goblet. In existing examples he never wears a fully plated tunic, although sometimes half of his tunic has platelets. The Rayed God probably never appears alone; he meets often with the Plate-shirt God, but rarely with the Snake-belt God. For a time he seems to have replaced the Snake-belt God.

The role of the Rayed God seems to be that of a royal sun god, with whom a ruler would want to identify. The concept of identification of a divine king with the sun is widespread. Also common in New World thought is the idea that more than one god is related to the sun: there can be different supernaturals for different facets or phases of the sun. In New World religions, the sun is often a warrior. The Rayed God can be accompanied by, or riding in, a rayed litter guarded by a jaguar (a frequent sun symbol) or other spotted feline. In the myths of many regions a solar god is conveyed across the sky in a litter or raft. In Figure 8.1, the Moche god's litter rests upon severed human heads, likely offerings that were the base of the god's power. Like the Aztec Sun God, this god may have needed human blood to traverse the sky. He is not a sacrificer, but the receiver of sacrifice. He foreshadows the time when Inca rulers, addressed as the Midday Sun, were sons of the sun and the manifestation of the sun on Earth.

The Rayed God was likely introduced into political manipulation of myth, religion, and ritual to meet the needs of a drastic situation, perhaps in the wake of devastation by severe Niños (one would want a strong sun god to outwit El Niño rains) or by severe drought (one might think that the sun needed more intense or specific respect), or because of disruptions and incursions from outside. One reason for the advent of the Rayed God as a replacement for the nonwarrior Snake-belt God might have been a need to emphasize the military side of ritual; the Plate-shirt God was also a warrior, but other significance or emphasis was needed. The fact that the Rayed God is dressed like a warrior king may be a way of communicating and stressing the power of a king at a time when the king was losing strength. The Rayed God, in at least one example, has two small disks on his headdress. The two-disk headdress is seen on distinguished, often-enthroned men in Phase III, and on eminent warriors in Phase IV (see Chapter 9). As a power garment it preceded the introduction of the Rayed God; its presence on the god would reinforce the power of humans wearing it.

If priests had assumed increasing power in Moche IV (Chapter 9), we might postulate that the Rayed God was introduced to counteract this power. As the Presentation Theme and other manifestations of the god became prevalent, priestly portraits disappeared. The so-called "revolt of objects" scene (see Figure 4.3) might be interpreted as revealing the triumph of the Rayed God when he faces the tiny priest before him.

THE HUACA RAJADA SIPÁN TOMBS

The Lord of Sipán, in Tomb 1, had grave goods related to war and sacrifice, evidence for military roles, priestly functions, and the assumption of divine identity or descent that the Moche ruling class must have claimed. The occupants of Tombs 1 and 2 have been equated with Figures A (the Rayed God) and B (the Plate-shirt

God) in the Presentation Theme (Alva and Donnan 1993; Castillo 2000a). The Sipán dead had been warrior priests, but I find little correlation with figures in the Presentation Theme (Benson [1993] 2003). The identification was made on the basis of southern iconography; I would like to use this iconography to argue against it. For one reason, the chronology does not work. Walter Alva and Donnan date Tombs 1 and 2 at ca. AD 300, a Phase III date. In the south, some motifs and concepts of later complex themes were present and beginning to come together in Phase III, but they did not yet appear in fixed complexes, as they did in Phase IV. Phase IV rituals had not yet been codified in the art, and the relative regularity of elements in the Presentation Theme and other Phase IV multifigure scenes is lacking. Some of the elements were there, but the iconographic grammar had not yet been formed. Moreover, there is no evidence for this southern iconographic development in the north, although some of its elements are scattered in the art, as they are in the south in Phase III (Alva 2001: Fig. 22).

What is particularly significant is the clothing. The grave goods in Tomb 1 include articles fairly common for high-status warriors in Phase III and later: a helmet with knife, bracelets, round ear ornaments, and backflaps (Alva 1994:43–145; Alva and Donnan 1993:55–145). Scepters from the tomb have subject matter that refers to capture but not to other elements of the Presentation Theme. A gold-platelet tunic was placed with the lord, as well as one pair (of several pairs) of ear ornaments featuring a central figure in a step-knife headdress and platelet shirt (see Figure 6.5), and many portrayals of the X Sacrificer with owl necklace and headdress ornament, featured on gilded backflaps and rattles. The iconography of Tomb 1 matches more closely that of the developing Plate-shirt God than that of the later Rayed God. The Rayed God does not wear very specific garments; however, in the known Presentation Theme examples, he never has owl accessories or a tunic completely covered with platelets. The headdress on the elaborate ear ornaments is also that of the Plate-shirt God.

The man buried in Huaca Rajada Tomb 2 (Alva 1994; Alva and Donnan 1993) was likely a sacrificer with at least some attributes of the Plate-shirt God. An elaborate, full-figure owl headdress with projections was found in the tomb, as well as a *tumi* and necklace beads that may represent trophy heads. Bowls and a copper cup are also suggestive. A rich tomb at the site excavated recently by Luis Chero included two gilded-copper goblets, like those that appear in the Presentation Theme, in the hands of the buried man (*El Comercio*, 2 September 2007a). Huaca Rajada Tomb 3 (Alva 1994; Alva and Donnan 1993), that of the Old Lord of Sipán, contained rattles and backflaps embellished with the X Sacrificer. Owl depictions are rare in Tomb 3, but a nose ornament includes a full-figure, frontal gold owl; this tomb also yielded a figure with a step-knife helmet. The tomb recently excavated by Chero contained a semicircular, two-pronged headdress with a seemingly human face (*El Comercio*, 2 September 2007a).

The iconography of the Huaca Rajada Sipán tombs is appropriate to Phase III in the north. It is significant that no evidence of the Rayed God has yet been found at Sipán or elsewhere in the north.

THE MOON GODDESS

Yuri Berezkin (1980:14–15) identified certain portrayals as a supernatural woman, and at the same time Hocquenghem and Patricia Lyon (1980) analyzed examples of the woman in detail; none of them names her as a moon goddess, although Hocquenghem (1987:82, 185) later mentions her moon associations. Having described her as a probable moon goddess (Benson 1985, 1988b:65), I now call her "the Moon Goddess"

(Figure 8.4). She appears in the Presentation Theme (see Figure 8.1) and in several other contexts (see Figures 4.3, 12.4, 13.3; Cordy-Collins 2001a; Holmquist 1992; Kutscher 1950:Abbn. 69, 72; Lieske 2001:23–27; Makowski 1996:81; Donna McClelland 1990).

There was a later male moon god, and the Moche figure used to be described as male, but the sex of the figure in Moche images seems clear (Figure 8.4). Moche women are generally identified by braids of hair and a basic one-piece dress, or tunic, which usually is dark and has a belt of contrasting color. In some early depictions a woman has a small captive or child and a sack or jar; her dentition is rarely supernatural, but her large size suggests special status. The Moon Goddess, surely the only Moche goddess, has a fanged mouth, and her braided, or spirally bound, hair ends in snake heads; she may have other snake appendages. The band of her headdress is usually decorated with circles, and rising at either side is an upward-curving or floppy element, sometimes with up-projecting elements in between; the projections can also end in snake heads. Variations occur, but the headdress is recognizably consistent. She usually wears a patterned dress and a cape or a headcloth that flows down behind her. Her garment often has bands of short, vertical lines or small circles (polka dots); the cape over a dotted dress may have markings like jaguar pelage, or the patterns may be reversed.

A nose ornament from Huaca Rajada Sipán Tomb 9 portrays a figure with some traits of the Moon Goddess—probably an early version—facing a plate-shirt

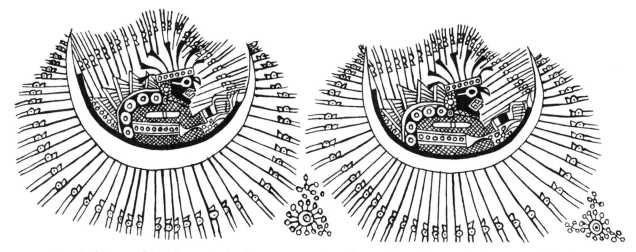

FIGURE 8.4 Dual image of the Moon Goddess in a crescent. *Museo Amano, Lima. Drawing by Donna McClelland.*

figure: she has a three-pronged headdress, a long braid, and a cape (Alva 2001: Fig. 22). The braid has no snake head, but there is an animal head on her belt, an unusual feature for this personage. Neither figure on the ornament has a supernatural mouth. They gesture to each other, and each holds a small vessel, while what may be a cloth bag floats between them. This portrayal, assigned to Phase III, was found in the tomb of an adult male along with war clubs, copper crescent headdresses, and other grave goods. It shows that elements of the Presentation Theme were present in Phase III, but not developed as in their later pattern or context: the Rayed God is missing, as are sacrifice figures and cups or goblets.

In addition to the Presentation Theme and the animated objects scene of Phase IV, the goddess is prominent in other late scenes of what is essentially a new iconography (see Chapter 13). In a net garment, she rides in a raft or a crescent, presumably as the moon traveling over the night sea (see Figure 8.4). In some raft scenes she holds a goblet like that in the Presentation Theme; when she lifts it to her mouth, she may have insect wings on her back. The crescent can project rays, which might show her radiance as the moon or reflections of moonlight on water. Alana Cordy-Collins (2001a: Fig. 3.13) suggests that the radiances represent the spines of a *Spondylus*. The goddess sometimes has wrapped objects with her, a bag often lies in front of her, and sometimes she holds a small staff or stick, probably a spindle or weaving tool. Krzysztof Makowski (1996) points out that she can be accompanied by weaving implements, as she is in the animated objects scene. In much folk literature of the Americas, the moon is a weaver (because of its movement in the sky), and this was probably true on the north coast of Peru.

This supernatural woman is shown also in the Burial Theme, a Phase V set of scenes with various supernaturals, as well as the same personages at different times in the narrative (see Figure 12.4; Donnan and McClelland 1979; McClelland, McClelland, and Donnan 2007; see also Benson 1985, 1988b:64). Figures appear in and near structures, notably a deep and complex tomb. Outside, a splayed, nude woman—nudes are rare in Moche art—is attacked by vultures; her masklike face resembles that of the woman in the tomb. The Burial Theme may depict a dark-of-the-moon or an eclipse; hence, the burial of the moon. María Rostworowski

(1992:27–28, 61–68) suggests that the theme may refer to a myth like that involving the later god Pachacamac, who killed a woman who had had a child by the Sun and then put her out for condors and other vultures to feed on. Donnan and McClelland posit that it illustrates a North Coast legend about putting to death an unsuccessful curer. However, the elaborate burial and the supernatural face on both the entombed figure and the supine nude imply that this is a major mythic being. In upper levels of the tomb, rows of small, female figures wear net garments and hold sticks or spindles like the raft woman's. They may be characters in myth, astral beings, priestesses of the goddess, attendants in the tomb, or some combination of these.

Grave goods in the separate tombs of two females at San José de Moro, Jequetepeque Valley (see Chapter 12), match depictions of the Moon Goddess, for whom the women must have been priestesses and whom they were imitating. The grave of the second priestess contained a bottle depicting the Burial Theme. While the first-excavated male burials at Sipán do not fit the Presentation Theme model, these late San José de Moro ones fit perfectly for the woman. The burials date to the early eighth century. The first-discovered female tomb, that of a woman a little over 40 years old, was excavated in 1991 by Christopher Donnan and Luis Jaime Castillo (Castillo 1996; Castillo and Donnan 1994b; Donnan and Castillo 1992, 1994). A goblet with a human-headed-club weapons bundle repeated around it was found in her grave. The following year the burial of a younger priestess was unearthed (Castillo 2000a, 2001; Cordy-Collins 2001a). The two women might have served sequentially as priestess. The burial suggests high status for the women.

Among the grave goods of the first priestess was a headdress with two projections of silver-copper alloy, similar to the goddess headdress. This tomb also held over-life-sized masks of silvered copper, prototypes of later masks of the style traditionally called "Lambayeque" but renamed "Sicán" (after the type site) by Izumi Shimada and others. (The second priestess had similar silver accessories.) In one tomb, among 73 ceramics, a Burial Theme bottle and two bottles depicting the woman in a raft were excavated, as well as jewelry of metal, bone, and shell, and turquoise beads. The first tomb also yielded a copper cup near the right hand.

FIGURE 8.5 Scene from a bottle showing Moche supernaturals who were prominent at various times but not usually seen together. *Private collection. Drawing by Donna McClelland.*

Judging from Early Moche ceramics, it seemed that women's duties were limited to sex, curing, and, rarely, nursing babies. By Phase IV women had a role in sacrifice and curing scenes, and they become prominent in Phase V iconography. Recent excavations in earlier contexts, however, give a different impression. Several quite elaborate tombs of women have been excavated: in a corner of Plaza 1 of Huaca de la Luna, as well as in the elite urban area near Luna (Chapdelaine 2001:80–81), and in the Huaca Rajada Sipán, where a woman was interred with an elaborate gold crown (Alva 2001:234–235). According to Franco, Gálvez, and Vásquez (1999b:50–51, 2001a:157–159, 167), some elite women formed part of the priestly class at Cao Viejo in Phase III. A possible wooden coffin belonged to one of them (see Chapter 13); her painted tomb was later disturbed by the arrival of another woman's body.

A recent discovery (2005) was the elaborately wrapped Phase III burial of the Lady of Huaca Cao

Viejo, who had within her mummy bundle a crown, a cloth or garment on which gilded-copper platelets were sewn, 31 metal nose ornaments, weaving tools, and other offerings (see Chapter 12; *El Comercio* 18 May 2006; Franco 2009; Franco and Gálvez 2010; Williams 2006). Her tattooed corpse was wrapped in 20 layers of shroud and flanked by two tall war clubs of wood encased in metal. She was probably a ruler; she was certainly a person of great power, and she has changed the conventional concepts of the status of women in earlier Moche society.

A SUPERNATURAL EVENT

One late Phase IV painted-bottle scene with Presentation Theme characters has two main levels, as several renderings of that subject do; the levels are separated by a skyband without animal heads (Figure 8.5). At the top a small Moon Goddess, isolated in a lunette, holds a cup. On the tier above the skyband an anthropomorphic hummingbird in a step-motif shirt sits in a rayed litter (hummingbirds are widely associated with the sun, war, and sacrifice [Benson 1989]), and three figures in platelet garments and semicircular headdresses are holding ropes attached to a ladder extending down to the lower world. Below, the Rayed God begins to climb the ladder. Behind him, on a throne, sits the Plate-shirt God. The Rayed God faces, on the other side of the ladder, the Snake-belt God, standing with upraised hands, one finger touching the ladder; he wears a step-motif shirt with fat snakes trailing behind. This is one of the rare scenes in which

the Snake-belt God and the Rayed God both appear. Behind the Snake-belt God is a splayed figure that surely refers to the X Sacrificer, but he lacks the X, and the raised hands are empty. He wears a semicircular headdress and a platelet shirt, with a platelet scarf hanging below; dots around circular ear ornaments may indicate the motifs that rim many such gold ornaments or may be a sign of shininess—or both. Two large snakes rise in front of him. Several smaller plate-shirt figures stand on this level. Supernaturals who were conspicuous at various times but are rarely seen together seem to present a brief summary of Moche iconographic history with a large cast of characters appearing in a complicated mythic scene.

CHAPTER NINE Rulers, Warriors, and Priests

WARRIORS ARE PROMINENT in murals, ceramics, and metalwork in Phases III and IV. Many carry a shield, a spearthrower and spears, or a club, or mace, which they often wield. Clubs and other weapons have been encountered in graves (Castillo and Donnan 1994b:125; Franco 2009; Larco Hoyle 2001, I: Fig, 236; Recuperación 2000; Strong and Evans 1952:157–158, Plates VIIB, XXIV). Clubs, full-sized and miniature, come from burials at Sipán; Walter Alva (2001: Figs. 5, 12) suggests that weapons found in one Sipán tomb may have been taken in ritual battle. Christopher Donnan (2001:71), excavating a high-status tomb at Dos Cabezas, noted that war clubs, spearthrowers, spears, and gold-plated shields found there lacked battle damage and were likely to be ceremonial. Clubs with a long, thin hilt, excavated at Huaca Cao Viejo, would not deal a heavy blow, and excavators Régulo Franco, César Gálvez, and Segundo Vásquez (1999a:20–21, Fotos 7, 8; 2001b:161–162) think that they were used in rites. The two large (nearly 2 m long) wooden clubs encased in gilded copper recently found in the tomb of the Lady of Cao Viejo would be more effectively used in ceremony than in battle (*El Comercio* 21 May 2006; Franco 2009; Williams 2006). The finely crafted clubs should be called maces, because they are significant symbols of office. However, a plain, hefty club excavated in Huaca de la Luna had human blood on it (Bourget 2001a:110–112; Bourget and Newman 1998). Clubs could also have serious practical use.

A *tumi* (a later word for a certain kind of blade) was apparently used only for sacrificial throat cutting. Warriors do not use it—it is held only by supernatural beings—but in ceramic scenes warriors frequently

wear a metal backflap made in the same shape, as do the two military figures in Figure 9.1, seen with captives and captured equipment; many of these objects were found at Sipán.

A knife of similar shape—or a model of one—rests atop the helmet of certain warriors, blade side up, perhaps as a sign that conflict led to sacrifice (Figures 9.1, 9.2, 9.6). The helmet knife is often flanked by step motifs, and a feline or fox head may be attached below. Few helmets have been found by archaeologists, but various types are shown in the art, surely conveying information about the wearer's status. Helmets were probably often of hide or thick, padded cloth; some were likely made of reeds, some of copper or copper alloy. In ceramic images, headgear tends to be simpler in painted battle scenes than in ritual scenes. The body dress of warriors could be two-piece—kilt or loincloth and short tunic or shirt—or a longer, apparently belted tunic; the garments seem

FIGURE 9.1 Scene showing the presentation of captives and captured gear. *Staatliche Museen zu Berlin—Preussischer Kulturbesitz, Ethnologisches Museum. Drawing by Wilhelm von den Steinen (Baessler 1902–1903).*

to have been made of thick cloth, sometimes with gilded-copper platelets sewn on.

THE NATURE OF WARFARE

Moche warfare—and Andean warfare, generally—has been much discussed, particularly the question of whether battle was "real" or "ritual," or both (Bourget 2001b; Castillo 2000a; Donnan 1997a; Golte 1994a; Hocquenghem 1978, 1987; Kutscher 1950; Makowski 1994b:131–135; S. Pozorski 1987; Quilter 2002; Rostworowski 1999; J. Rowe 1946:308–309; Shimada 1994a:108–110, 239–240; J. Topic and Topic 1987, 1997; T. Topic 1982; Verano 2001c). Inca ritual warfare is described by Spanish chroniclers, but the enormous Inca empire was not built and held entirely by diplomacy and religious conversion. Moche images show duel-like, one-on-one combat: this may have been the nature of battle, but it may be an artistic device for indicating conflict of larger scale. Battle was probably waged for religious, astronomical, and calendrical reasons, as well as for what are, to us, more political or economic aims. Death was not the purpose of combat; no one is shown dead in battle. Taking captives for ritual sacrifice, however, must have been a major motivation. Some battle rites may have reenacted wars of the past, which would have attained mythic, as well as commemorative, character.

Displays of military, otherworldly power served a purpose in the Moche political world. Although warriors do not seem to have gone into the field purely for territorial conquest, the Moche did gain control of some new valleys, and asserted power in other valleys that they shared with other peoples. They controlled water sources and distribution; they had access to raw materials, and transmontane and coastal trade routes; they controlled valley land, and perhaps maintained upland growing and grazing areas; they had some control over offshore resources. Moche well-being seems to have depended on displays of military aggression and defense against neighbors seeking Moche assets or rebelling at Moche control.

Some ritual battle would likely have taken place between members of the same community, or communities close to each other, with both sides wearing essentially Moche dress. Some DNA evidence suggests that those sacrificed came from the same group as the sacrificers. Less-ritual battle likely took place between Moche communities or with peoples of other groups. Multiethnic situations in some valleys have been posited by Krzysztof Makowski (1994b:131–35l) and others (Bourget 2003; Castillo and Donnan 1994b; Shimada 1994a:53; Shimada and Maguiña 1994; Verano 2001c:116–117). Moche and Gallinazo populations often lived close to each other (Millaire with Morlion 2009), and Cajamarca and Recuay peoples were sometimes close to them. It seems unlikely that the Moche could have inhabited and controlled parts of the distant Piura Valley without a show of strength, or that they could have established, without some force, the great center of Pañamarca in a southern valley occupied largely by the Recuay (Proulx 1982).

Sacred hills, caves, and rocks might have been fought for. The Moche presumably took from the Gallinazo people the early structures that became Huacas del Sol and de la Luna, causing the Gallinazo to lose sacred space. Ritual battle may have protected or acquired sacred places that also had practical value. Offshore islands, for example, were sacred places, but also fishing stations, home to a wealth of sea lions and birds, and a source of guano for fertilizer (see Chapter 11). Sources of precious metals must have been sacred for what they held.

Surveys in the mountains above valleys occupied by the Moche indicate fortified villages and hilltop bastions from various periods. John and Theresa Topic, after examining mostly Early Horizon, northern valley sites that look like fortresses (with defensible locations, parapets, moats, and sometimes slingstones), argue that these were sites for ritual war, because there is no water in these places for those under siege, because gates are latched from outside, and so on (J. Topic and Topic 1987, 1997; T. Topic 1982; see also Moseley 1992:162–163; Netherly 1984:231). Topic and Topic do not see conquest and territorial expansion, but cultural expansion and long-term relationships that involved ritual warfare, much of which affirmed the bonding of specific opposing groups in a community—known in Inca times as *parcialidades,* or *ayllus* (lineages).

A framework for interpreting Moche warfare might be provided by Classic Maya glyphic and archaeological evidence for intersite alliances and arranged marriages, as well as for intersite battles (Martin and Grube 2000:7, 14–18, 20; Schele and Mathews 1998; see also Benson 1983, 2004, 2010; Carlson 1993; Verano 2001c:122–123). Maya rulers can appear as conquerors or captives of other Maya rulers. One king might attack another, or put a ruler on the throne of another site; upstarts founded power bases that threatened other kings. Some attacks, controls, and relationships took place over considerable distance. Candidates for kingship had to prove themselves in battle, for a primary royal duty was to lead forces against rival kings, and captive taking often preceded elevation to office. Maya battle scenes are rare, but many stelae portray a king in war regalia with a captive at his feet, and temple steps are carved with images of captive kings and their names to be trodden upon. This warfare was performed with ritual. Simon Martin and Nicolai Grube (2000) note that political expansion among the Maya did not mean acquiring territory, but extending elite networks, and just as rivalry existed between Maya cities and their kings, there was likely competition between Moche cities. Naked Moche captives pictured in litters, a means of transportation available only to those of high status, might be evidence of similarities to Maya activities.

Blood was ritually fed to the earth in many places in the Americas, so that the earth would provide good crops and other benefits. Maya captives dripped blood, and Maya royalty engaged in a penis- or tongue-piercing rite. Blood often drips in Moche battle and sacrifice scenes, and the Huaca Cao Viejo mural reliefs include a line of nude captives, one or more of whom has a cut penis. All battle was surely related to the importance of blood.

Such a high proportion of Moche subject matter concerns combat and the sacrifice of conquered warriors that it is not surprising that recent archaeological excavations have uncovered substantial physical evidence for these related activities (Bourget 2001a:100–103, 2001b; Orbegoso 1998; Tufinio 2004a; Verano 1998, 2001a, 2001b:178, 2001c:120–121; Verano, Tufinio, and Lund 2008). The sacrifices of Plaza 3A at Huaca de la Luna seem clearly related to El Niño events; the group of sacrifices excavated at Plaza 3C implies a different cause. There, the remains of adolescent and adult males show cut marks that correspond

most often to areas of muscle attachment, suggesting dismemberment and flaying (see Chapter 10).

IMPORTANT PEOPLE

Judging from apparel, accessories, scale, and context, the most important personages depicted in Moche effigy ceramics are men with generic faces who wear fairly specific dress: military garments with bracelets and necklaces, pectorals, ear ornaments, and sometimes nose ornaments (Figure 9.2). Some of them, like some portrait heads, have partially painted faces. They sit alone with hands on knees, sometimes on a stepped platform or throne; some enthroned men have one hand on the head of a small feline, surely a power symbol. Stepped thrones are apt to be occupied by a man

FIGURE 9.2 Bottle portraying a probable ruler sitting on a platform and wearing a *tumi* headdress. *Courtesy Museo Larco, Lima, Peru, XXC-000-190.*

in a conical helmet, but some men wear headgear with a disk at either side of the brow. The disks—apparently made of metal, wood, or hide—can be concave or convex; occasionally, they resemble a tight bunch of feathers. A man wearing the two-disk headdress often has the primary role in fine-line scenes where warriors present captives to him (see Figure 9.1). In this instance he may sit on the ground, or sit or stand in a house on a stepped platform near an ongoing sacrifice. On a silver spatula-scepter from Sipán Tomb 1, he stands in full regalia over a kneeling captive (Alva 1994:86–87; Alva and Donnan 1993: Figs. 105, 106). He may also be shown as the largest figure in a ritual dance scene (see Figure 6.9; Donnan and McClelland 1999: Fig. 4.84) or as the most prominent figure in a Dance of the Dead scene (see Figure 12.6).

How did these men achieve such power? Various authors have discussed the likelihood of dynastic succession on the north coast of Peru, and the idea that chiefly roles—and perhaps priestly ones—were inherited, not always lineally but also brother to brother (Donnan 2001; Chapdelaine 2001:76–77; Larco Hoyle 1939:132–136; Netherly 1977:112–124, 1993:25–31; Ramírez 1995; Rostworowski 1990:449–450, 457, 1999:97–101; J. Rowe 1948:28; Russell and Jackson 2001:161; Salomon, in Salomon and Urioste 1991:18; T. Topic 1977). The position may also have been achieved through a remarkable talent, or even a grab for power.

PORTRAITS AND RELATED FIGURES

The Moche had a propensity for portraiture in modeled ceramic bottles portraying men with individualized faces and soft, cloth headgear, tied and/or wrapped like a turban, which appear in quantity in the southern region in Phase IV. It seems that the traditional elite did not need personalized portraits; a man on a throne has the austere, impersonal power of office and heritage, displayed by dress and paraphernalia.

Of a different category are portraits. A few Early Moche depictions of old men seem to be portraits, but there was no extensive portrait production before Phase IV, which produced the most realistic portraiture in all pre-Columbian art. The same man can be

recognized on many bottles, at different ages or in somewhat varied clothing (Donnan 2004; see also Benson 1997b: Nos. 67, 68; Larco Hoyle 1939: Fig. 135, 2001, I: Fig. 134). Some bottles are made from the same mold but differently embellished. Few have been found in controlled excavation, and their provenience is rarely known. A man whose plump cheeks press the strap of his headcloth is seen in a number of examples; Larco Hoyle reported this subject to be common in the Santa Valley, and he identified other faces with the Chicama, Moche, and Virú Valleys. A youngish, handsome man with a scar over his lip is also recognizable in many portrayals (Figure 9.3). Most portrait bottles are heads only, but some of these men can be

FIGURE 9.3 Portrait bottle depicting a young man with a scar above his lip and a faintly visible fold in his cloth headdress. *Staatliche Museen zu Berlin, Preussischer Kulturbesitz, Ethnologisches Museum, VA 17989. Photograph by Claudia Obrocki (4/2011).*

FIGURE 9.4 Full-figure portrait bottle depicting a priestly figure holding a staff, and wearing tied headgear and a "badge" on his garment. His left foot is missing. *Courtesy Museo Larco, Lima, Peru, XXC-000-051.*

A ruler would probably have been chief priest and military officer, but the proliferation of portraits of priestly figures in the south during Phase IV implies the rise of a cult of charismatic, puissant priests who worked with the rulers—but may also have eroded their control. The priests perhaps gained power through emphasis on themselves as individuals. Portraiture is extremely rare in pre-Columbian art, and northern Moche ceramics show no obvious sign of individualism, so its existence in southern Moche art seems to exhibit very special status. The Rayed God may have been introduced in the south by perhaps hereditary rulers as a way of combating priests who were upsetting the balance and cohesion of power, or perhaps the priests were not effective in coping with drought and El Niño conditions, and the godly warrior was thought to be more effective. In any case, the portraits of priestly figures go out as the godly warrior comes in.

Donnan (2004), who has published many of the portraits, points out that some of the individuals identified in portraits may also be depicted as captives. This might relate to their special value as sacrificial offerings—or to their having fallen out of favor. Donnan (2004: Fig. 7.40) interpreted an unusual vessel excavated in a tomb in the urban area near Huaca de la Luna as a possible captive. The portrait head has no headcloth or ear ornaments, and the body is an unusual egg-shaped bundle, perhaps indicating that the body and its grave goods had been wrapped in preparation for burial (see Chapter 12).

recognized in full-length, seated, effigy figures wearing a long cloth garment with various accessories (Donnan 2004:126–128). Some of the less elaborately dressed figures have a small, woven patch at the chest that suggests a badge of office (Figure 9.4). Remains of garments with this patch have been excavated at Pacatnamu and Dos Cabezas (Donnan and Donnan 1997:226, Figs. 3, 27; Jiménez 2000). The simple cloth garments look unimpressive compared to the "hard" ones, but given the symbolic value of cloth in the Andes, they express high status. Full-figure effigy portraits often sit with hands on knees; sometimes they hold a flute, a lap bag, a scepter, or an implement. These men surely had a priestly role.

THE ACTIVITIES OF PRIESTS

Religion was likely shamanic; however, I prefer the term *priest* to *shaman* because it is a broader term, allowing flexibility in definition for a role in a religion that is not fully understood.

Portrait headcloths vary, but those with a decorative edge, and sometimes a chin strap, would seem to belong to men of the highest status in a large, hierarchical group of "soft-dressed" men. I call the soft-dressed figures "priests" because they are often depicted engaging in what appears to be priestly activity. Most other such figures who are seen as portrait-head and full-figure bottles, and drawn on fine-line vessels, have a headcloth with a tied, diagonal fold over the brow, indicated by a line slanting across the front, drawn even on sketchy figures in large scenes. This diagonal surely points to a symbolic language of costume and ritual wrapping of cloth (Benson 1975, 1979; see also 1976a). Priestly figures represented by effigy bottles wear a long garment; men in fine-line scenes with the same headdress and other similar details wear a short tunic, which seems to indicate action (see Figure 4.1). Many have headcloth ties and shorter tunics with vertical, fringelike lines at the bottom (see Figure 9.4). Remnants of clothing with fringe were excavated at Dos Cabezas (Jiménez 2000:82–83). Some men wear a carefully tied cape or shawl. On lesser priests a bundled carrying cloth, tied around the body, may contain shamanic objects or material for planting, divining, or placing in graves (Benson 1975:134, 1987a, 1995a; Donnan and McClelland 1999: Fig. 4.84). It suggests sacred bundles or the *mesas* (curing or divining material) of many contemporary indigenous groups. The priestly iguana who accompanies the Snake-belt God wears the cloth regularly (see Figure 7.7), and a man with a scarf tied at the shoulders and a chin-strap headcloth appears with offerings in a little house of a kind that seems to be sacred space in many scenes.

Important positions in the priestly hierarchy might be: someone in charge of huacas; an expert in the liturgy and the calendar; someone to carry out funerary rites; a supervisor of sacrificial rites; and someone in charge of victims before the rite (Arriaga 1968 [1621]:32–37, 121; Arsenault 1993; Donnan 1990). Other men might oversee preparation of offerings and the care of sacred objects (see Figure 4.1). Also, in sacrificial and funerary ritual, music and dance were organized. Makowski (1994a) compiled a somewhat different list based on an excellent analysis of the activities of these figures in fine-line scenes.

Those depicted in priestly dress, especially in Early Moche, are often old men, who were perhaps thought of as approaching the status of sacred ancestor. Other priests are blind or have a drooping eye. Early chroniclers observed that in the Piura Valley, some native people were "one-eyed," and acute eye illness was endemic (Cabieses 1974, II:122–129). Some depictions seem portraitlike because they portray such disabilities. In many cultures, people with physical oddities

are believed to have special power, such as the "second sight" attributed to the blind. It seems likely that Moche men with diseased or distorted faces had special qualifications as curers or guides for the dead. In modern times, guardians of some of the best potato fields upvalley in the Peruvian Andes were required to be afflicted with leishmaniasis (uta) (Weiss 1961; see also Benson 1975:114). Faces disfigured by leishmaniasis or verruga, two diseases endemic in the Andes, look like faces of the dead and have a sympathetic magic connection with ancestors. Steve Bourget (1994a:94–95) believes that the Moche deliberately mutilated some faces to make them resemble skulls, and he observes that faces of those who have drowned and been in salt water for a long time show mutilations similar to those caused by the illnesses.

Bourget puts men with a missing foot in a class of specialists dedicated to preparing offerings or performing other ritual tasks; similarly, Daniel Arsenault (1993) places soft-dressed men with only one foot in a group of "stewards" who served the ruler (see Figure 9.4; see also Chapter 12; Benson 1975; Cabieses 1974, II:83; Verano 2003). A one-footed man in priestly dress may have a staff, which would not only have steadied the man but could also be used for agriculture and grave digging (see Figure 9.4). Arsenault's "dance of the dead" scenes include a prominent figure with a foot prosthesis (see Chapter 12) believed to have escorted high-status dead to the underworld.

THE LIBATION RITE

Warriors, priests, and captives are all shown in the Early Moche ceramic corpus, usually depicted alone in individual, sculptural form. Complex fine-line renderings of battles and the presentation of captives were being created at least as early as Phase II (Donnan and McClelland 1999: Fig. 2.18), with battle and sacrifice becoming the primary themes by Phase IV. Sacrifices were probably meant to empower the priests, as they perhaps promised environmental improvement and increase in royal power. The mythic sacrifice of the Presentation Theme (Figure 9.5) likely had a human version and shared elements indicate their relationship. Donnan and McClelland (1999) call this, in part, "the Warrior Narrative"; I call it "the Libation

FIGURE 9.5 Captives being transported through the desert in litters to a ruler seated on a roofed platform and holding a goblet (*left*). A plate-shirt warrior, also holding a goblet, stands in a house with clubs (*upper right*) as an anthropomorph prepares to behead a captive. *American Museum of Natural History, New York. Drawing by Donna McClelland.*

Rite," after Makowski (1994a; see also Arsenault 1994; Bonavia and Makowski 1999).

The sequence of the rite is uncertain, but it may begin with a procession of warriors in a landscape with plants; often a hummingbird, hawk, or falcon (all aggressive species) flies among them. Battle is shown between pairs of men in Moche dress in a landscape that sometimes has upvalley plants such as cacti and tillandsia. One warrior hits another's head with a club or grasps his hair in conquest. A defeated warrior's garments and gear fly off, and his weapons and clothing then hang on the victor's club, usually with the captured club hanging downward. Captives, stripped of clothing and weapons, are presented to one or more well-clad men, out in the open, apparently upvalley (see Figure 9.1). The roped captives are then led through landscape from the battlefield to the center, where the procession enters the courtyard of the huaca, presided over by a ruler occupying a stepped or ramped, roofed space. Captives run past or are presented to him. Sacrifice can be depicted in front of another building in the sacred precinct.

On the basis of excavations in Huaca de la Luna, Uceda (2000a:214) surmises that a throat-slitting rite took place on the lower level of Patio 1, Platform 1, in front of the painted-relief god faces (see also Franco 1998; Morales Gamarra 2003). Uceda mentions a sacrificial altar where blood was collected for presentation

to the gods. Ricardo Morales calls a construction in Patio 3C "an altar" based on remains found there that probably indicate sacrifice (Tufinio 2004a). From the upper space the ruler could have looked out on the procession, but perhaps not the sacrifice.

John Verano (1995:219; 2001b:172) has observed that "decapitation at the hands of supernaturals appears to be the most pervasive metaphor for ritual death." Given apparent Moche reluctance to picture a human sacrificer, it has not been clear who did the deed, but some recently excavated tombs may be those of sacrificers. An elderly man was found buried at Dos Cabezas with gilded copper ornaments around his head and chest, and a copper knife in his left hand; a ceramic human head, broken from a jar, lay by his right hand (Cordy-Collins 2001b:30–33). Two men buried with a bloody club near a sacrificial site at Huaca de la Luna are also thought to be sacrificers (Bourget 2001a:110–112), and Sipán has yielded tombs of officials who might have presided over sacrifices (Alva 2001:240).

Women sometimes appear in Phase IV sacrifice scenes, most often bare-headed with a braid (or two) hanging down. In some scenes two women are pictured sitting in a ritual house, and in others a woman is shown moving toward the sacrificee carrying a jug and cup, or holding the victim's hand (see Figure 9.5; Donnan and McClelland 1999: Fig. 4.85; Kutscher

1983:Abbn. 120, 123, 124). The women might be those entombed with the dead (see Chapter 12), or they may have had a priestly role. Anthropomorphic vultures sometimes stand with the women, and actual vultures would have been nearby on the occasion of a sacrifice, but Anne-Louise Schaffer (1983) sees these as women in vulture masks.

A complex scene of battle and the taking of captives is seen on a globular bottle in the Übersee Museum, Bremen (Donnan and McClelland 1999: Fig. 4.106). Two men are seated, ready to receive captives, on the upper curve of the vessel; at the top of the spout, high above the action, stand actors from the Presentation Theme, but in unusual forms: the Rayed God without rays, and the Plate-shirt God with rays (Donnan and McClelland 1999: Fig. 4.106). In some scenes a ruler on a stepped platform is holding or being given a goblet. At least some goblets held human blood (Bourget 2001b:95, 2006:14–19; Bourget and Newman 1998), but we do not know if someone drank it or it was fed to a god or to the earth. Participants may have consumed chicha and offered the collected blood, and it is possible that humans, as incarnations of the gods, drank the blood themselves.

THE INTERACTING FIGURES

In captive taking, presentation, and sacrifice, the activities of men in hard and soft dress are integrated. Some men wear mixed military and priestly clothing. A warrior may have a headcloth, a man in soft garments may wear a feline or bird headdress or hold a club or club-shaped scepter, or a man may have a knife painted on his headcloth. In an early instance, a priestly figure holds a rope around the necks of two nude captives with tattoos; behind the captives are three soldiers (Donnan and McClelland 1999: Fig. 3.51; see also Franco and Vilela 2004; Kutscher 1950: Fig. 25; Schaedel 1951:154). Scenes, and actual burials, often include both martial and shamanic traits.

As mentioned above, priestly portrait faces are sometimes scarred, but not the faces of those depicted as warriors. Perhaps the priests were former warriors or scarred from ritual battle. In any case, priests were seen as individuals, and warriors were not. Donnan

(2004:141 ff.) has observed that some scarred faces are those of boys or very young men.

DANCE

Processions of distinguished dancers—chieftains, warriors, priests, and, occasionally, a god—appear in fine-line scenes on globular bottles accompanied by various instruments and sometimes moving up in a spiral (see Figures 6.8 and 6.9; Donnan 1982; Donnan and McClelland 1999; Jiménez Borja 1955; Muelle 1936). Murals across facades at Huaca Cao Viejo and Huaca de la Luna show a probable line of dancers holding hands. Joseph Bastien (1987:70; see also Zuidema 1992:72) has described modern dances at the major agricultural festival in a Bolivian village where flute players spiral inward counterclockwise and move out clockwise. Inca youths, after ritual combat, would take a long rope and spiral around the king. Moche dancers may sometimes have moved up a ramp allowing a ritual ascent from the large, main courtyard to the upper, sacred spaces of the huaca. They could not have literally danced in a spiral, but they would have changed angles as they moved up the ramp.

Lurking in one of the ceramic dance scenes is a captive, and a goblet is held in several others. In one, a small warrior offers a bowl or cup to the major figure, and at the top of the picture is a little house under a severed head, with jugs outside and a stirrup-spout vessel on the platform inside. In another complex scene one of the dancers seems to have nicks on his legs, whereas other figures have some sort of tied leggings (Figure 9.6).

Less clear depictions show prickly-looking legs, which may indicate leggings or rattles, or perhaps blood. An oversized figure being elaborately dressed in plate-shirt garments may portray a sacrificer preparing for the event as other leaders, soldiers, and priests dance up the ramp, perhaps led by the ruler. The scene may, however, depict funerary preparations for the large figure. In another scene, hand-holding priests, led by a drummer, face an elaborately accoutered man— perhaps the hereditary ruler—in a striped cape, nose ornament, and headdress with two disks, a *tumi*, and an animal head (see Figure 6.9). The presence of a dog may suggest a mortuary rite.

FIGURE 9.6 Priestly and military dancers and musicians move toward and below a large warrior with a *tumi* headdress. *Museo Colchagua, Chile. Drawing by Donna McClelland.*

Dancing might also have been part of a rite involving well-dressed captives. Trumpets are often decorated with a relief figure wearing the garments of the Plate-shirt God (see Benson 1978; Menzel 1977:38–39). The man in the two-disk headdress is shown as a recurved trumpet. Well-dressed warriors or captives play instruments, which are adorned with their figures, and they *become* trumpets and whistles. Whistles can take the form of an anthropomorphic owl playing panpipes.

The entire Libation Rite may have been choreographed. Some battle and procession scenes look like dances, and even the skeletons of those sacrificed at Luna Plaza 3A look like those of dancers (see Figure 10.9; Bourget 2001a: Fig. 5.21, 1997a: Plates 4, 5, 8, 9). Ceramic depictions of dances of the dead exist, and it has been suggested that the bones found in Luna Plaza 3C may have been rigged to perform a puppet-like dance.

THE TINKU RITE

John and Theresa Topic (1997) have surmised that a specially chosen group fought occasional battles to ensure a good harvest, and Anne Marie Hocquenghem (1987:55) sees the Moche military as similar to that of the Incas—part of an elite group charged

with carrying out rites for the general good. Spanish chroniclers recorded ritual battles between two sectors of a closely related Inca community, describing them as rites of passage in which young warriors proved their aptitude for defending the community. Called *tinkuy* by the Incas, and usually known as *tinku* today, the rite was held between the summer solstice and the autumn equinox, when the rainy season was under way, rivers were high, and plants were growing. Tinku is still performed, usually closer to Carnival than the solstice, although it can be held at other times (Allen 1988; Bastien 1987:70; Gose 1994:194–224; Hocquenghem 1987; Joralemon and Sharon 1993:271–272; Makowski 1994a:64; J. Rowe 1946:308–309; J. Topic and Topic 1997). The rite is now often used for crop prediction, with the harvest of the winners expected to be better than that of the losers.

Tinku has many meanings and various spellings, and there are also other Quechua words for the rite. The simplest definition is "meeting or encounter in opposition," whether of warriors, lovers, or rivers. It can also refer to a dangerous meeting place. Tinku has an element of sexuality, and "ritual battle" can be a metaphor for copulation, reinforcing the rite's fertility associations. Tinku can also be described as a dance; the Topics (1997) found tinku defined as "a game in which legs are whipped"; Peter Gose (1994) notes that the word means "to sprinkle or libate."

Mock battles in which blood is drawn were performed in Colonial times and are still carried out by many Andean peoples with fields or herds. Those who have witnessed tinku in the southern highlands emphasize a need for the rite to produce blood. If tinku is bloody, the coming crop will be good; in some communities, if someone dies, the earth is the beneficiary of that death. The participants are not considered guilty in the event of injuries or deaths because it is believed that the battle results are foreordained by higher powers.

José María Arguedas (1978) described ancient heroic songs and music being played as ritually drunken participants worked themselves into a singing and dancing frenzy. As some sang and played, others whipped themselves to bleeding; afterward they wept in the shadow of lofty mountains, near chasms and cold lakes. The snow-covered mountains, places of origin and homes of ancestors, were thought to recognize the valor of combatants and to concede them good crops, but the ritual battles were often fought away from cultivated fields.

Carnival clowns and village elders wage mock battle in tinku in the court of a shrine in the center of a Bolivian hamlet (Bastien 1978:57–58), with the clowns sprinkling each other with water, and the elders slinging ripe fruit. Women sometimes invade the courtyard and beat the males to the ground with cornstalks. One man in the village proudly pointed to a tinku scar on his forehead. During Carnival in Pacariqtambo, near Cuzco, Gary Urton (1993:126–129) observed a headman from one moiety fight a headman from the other, each with musicians and dancers to accompany him. A support group of women carried jugs of chicha and cups. This ritual battle takes place just before plowing for the potato crop.

MOCHE RITES AND TINKU

Although tinku and Moche ritual battle cannot be considered exact equivalents, scenes of ritual battle on Moche ceramics contain elements that exist today. In some tinku fighters try to take the competitor's hat, jacket, or weapons, just as Moche victors are depicted collecting a captive's garments and weapons (Figure 9.1). Tinku participants and Moche captives sometimes drip blood. Women often carry cornstalks or

chicha in modern tinku, and cornstalks are pictured in some Moche scenes, as are women holding jugs, probably filled with chicha (it would be hard to collect blood in them) (see Figure 9.6). Some tinku descriptions mention a whip, an object sometimes carried by Moche priests (see Figures 4.1, 10.2; Arsenault 1993: Figs. 1–4; Donnan 1982: Figs. 6, 7b, 14; Donnan and McClelland 1999: Fig. 4.69; Hocquenghem 1987:104–105, Figs. 11, 51; Larco Hoyle 1939: Lám. XXXI; Makowski 1994a:64–65). The Moche whip holder is often near a platform or throne, but two priests, also carrying whips, can stand in the middle of a dance, and low-relief scenes of apparently dead people dancing can include a man with a prosthetic foot holding a whip. In a scene with vessels that tip themselves for pouring, two small priests, each with a whip, stand nearby (see Figure 4.1).

Post-battle sacrifice is indicated in Moche archaeology and art, and rumors suggest that deliberate killings occasionally take place after tinku (Tierney 1989). From early Colonial times, conversion to Christianity would have worked against the sacrificial rites found in many pre-Hispanic cultures, but customs die hard in the Andes.

Dance was likely part of the Libation Rite sequence, but it is unclear whether it came before or after the sacrifice. It may have celebrated the incipient rite, the accomplished offering, the journey to the other world of the sacrificed one—or all three. An Inca dance was held after an initiation rite mock battle, and sacrifice was made after dancing and drinking (J. Rowe 1946:309). The Huarochirí manuscript (Salomon and Urioste 1991:120; see also Gose 1994:219) mentions "a dance of origin," performed after conquest in war (with no mention of sacrifice); a modern tinku ends with music and dance, in the course of which there can be fatal injuries. Dancing skeletal figures with music instruments, shown on Moche ceramics, imply that dance is related to death and probably took place at the end of the ritual (see Chapter 12).

RULERSHIP AND DUALISM

Given the inherent dualism of the Andean landscape, and its physical incarnation in the Moche placement and use of buildings, the Moche may have had dual kingship. Dualism, expressed as two complementary parts of a whole, can be seen in the reciprocity and exchange systems that were basic in the Andes. Duality is also often found in smaller things; for example, Richard Burger and Lucy Salazar-Burger (1993:106; see also Bourget 2006) see the stirrup-spout form as indicating duality. Ceramic vessels were probably always made in pairs (although they are never exact duplicates), and figures depicted on them are often two men, both dressed well but differently, facing each other, perhaps a man and a captive. There are often two pairs of these figures on a bottle. In a continuing scene, two captives are often presented to two men in slightly different dress. As mentioned previously, captives can appear in two types of fine dress. Priests are often paired, and there are usually two women at sacrifices. An anthropomorphic deer is depicted as both warrior and captive; deer are prey and sacrificed animals, but they also have warrior attributes (see Chapter 10). Snakes are usually paired or two-headed, with one head larger than the other. Certain offerings are shown on ceramics in twos, tied together but not exactly alike. Panpipes are played in twos (with complementary notes). Anne-Louise Schaffer (1985:101–102) has observed that Loma Negra metal objects come in pairs. Metal objects are sometimes half-gold, half-silver, and nose ornaments frequently comprise a pair of motifs—one gold, one silver. Innumerable examples of contrast, splitting, and pairing exist.

In addition to civic administration, rulers likely did double duty, at least nominally, as chief warrior and chief priest. These elements were always present, but a particular pattern of this form of power and political organization likely developed in Phases III and IV, or Middle Moche, as their society became larger and more complex. Each city or state may have had a military and priestly pair, or a single ruler who combined the two roles. In some ceramic scenes, both kinds of figure appear, but in others the costume suggests that one person took on both roles.

Claude Chapdelaine and others (1997:86; see also Alva 2001; Bawden 1996:144–149; Rostworowski 1999) have inferred a concentration of power in a priestly military elite in Andean states based on intensive agriculture. Over and over scholars find in the ancient Americas evidence of a ruler's obligation to feed his people, and both religion and technology were required to ensure successful agriculture. Good land usage and water distribution were needed, as well as good relationships with gods, ancestors, otherworldly powers, and forces of nature—all closely interrelated. The Inca ruler was a priest, warrior, and farmer or herder, and in each community these functions had to be performed (see Hocquenghem 1987:29). Tinku exemplifies dualism as ritual confrontation between two parts of a whole, fought with military and priestly elements, to lead to agricultural fertility.

Patricia Netherly (1977:230–233, 1990, 1993; Netherly and Dillehay 1986) and others (Bourget 2006; Moseley 1990:5, 22–24; Rostworowski 1990:448–449, 1999:138–147; Urton 1993) argue that polities were characterized by integrated "dual corporate organization"; at any level, each unit could be subdivided into two unequal groups, with one person or group outranking the other in social, economic, and religious systems. Lords of different levels represented groups for whom they were directly responsible.

It is difficult to know how day-to-day administration would have worked in such dual hierarchies. Ceramics and grave goods do not spell this out, and archaeology is unlikely to give specific answers, but evidence for moieties and dual rulership in later North Coast cultures suggests considerable time depth. Jerry Moore (1996:178) makes the point that legend about the founding ruler of the Lambayeque/Sicán culture indicates that royal servitors did not have general administrative tasks, only duties focused on the leader, and Susan Ramírez (1995:302) has noted that in the sixteenth century, the chief of the fisherfolk in a part of the Chicama Valley was directly responsible to the principal lord. The Moche likely followed similar patterns.

CHAPTER TEN

Ritual Life

RITUAL IS A MEANS OF SOCIAL CONTROL and an attempt at supernatural control. Moche rites based on skywatching, natural events, myth, history, and funerary procedures were likely performed throughout the year in spaces of landscape or architecture that were sacred or being sacralized. A Moche ritual calendar, which surely is implied in many art depictions, must have some correlation with the Inca calendar described by Spanish chroniclers (Guaman Poma 1980 [1614]; Urton 1982; see also Franco and Vilela 2004), and was likely based on solstices, equinoxes, the rise of the Pleiades, certain Venus events, the dark of the moon, and/or the zenith and nadir of the sun. Rites would also have been performed in association with planting and harvesting, canal cleaning and the seasonal flow of water, the running of fish in the sea, and other significant events. (Anne Marie Hocquenghem [1987] has explored this in detail, so I will not reconsider it here.) Other motivations for ritual might have been religious-political events (a ruler's accession or death, an important anniversary) or natural catastrophes (El Niño, drought, or earthquake). Most Moche rites would seem to have been propitiatory or celebratory.

Some Moche scenes depict only mythical beings, some all humans, and a few a mixture. Not all important rites were illustrated in obvious ways. For example, an accession ritual may be shown in a way that we do not recognize. Do effigy portrayals of a man on a low throne, with or without a small feline, record the seating of a ruler? Is the Libation Rite a part of kingly investiture in Phase IV? Clues for funerary rites come from the Burial Theme (see Chapter 12), a probably mythic-astronomical subject that seems to show some practices from mortal interment rites (Donnan and

Castillo 1994; Donnan and McClelland 1979; see also Benson 1985, 1988b).

Some rites would have been held in daylight, others at night: day is for humans and the visible world, night for communication with the other world. Modern Peruvian divination and curing rites occur at night, as they did at the time of Spanish contact. On the Central Coast, "people used to go to consult Paria Caca at night, taking along llamas or other things" (Salomon and Urioste 1991:118; see also Joralemon and Sharon 1993; L. Larco 2008:22; Narváez 2001; J. Rowe 1946:302; Sharon 1972). Moche curing rites are usually depicted on modeled bottles, where darkness cannot be shown, but a covering or garment with a star or plus design might symbolize night. In fine-line coca rites (see below), black sky shapes suggest night. Sacrifice scenes do not show night, but sacrificers are often based on nocturnal creatures: owls, bats, and jaguars.

RITUAL INDICATORS

Architecture is a telling element in ceramic scenes. Roofed, stepped structures are usually settings for a seated, well-dressed ruler to witness a presentation of captives or another rite, but sometimes such structures are unoccupied. A few rites show open platforms. Simple structures generally shelter figures in priestly dress.

War clubs were important symbols for the Moche, appearing as ceramic designs, maces, and roof ornaments for certain buildings. Knife shapes are incorporated in many of their special objects and garments (notably helmets and backflaps), as they are in other parts of the Americas—for example, Olmec polished

FIGURE 10.1 Deer hunt scene. *Museo Chileño de Arte Precolombino, Santiago, 0676PCIB. Drawing by Donna McClelland.*

jadeite blades and carved Veracruz stone *hachas* in Mexico. Stirrup-spout bottles float in space in Moche imagery to indicate the status or sacredness of a person or place. Jars, likely holding blood or chicha, seem to designate scenes as sacrificial or funerary. Woven bags of several types are significant; they probably contain materials for ritual (Donnan and Donnan 1997; see also Benson 1978, 1984b).

Ropes and cords have many associations, often funerary and sacrificial (Benson 1975b:108–109; Orbegoso 1998; Tufinio 2001c, 2004b; Verano 2001a, 2001b, 2001c). Ropes can appear on skeletal remains; a coffin can be lowered with rope; and panpipes played by two skeletal figures in a fine-line ceramic scene are usually shown tied together. Rope is also related to offerings. In fine-line scenes a rope is tied around the neck of a jar—or a captive—and a cord motif is painted at the neck of many actual jars. Offering bowls are frequently tied in twos, both in real burials and in ceramic scenes of grave goods. One man seen in effigy vessels is identified, in part, by a V on his headdress and a loose rope around his neck with one end dangling (Benson 1982a; Franco, Gálvez, and Vásquez 2001a: Fig. 42a). The rope appears to be worn as a symbol of office, so perhaps he had the duty of tying captives or offerings.

Many garments, especially headdresses, are rite-specific. The iconographer must try to ascertain when a given person or someone of given rank wears different garments in various rites, and when different people celebrate the rites. Excavated burials give clues but rarely—if ever—do they provide definitive answers about which garments were used in which rites. Some grave offerings may not reflect rites undertaken by the deceased. On ceramics, victims of different rites are also distinguished by dress, attributes, and face paint.

THE DEER HUNT RITE

Deer are not significant in Early Moche art, but excavations at Ventarrón, in the north, have revealed very early, pre-Moche murals showing nets and deer (Alva and Alva 2008; *El Comercio*, 11 November 2007), and in Phase IV Moche art the hunting of a white-tailed deer by a figure who sometimes has a god's mouth is a frequent theme—and surely part of a critical offering rite (Figure 10.1). Christopher Donnan (1997a) properly relates the hunt to rulership and war (see also Benson 1988a, 1997a; Bourget 2001a:104–112; Donnan 1978:179–181; Netherly 1977:78–79). The Classic Maya also associated deer hunts with rulers, war, and sacrifice (Benson 1988a, 1997a; Kerr 1989; Reents-Budet 1994: Fig. 6.35). Maya cylinder vases show gods with a stag and its antler at a rite held when the antler detaches, leaving a bloody pedicel to be seen, a reference to blood-letting. The deer was also a sacrificial animal for the Moche.

Hocquenghem (1987:86–93, Figs. 39–41) argues effectively that the Moche Deer Hunt Rite provides an offering to the ancestors for water. During the dry season in the Andes (June to November), deer descend to the *lomas* vegetation of the then-moist lower slopes. Moche ceramic scenes often show priestly figures using clubs to drive the deer into a netted area, and well-dressed figures spearing them. A big net is sometimes tied with cloth knots (Donnan and McClelland 1999; Kutscher 1983: Abbn. 68–87), and one or two richly dressed hunters follow the deer, carrying spears. Their clothing combines military and sacerdotal attributes, often with traits fairly specific to the deer hunt. Headgear is often helmet-shaped but soft; it may have a feline head and a knife; it can be the portrait headcloth; and sometimes one of two hunters wears hard headgear and the other soft.

Deer hunters appear to have been at the top of the social structure, and some were probably rulers. A few deer hunt scenes include an unoccupied litter, which is surely not for the ranking hunter but for the carcass. Given that use of litters was restricted to those of high rank, it is clear that the deer was a valuable offering. Small priestly figures like those in the Libation Rite are active in some versions of the hunt. A dog near the primary figure may be an underworld guide as well as a hunter.

A variety of different plants appear in Moche deer hunt scenes, but usually only one species in each. The deer's ears and tail often look leaflike, and deer are widely associated in myth with agriculture and with ancestors as early hunters, gatherers, and farmers. Vegetation can get caught in a stag's antlers (Figure 10.1), and the resemblance of antlers to branches is a folklore theme. The white-tailed stag grows antlers every year; when new, they are covered with blood-veined "velvet." Often the growth of the antlers—one of the fastest-growing animal tissues—begins at the time of planting, and shedding of antlers coincides with harvest. Male genitalia are usually shown in deer drawings, a likely reference to fertility.

Effigy bottles can portray a stag sitting like a human with hands, but with a deer head and antlers, hooves, and tail; sometimes this stag is a warrior (Donnan 1997a: Figs. 1, 13). Deer have attributes helpful to warriors: alertness, sharp vision, and good hearing. They can run fast for a short distance; their hoofs can kill a small animal; antlers resemble weapons; and stags fight mock battles with antlers. In the seated position, an effigy stag can also appear as a distinguished person, as a captive with a rope around its neck (Berrin 1997: Fig. 104), or as a priestly figure playing a musical instrument. Occasionally a human musician or dancer wears clothing that suggests deer hunt dress.

Deer remains are rare in the refuse of Moche archaeological sites; deer hooves, however, appear in modern shaman's mesas and in ritual bundles at tinku time (Vásquez and Rosales 1998:181, 2004: Cuad. 58; 2008:182; Joralemon and Sharon 1993; Gose 1994:209).

THE WATERLILY, OR "BADMINTON," RITE

Gerdt Kutscher (1976) called one Moche rite "ceremonial badminton" because participants are depicted using staffs or spears with flowery attachments resembling badminton cocks. He suggested that this ceremony and the deer hunt were fertility rites (Figure 10.2; see also Donnan and McClelland 1999: Figs. 3.31, 4.50, 4.91; Golte 2009:243–254; Hocquenghem 1987: Figs. 1–7). Edward de Bock (1998) identified the

FIGURE 10.2 "Badminton" scene with the Snake-belt God atop a platform, an owl-priest in front of him, and anthropozoomorphs with spear throwers and priestly headdresses. *Museo Nacional de Arqueología, Antropología e Historia del Perú. Drawing by Madeleine Fang.*

attachments as waterlilies and renamed the activity. Hocquenghem (1987:47–62, Figs. 1–7) believes that these are flowers of lakes and sweet-water lagoons, whereas de Bock assumes a river location. Observing that water flows too fast for waterlilies during the rainy season, he places the rite between April and October; Hocquenghem puts it in September. If these are indeed flowers—they sometimes resemble feathers— the rite was likely performed after the deer hunt and shortly before seasonal water came to the coast.

Several waterlily rites show anthropozoomorphs who probably never appear in hunts, but the relationship of the rites is attested by the prominence of a deer in some of these scenes, and of a waterlily rite in which two severed deer heads rest on separate bundles (Donnan and McClelland 1999: Fig. 4.50). The rites also frequently have in common the dress of high-status participants (Benson 1975, 1976b, 1979; see also Donnan and McClelland 1999: Figs. 3.17, 3.19, 3.46, 4.50). Elite hunters and waterlily ritualists often wear a short tunic with vertical panels, and, projecting from the rear of the waist, two dark, rectangular backflaps. A "kilt" with patterned squares at the bottom, separated by slits, is common in both rites. The kilt can be worn by warriors, but the shirt and the waist projections probably appear only in these and related scenes.

The Waterlily Rite has both mythic and ritual versions—that is, human or supernatural participants— and there appears to be some connection with the Libation Rite, for white-garbed priests are prominent, and jars usually are pictured. In one example an owl-priest stands with a whip. Both rites were held in, on, or near architecture, and the celebrants have likely returned to the center from the countryside after a deer hunt.

A platform at the Cerro Blanco Complex excavated by the Moche Valley Project yielded only high-status, adult, male burials, one of which included a long copper tube. The tube probably enclosed a wooden shaft, a contraption like those held by Waterlily Rite participants (Donnan and Mackey 1978:154–158; Donnan 1995:154–154).

THE RUNNER RITE

Men running in line through a sandy landscape, each carrying a bag or folded cloth, constitute another

FIGURE 10.3 Ceramic dipper depicting bird-headed runners holding bags. At the end of the handle is the headdress for a face on the other side, where there is a round hole for dipping in the body of the vessel. *Courtesy Museo Larco, Lima, Peru, 066-005-00*8.

common subject of Phase IV fine-line ceramics (Figure 10.3). They carry no weapons and lack warrior dress; they wear a loincloth or "kilt" but no shirt or tunic. The typical runner headdress has the head of an animal, usually a fox, in front of a vertical plaque; headdress plaques usually alternate round and trapezoidal shapes. This headdress can appear alone as a ceramic motif. A frequent deck figure is a seated runner, apparently tying his headdress; his head may be that of a fox (see Figure 1.4 for a headdress fox head). Sometimes the runners are anthropozoomorphs, and the deck figure can be human.

The animal-human runners have been described as "ritual imitators" of eagle, jaguar, fox, and other animals, which may be accurate, but folklore, some of it from the North Coast region, is full of accounts of shamans and witches turning into animals (Glass-Coffin and Vásquez-Guerrero 1992:103; Sharon 2000). If the runners are shamanic, the creatures may show transformation. Wearing an animal mask or attributes might be considered to cause transformation, but if both anthropozoomorphs and humans are engaged in the rite, why is one group transformed, or imitating, and the other not? Perhaps the scenes show separate moments in a rite, or indicate that the zoomorphs are allies of the Moche, or simply ascribe to the Moche attributes of swift and clever animals. Running anthropozoomorph warriors often take different animal forms than those of these runners; the runners can have fish or insect traits, but I have never seen these traits in warriors.

Possible examples of round, metal headdress plaques, and/or of the metal animal heads that accompanied them, were found in burials at the Cerro Blanco Complex (Chapdelaine 2001:79–80; Chapdelaine et al. 1997:81–82; Donnan 1995:153; Donnan and Mackey 1978:144–158, 208; Jones 1979: Fig. 19), at Huaca Rajada Sipán (Alva 1994: Lám. 323), and at Huaca de la Cruz (Strong and Evans 1952:160, Plate XXVI-D); others are of unknown origin (Jones 1979: Figs. 1–3, 20). In the Cerro Blanco burial group that produced the waterlily staff, one burial contained a bottle with runners, and three burials had, over the heads, a large copper disk, possibly from a runner headdress, although a means of attachment seems lacking. No connection between runners and Waterlily Rite participants is obvious, but the same men may have taken part in both rites.

The running men have sometimes been called Bean Runners because beans float in the air in some scenes, but other vegetation is often present as well. Beans and plants suggest that bag contents were used in planting or crop divination. Some authors suggest that the floating beans reveal contents of the bags (see Kutscher 1951); Rafael Larco Hoyle (1939:83–124, 1942, 2001,I:145–175) proposed that the bags might contain beans marked with a form of writing. (It is usually believed that the Moche left no written records; if markings on beans were deliberate, they would surely have been limited in form and use.) Bags found by Larco Hoyle in the Santa Valley held white powder and a piece of quartz. A bag encountered below a

burial at Huaca del Sol contained quartz crystals, stones, beads, an animal bone fragment, and plant remains (Donnan and Mackey 1978:68), and near a man's body at Huaca de la Luna lay remains of an apparent bag with bits of quartz, pieces of hematite, and elements possibly from a necklace or pectoral (Bourget and Millaire 2000:50). Similar materials, likely with shamanic meaning, were used in Inca agricultural rites.

Questions about the identity and activity of the runners persist. Are they perhaps warriors in a prelude to ritual battle? Runner compositions resemble running warrior scenes. Inca *chasquis* ran bearing oral messages or those recorded on the strings of a *quipu* (Hocquenghem 1987:100–108, 176; J. Rowe 1946:310). Inca running rites were also associated with ritual combat and youth initiation, and with planting and ancestors who cared for growing plants (*mallqui* in both senses [see Chapter 4]). Perhaps the Moche runners' participation in ritual activity related to agriculture also served as an initiation.

Interpretative complications arose with Claude Chapdelaine's (2001:80) discovery, in the Cerro Blanco Complex urban sector, of a possible headdress disk in the grave of a woman with a copper knife in her left hand, and in another female burial, in Plaza 1 of Huaca de la Luna, of a bottle with a runner deck figure. Like the clubs found recently in a female burial at Huaca Cao Viejo (Franco 2009; Williams 2006), these finds indicate that objects were not as sex-specific as once thought.

BEAN DIVINATION

In Moche art a human face and accoutrements of warriors can be found on beanlike bodies; in fact, a helmet fits a bean "head" neatly. Beans seem to be enlivened as a part of military display, for animated, warrior beans often appear running, battling one another, or sitting emblematically before a weapons bundle (Donnan and McClelland 1999; Golte 2009:209–243; Kutscher 1983: Abbn. 203–212; Larco Hoyle 1942; Lieske 2001:193–195). Bean creatures are also seen holding beans and sticks, with beans in the air around them. Various supernaturals—most often the Snake-belt God and Iguana or another

FIGURE 10.4 Bean warriors with *tumi* headdresses confronting stag warriors with foliage caught in their antlers. All of them are wearing tumi-shaped backflaps. *Private collection. Drawing by Donna McClelland.*

partner—are featured in a "game" that may relate to crop divination, for beans and sticks are widely used for Andean divination and problem solving (Donnan and McClelland 1999:4.73–4.76). In the sixteenth century, Cristóbal de Albórnoz (see Hocquenghem 1987:155) observed a "game" played by the Inca and priests to determine territorial redistribution of huacas, and Bernabé Cobo (1990 [1653]:110) wrote that "the type of sacrifice depended on the will of the conjurers and sorcerers," who cast lots to choose which form to use. All Moche players seem supernatural (Figure 10.4), but there must have been such a rite in the human world.

CURING RITES

Although diseases may be thought to have supernatural causes, plants used in curing in the Andes often have real medicinal effect (Cabieses 1974; Cobo 1990 [1653]: Bks. 4–6; Gillin 1947:123–142; Hocquenghem 1987:132–138; L. Larco 2008; Schultes and Hofmann 1979:27–36; J. Rowe 1946:312–313). Some plants are hallucinogens taken to send the curer to the other world to discover causes of illness; the San Pedro cactus, for example, long used in North Coast curing, is said to enable a curer to ascertain a patient's illness (Cordy-Collins 1998; Donnan 1978:124–130; Glass-Coffin and Vásquez-Guerrero 1991:103; Joralemon and Sharon 1993; Sharon 2000; see also Bourget

1990; Sharon and Donnan 1974). The North Coast is known today for curing rites, as it apparently was in Colonial times. Illness is treated naturally and supernaturally in nocturnal rites, which typically end with the rising sun, an appropriate symbol for a healing rite. A modern curer, male or female, prepares a mesa with "power objects." Some markets carry plants and objects for mesas. Curers engage in a kind of tinku, fighting to rid a patient of evils and combating witchcraft, as well as divining. They "cure" fishermen's nets before boats go out, help people find lost or stolen property, and ensure success in personal affairs (Gillin 1947:33).

In Moche art, curers and diviners are often women (Uceda and Armas 1998: Fig. 8; see also Benson 1987b:78; 1988b:66; Larco 2001,II: Figs. 253, 254; Russell, Leonard, and Briceño 1998: Fig. 10). They often wear a cocoon-like cape, and most have closed eyes and hold a piece of San Pedro cactus. The women curers appear with patients, hold rattles, make chicha or San Pedro brew, or prepare grave goods. Helping sacrificial victims may have been another duty. Anthropomorphic owls in priestly garb can be male or female. Douglas Sharon (2000:8, 13) has noted that the nocturnal raptor is the animal "familiar" of modern curers, helping them to "communicate with the underworld and the ancestors to facilitate the fecund interaction between earth, water, and sky." Moche curers sometimes have an owl head. Bottles showing a female owl curer with the Snake-belt God supine at her side display objects that suggest a curer's mesa (Figure 10.5). Grave goods in important burials were surely arranged in a pattern resembling a shaman's mesa.

Other curing plants were possibly used. Two closely related genera of the family Solanaceae are *Datura* and *Brugmansia*; the latter has half a dozen species in the Andes (Cabieses 1974 I:354–357, II:7–11, 1981; Schultes and Hofmann 1979:117; Constantine Torres, personal communication, 2000). The large, bell-like flowers of both plants open at night. *Brugmansia*, with pendant blooms, was probably brought to the coast, where it appears in gardens and sometimes grows wild. It can provide medication for asthma, visceral ailments, and some nervous system illnesses. Its narcotic action combats insomnia. (One sleeps pleasantly with *Brugmansia* blooming outside an open window.) Used improperly, however, the plant can cause ailments and sometimes death. Possible Moche use of it has been discussed, but there is no obvious evidence.

A frequent motif in many scenes of sacrifice and coca rites is a fruit known as ulluchu (see Figure 8.1; Larco Hoyle 2001,I:149–151; McClelland 2008; McClelland, McClelland, and Donnan 2007:149). On one Phase V bottle the Plate-shirt God with owl face and animal headdress floats in space surrounded by floating ulluchu fruit (Sawyer 1966: Fig 64). Before actual ulluchu fruits were identified, they were thought to be an anticoagulant used to keep sacrificial blood flowing, but the fruits, much smaller than expected, were found for the first time in Sipán tombs, under a hammered-relief border depicting them, on a banner of gilded-copper platelets (see Figure 7.6; Alva 1994, 2001:226–227, 244 n.3), and in a burial offering at Dos Cabezas (Donna McClelland 2008:61). Apparently not an anticoagulant, ulluchu is now identified as a member of the Meliaceae family. A plant in some deer hunt scenes is vilca (*Anadenanthera colubrina*); a hallucinogen produced from its seeds is

FIGURE 10.5 Stirrup-spout effigy bottle depicting an owl curer (probably a woman) sitting with a *florero* above a ritual arrangement of objects. The Snake-belt God lies beside her. *Peabody Museum, Harvard University, Cambridge, F-729. Photograph by Christopher B. Donnan.*

used in curing (Cabieses 1974 II:9; Glass-Coffin 1992; J. Rowe 1946:292; Schultes and Hofmann 1979:117; Sharon and Donnan 1974). Pungent, dried espingo seeds, apparently from several varieties of plants on the far side of the Andes, occur in coca rite contexts and have been found at Moche sites (Arriaga 1968 [1621]:44; Bourget 1990; Donnan 1978:127, 191 n.3; Gumerman 1997; Sharon and Donnan 1974:53; Shimada 1994b:43; Wassén 1979). In the sixteenth century the seeds were added to chicha for medicinal use. Used by curers today, they are apparently psychoactive and are plentiful in markets. A nonvegetal, psychoactive medication comes from sea snails of the highly toxic genus *Conus*, whose shells have been found in Moche ruins. Past use is uncertain, but a *Conus* peptide has been formulated into a painkiller, and another is being developed for use by epileptics (Sreenivasan 2002; Vásquez et al. 2003).

THE COCA RITE

In the Andes, coca leaves have been chewed, brewed, burned, and placed on sacred stones as a revered offering. The leaves are still presented to mountain shrines, and quids from modern rites can be found at ancient sites. Leaves of the sacred plant—containing calcium, iron, phosphorous, vitamin A, and riboflavin—are used to alleviate fatigue, altitude sickness, aches, and pains by drinking coca "tea" or chewing a leaf or two with an alkaline (to facilitate extraction and absorption of juices) and sucking the quid as it is held between gums and cheek (Plowman 1984; see also Benson 1976b, 1979; Richardson 1994:43–44). In art from Ecuador and Colombia, a bulging cheek may be the only indication of a coca chewer. Moche artists were more interested in signifiers of the rite than in the quid, although there are a few protruding cheeks (de Bock 1988: No. 41; Donnan 1978: No. 181).

The Coca Rite (or elements from it) appears in Phase I ceramics and was prominent through Phase IV. Effigy coca takers and those in fine-line scenes carry a gourd or other container to hold lime, as well as a stick to remove it, and some figures have a bag, likely for coca leaves, on a cord around the neck, hanging most often against a shoulder (Figure 10.6; see also Figure 1.5). On earlier ceramics ritualists are depicted alone, but Phase IV scenes show several figures. The major human personage is likely the prominent man seen in the Libation Rite and other rituals. Phase IV ceramic scenes show the rite being performed on the ground, presumably under a night sky. Jagged lines suggest a rough landscape, and cactus plants may indicate an upvalley site. The Moche perhaps used coca to communicate with sacred mountains and achieve a sacred state of being for divination.

As patron of the Coca Rite, the Plate-shirt God stands alone on one side of several fine-line bottles, while the human participants sit on the other side (Figure 10.6) (Uceda 2008). This division may express time as well as human-versus-supernatural space. In the Huarochirí manuscript (Salomon and Urioste

FIGURE 10.6 Depiction of the Coca Rite showing the Plate-shirt God under an arching skyband and three elite humans using sticks to put lime on the coca leaves in their mouths. *Linden-Museum, Stuttgart. Drawing by Donna McClelland.*

1991:69), the god (or son of the god) takes coca first; then the people engage in the rite. In the Moche scenes the god wears the ulluchu headdress or the one with curving projections. A large, animal-headed, metal-platelet attachment hangs from his shoulders, flying out in fine-line scenes or lying flat on effigy figures. The elaborate, multimedia object excavated in a funerary offering in Huaca de la Luna was the first known example of the actual object, and one has been found also at Huaca Cao Viejo (see Figure 6.6). The hanging is depicted on a number of bottles, a few of which show it on a mortal with coca traits (Asmat and Fernández 2002; Benson 2008:3–6; Donnan and Donnan 1997: Fig. 43; Makowski, Amaro, and Eléspuru 1994: Fig. 150; Morales Gamarra 2004; Asmat, Morales, and Fernández 2000: Fig. 8; Uceda 2004, 2008).

In this much-depicted ceremony, with or without the god, the men—no women appear—are, I believe, Moche, although, on the basis of dress in some scenes, it has been argued that they are Recuay "foreigners" from the Callejón de Huaylas (Lau 2004; see also Lau 2000; Makowski and Rucabado 2000). A squarish bag on a cord and a headdress with upraised jaguar paws or human forelimbs appear on Huaylas sculpture, and elite Moche coca ritualists often wear a headdress with two vertical elements or two upright hands or jaguar paws. A variant headdress displays two ulluchu fruits—for example, that worn by the Plate-shirt God in Figure 10.6. The ulluchu headdress and the pendant-disk ear ornaments, usually seen on Moche coca ritualists, have not been found in Recuay art (Joan Gero, personal communication, 1999). In Moche art, faces of participants are often marked with a Maltese cross (see Figure 1.5). Shirts or tunics with a banded vertical panel or a checkerboard motif are distinctive coca rite garments; a bundle with a checkerboard motif carried by a llama may contain coca leaves (Berrin 1997: No. 27). Less richly dressed figures have a cap or bare head and a bag at the shoulder; some hold up a tunic, usually with one of various designs worn in the rite.

Combat was associated with the Coca Rite (Benson 1976b, 1984b; Donnan and McClelland 1999; Kutscher 1983: Abb. 129; Proulx 1982:89–90). In these scenes typical Moche warriors club the heads of men in a raised-hand (or paw) headdress with a bag

or banner flying out behind. The weapons bundle in coca scenes can show captured weapons and garments, sometimes of an unusual kind. Naked captives in the rite tend to have Maltese-cross face paint or pendant-disk ear ornaments; sometimes the dress or body-tattooing of the defeated simply looks foreign. A man with a moustache, small beard, stippled brows, pale skin, pendant-disk ear ornaments, and a tuft of hair appears as a captive or as a warrior in distinctive garments; he seems to have been a foreigner captured in battle related to the rite (Donnan and McClelland 1999: Figs. 3.4, 3.52). A long, white beard and upraised headdress typify a seated effigy figure—the only heavily bearded man in Moche depictions—who sometimes holds coca equipment. Portraits of him without coca attributes surely belong to the complex, although he does not appear in scenes (Donnan 2004: Figs. 1.7, 7.11, 7.12; Larco Hoyle 2001,I: Figs. 135, 151). These unique personages—they have facial hair—may be historical/legendary characters. The bearded man seems to have been a coca ritualist.

The battle related to the Coca Rite seems to imply highland-lowland interaction. It may commemorate the conquest of coca fields and the gaining of the right to wear clothing of the conquered. It may reenact warfare that set and maintained boundaries with Recuay or other peoples. As ritual battle, it might celebrate the coca harvest and venerate the sacred plant. If the Moche were fighting highlanders or commemorating a highland war, coca might have been chewed before battle to combat altitude sickness, to give combatants extra vitality, or to vitalize weapons.

A Phase IV tomb constructed in fill in Huaca de la Luna and excavated in 1992 by Santiago Uceda (1997d:178–181) contained the intact burial of an official with offerings that included a lime container of gilded copper, a copper spatula or stick, and some coca seeds (see Chapter 12). These were the first such objects to be excavated in a Moche burial, although seeds have been found on a bench in front of a mural in Plaza 2, suggesting an offering.

A gastropod trumpet, or *pututo*, usually of *Strombus* shell, is often held by a man in coca rite dress in Phase IV ceramics. Such trumpets were sacred in many pre-Columbian cultures, often decorated with incised, inlaid, or painted designs. In the art of earlier Moche phases they appear randomly, sometimes in warfare scenes. The use of shell for the lime of coca taking is a possible link. Coca seems to have a sea association: some held-up tunics display a waterbird or a ray, and the two-projection headdress may relate to the two-pronged headgear of fishermen. The trumpet might announce a journey through the sea to the other world. Uceda (2000a:213) sees the rite as associated with water and fertility.

Monkeys are the only animals or anthropomorphs shown with coca paraphernalia, possibly because monkeys and coca likely came from the same regions (Donnan 1978: Figs. 95, 96, 182; Larco Hoyle 2001, I: Fig. 65; see also Kutscher 1950: Taf. 48). In one example a monkey with a topknot holds a lime gourd and stick, and wears a long, white garment; a coca bag hangs by a cord at his back. Both coca humans and coca monkeys sometimes appear in pairs, side by side, with pendant-disk ear ornaments and a coca bag in front. Monkeys are also seen with ulluchu fruit.

PILGRIMAGES

At Chavín de Huántar, pot sherds from various regions indicate visits by pilgrims (Keatinge 1981:179–184; Lumbreras 1993; Burger 1992:226; Quilter 2001:29–31; Rick 2008). It has been suggested that there was an oracle there. An early-seventeenth-century Spanish source tells us: "Near this village of Chavín there is a large building of huge stone blocks very well wrought; it is a *guaca*, and one of the most famous of the heathen sanctuaries, like Rome or Jerusalem with us; the Indians used to come and make their offerings and sacrifices, for the Devil pronounced many oracles for them here, and so they repaired here from all over the kingdom" (Vásquez de Espinosa 1948 [1616]:491).

Moche pilgrims may have journeyed to that earlier site, although there is no specific evidence for this. Were the Coca Rite and battle parts of a pilgrimage to the Recuay border on the way to Chavín? Were pilgrimages made to Cupisnique sites near the coast—Caballo Muerto, for example?

The Moche, moving through and marking landscape they controlled, surely felt a need for timely pilgrimage to a series of shrines. Some rites took place in a ceremonial center; others in the open—often in uplands, sometimes at sea. Pilgrimages were

movements through time and space, and landscape and architecture had roles in the procedure. In two examples of the Runner Rite, participants arrive at an unoccupied structure, the likely goal of pilgrimage, possibly Huaca de la Luna. Activities outside centers would be held at various places, each for its own reasons. Mountain sacrifices may have climaxed a myth-related pilgrimage. Remnants of ritual activity on offshore islands strongly suggest pilgrimages (see Chapter 11).

Huaca de la Luna was probably a, if not the, major shrine. Uceda and Elías Mujica (1998:9–19; see also Gwin and Block 2004) propose that it was dedicated to a fertility cult, with rites involving the taking of captives and their preparation and sacrificial offering to the gods, as well as ritual interment and regeneration of the structure itself (see also Moore 1996:124; Rostworowski 1992:102–103; J. Rowe 1946:302; Verano 2001b:182). Régulo Franco (1998:101, 104) has argued convincingly that human sacrifice, offering presentations, ceremonial dances, and other ritual activities took place within sacred precincts of Huaca Cao Viejo. Both huacas must have been goals of pilgrimage, as well as starting points for journeys elsewhere on calendrical or urgent occasions. Pilgrimages would have been vital to political, social, and commercial—as well as religious—life.

Pilgrimages to ancestral and oracular shrines are described in ethnohistoric and ethnographic sources, and these are still undertaken at times and places of "special potency" (Allen 1998:14–15; Moore 1996:124–131; Urton 1981:201–202). John Gillin (1947:27) noted that a statue of San Isidro, the patron of agriculture, was taken out of a Moche village church on a pilgrimage through the countryside. Rites are now carried out, for example, in a special place at Galindo, in the Moche Valley where the mountains begin; remains of fires, coca quids, and a certain kind of modern bottle are found in quantity. Gold banners excavated from Tomb I at Huaca Rajada Sipán might have been displayed in pilgrimages, rites, or battle (see Figure 7.6). The splayed, gold figure on Sipán banners likely represented the ruler or ancestor in the pose of the X Sacrificer (see Figure 7.6; Alva 1994; Alva and Donnan 1993: Figs. 57, 62). A banner carried publicly would proclaim the sacredness and power of the ruler and the people. Banners were found also at Loma Negra

(Jones 1993), and a roughly contemporary cloth banner with feather trim was excavated in a burial offering at Huaca de la Luna in 1999 (Morales, Asmat, and Fernández 2000:53).

"Offering rooms" at Pacatnamu and Dos Cabezas are described by Alana Cordy-Collins (1997). One room in the center of Pacatnamu was the apparent site of a rite carried out with human skeletons and animal remains, along with 400 small, unslipped pots arranged in eight clusters, as well as other pottery, pieces of copper, textiles, and shell objects; liquid had been poured into the room, which was burned at least once. Were these rooms used by pilgrims, or were they for local rites? Ritual fires are little discussed, but there is evidence for them (Franco and Gálvez 2010:81; Franco, Gálvez, and Vásquez 2001b:140, 167). Fires were part of the program of architectural change and of burials, offerings, sacrifices, disinterments, and other activities.

THE SNAIL HUNT RITE

Snail hunters carrying a woven bag or basket and a stick to remove a snail clinging to a plant are featured on some Phase IV bottles with peaks (Figure 10.7). They wear the headcloth, tied cape, and short, fringed tunic of priests, but the double backflap of deer hunters. Jürgen Golte (1985) points out that both snails and mountain sacrifice are associated with agricultural fertility.

Land snails have formed part of the North Coast diet for 11,000 years, according to Gálvez, Castañeda, and Becerra (1993); snail remains have been excavated in Paiján middens. In moist winter months large snails are found on isolated hills near the sea, in the first foothills, and along a narrow band at about 2,600 m elevation, where remnants of forest cover remain. With sufficient fog for lomas vegetation, snails feed on tillandsia, cacti, and small trees; they also cling to rocks. Gálvez and others (1993), as well as Alan Craig (1992), exploring the association of snails and tillandsia, note that El Niño conditions encourage rapid proliferation of snails, and many recipes exist for preparing them as food. Cristóbal Campana (1994:74) describes sprinkling ground maize on snails to purge them, cooking them in salted water, and taking them from the shell with a long spine (see also Gillin 1947:26).

FIGURE 10.7 Effigy bottle depicting snail-topped mountain peaks and figures gathering snails in the uplands. *Museo Nacional de Arqueología, Antropología e Historia del Perú. Photograph by Steve Bourget.*

Steve Bourget's (1990) investigations indicate that snails feed on San Pedro (*Trichocereus pachanoi*) cactus, which contains mescaline and other alkaloids (see also Cordy-Collins 1998; Sharon 2000). The Moche not only gathered a delicacy, but were perhaps also finding an effective substance for use in rites. If the Conch Monster is based on the land snail as well as on the larger *Strombus*, it might be easier to imagine after eating cactus-fed snails.

MOUNTAIN SACRIFICE

Unadorned mountain bottles, or those with plants painted on them, began to appear in Phase III and

FIGURE 10.8 Effigy bottle showing a mountain sacrifice. *Staatliche Museen zu Berlin—Preussischer Kulturbesitz, Ethnologisches Museum, VA 48095. Photograph by Claudia Obrocki (4/2011).*

became common in IV. Bottles can have one to seven peaks, but many have five and resemble a fist, which is also a Moche motif in wood and bone (Figure 10.8). Phase IV examples of the bottles with high-relief figures usually display a sacrificial victim bent face down over the central peak, hair and blood flowing like water—or becoming water (Zighelboim 1995; see also Bergh 1993; Bourget 1995:89–98; Cordy-Collins 1998: Figs. 6.11–6.13; Donnan 1978:144–155; Golte 1985; Hocquenghem 1987:182–186, 189). Human attendants—and often a deer or other animal—are depicted. A second victim may lie supine at the base of the peak, sometimes beheaded, although there is no obvious sacrificer. One bottle excavated in the Uhle Platform at Huaca de la Luna depicts a deer lying

alone at the base of the peaks (Chauchat and Gutié-rrez 2008: Fig. 82a).

Mountain sacrifice scenes combine human and divine figures. The old Snake-belt God is often seated like a sculpture on a low platform; he may also emerge from a cave. A variant form shows an abstract step-wave with a victim prone on top, like a swimmer riding a wave crest, hair flowing like water. Often the active version of the Snake-belt God leans in on one side, while Iguana stands on the other, in what is likely a rite to invoke water for fields. If regularly scheduled, this sacrificial nourishing of a water source to ensure a good supply would likely occur just before the mountain rains were due. The rite might also have been a response to severe drought or some other drastic situation.

A careful study of mountain bottles by Ari Zighelboim (1995) proposes that mountain sacrifice was performed at Cerro Blanco to reenact a mythical event. The bottles do not show architecture—only the god's throne—and the mountain setting is emphasized, so it seems likely that the rite took place at a critical upland water source. Several scenes show the snails and San Pedro cactus of the upland lomas. One scene with many skeletons resembles sacrifices found at Huaca de la Luna (Hocquenghem 1987: Fig. 186).

HUMAN SACRIFICE

Sacrifice is not always easy to identify in archaeological remains, but the practice of offering humans, animals, and other valuables is ancient in most of the world (Benson 2001). Moche art pictures blood and detached human heads and limbs, and sacrifice is implied by battle and captive taking, and by scenes in which an anthropozoomorph holds a knife to a human throat. Evidence of large-scale sacrifice of warriors has come from recent excavations at Huaca de la Luna (Bourget 1998, 2001b; Bourget and Millaire 2000). Sacrifices were part of elaborate funerary rites at many sites, as Verano (1995) has observed (see also Verano 2001a, 2001b, 2001c; Cordy-Collins 2001b). Although women do not appear in mass sacrifices, women and children accompanying the high-status dead can be considered sacrificed (see Chapter 12).

Child sacrifice was prevalent in much of the ancient world, and at Moche sites and elsewhere, children were sacrificed at the time of building dedication or reconstruction (Franco, Gálvez, and Vásquez 2003:153). Evidence of an apparent child sacrifice was found at Huaca de la Luna near the mass sacrifices of warriors (Bourget 1997c, 2001a; Tufinio 2001c), and Antonio de la Calancha (1974–1982 [1538]) described a Jequetepeque Valley temple where child offerings were made in Inca times. The Capac Hucha rite of the Incas turned children into huacas by burying them with offerings in sacred places, often on high mountains (Reinhard 1996, 1999). Several kinds of Moche figures hold a small being that is likely a child and probably sacrifice-related. Hocquenghem (1987:111–113) sees a Moche whistler with a child as an early version of Capac Hucha.

Large figures apparently associated with child sacrifice are shown whistling or holding rattles, which are shamanic implements (Sharon 2000). Whistles appeared in a child's burial in Huaca de la Luna (Bourget 2001a), as well as in the graves of an important woman in Huaca Cao Viejo (Franco, Gálvez, and Vásquez 1999b) and of a woman at Huanchaco (Donnan and Mackey 1978); rattles and sacrificial knives also occurred in a tomb at Huaca Rajada Sipán (Alva

2001). Today a rattle is used, with whistling and songs, to activate supernatural forces, attract guardian spirits, and ward off evil (Joralemon and Sharon 1993; Sharon and Donnan 1974:52; Olsen 1992:81). Frank Salomon (1995:323–324) describes a Contact-time night visit to ancestral mummies in a cave: "Arriving at the cave mouth, the worshipers whistled to ask entry."

In Platform II of Huaca de la Luna, tombs of two old men, thought to have been sacrificers because of knives in their burials, were excavated above Plaza 3A, where 15 strata of sacrificed human remains included at least 70 persons in at least 5 rites; there is evidence of heavy-rain sedimentation between levels (Bourget 1997b, 1997c, 1998, 2001a, 2001b, 2006; Bourget and Newman 1998; Uceda 2001a:63; Uceda and Tufinio 2003:200–202; Verano 2001c:117–120). The victims were healthy, active males, aged 15 to 39, with healed fractures and wounds as well as fresh injuries; skulls were fractured by blows from blunt objects, and throats were cut deep enough to mark vertebrae (Figure 10.9). There were signs of torture and dismembering. Ongoing DNA studies may suggest that the men were not foreign (Shimada et al. 2008). Uceda (2000a:214) points out that if sacrifices were

FIGURE 10.9 A few of the skeletons of sacrificial victims in Plaza 3A, Huaca de la Luna. *Photograph by Steve Bourget.*

propitiatory offerings, the rite should involve groups within the society, meaning that local warriors would be sacrificed for the community. This rite appears to have been performed in desperation in the last phases at Luna. Metal grave goods with the two old men had been looted, but the accompanying ceramics depict warfare, captives, and sacrifice, and a wooden mace covered with human blood was unearthed in one tomb.

An earlier and different kind of sacrifice was found in nearby Plaza 3C (Orbegoso 1998; Tufinio 2001c; Uceda and Tufinio 2003:192–197; Verano 1998, 2001c:120–121, 2008; Verano, Tufinio, and Lund 2008). The largely disarticulated skeletons of seven adult and adolescent males showed evidence of throat slitting and cuts that often correspond to areas of muscle attachment, suggesting dismemberment and flaying. Some bones were tied with cord. The bones may have been deposited in rites in which skeletons

were made to dance (see Chapter 12). At the time of death some victims had healing injuries, possibly inflicted during their capture.

The head, the most important part of the body, was a special offering (Verano 1995, 1998: Fig. 165, 2001b:172, Fig. 8.4). A cache of 18 skulls was found at Dos Cabezas (Cordy-Collins 2001b; Donnan 2001); the tomb at La Mina yielded a cranium cut into a plate (Narváez 1994:66); and two crania in niches in a residential unit near Huaca de la Luna were cut open at the top and had holes drilled for attachment of the lower jaw; they could have been used as vessels (Verano 2001b: Fig. 8.4).

There are many questions about sacrifices. Who were the victims, and how were they chosen? Why were some bodies carefully buried, and others left on the surface? And why were some beheaded and others cut into pieces? What was the significance of later use? Why was what done to whom on what occasion?

CHAPTER ELEVEN

The Sea

ABSTRACT WAVES, CATFISH, and rays are motifs on Early Moche ceramics. Later, murals with similar marine patterns appear in Huaca de la Luna and Huaca Cao Viejo (see Figure 5.6). Sea and shore birds, sea lions, and crustaceans are ceramic subjects. The Snake-belt God fights supernatural sea beings, takes the guise of various marine creatures, and makes love to a woman, possibly on an island in the sea (see Chapter 7). Pelagic resources and symbolism were important to the Moche, realistically and religiously.

THE RAFTS

Rafts made of bundles of rushes tied together were described by José de Acosta (1970 [1608], Bk. 3, Chap. 15:150; see also Hocquenghem 1987:127). Fishermen carried them on their shoulders, put them in the water, jumped inside, and using long cane paddles, the men went to sea with nets and cords. Moche fishermen used something like the present-day *caballito*, the "little horse" of a raft, about 3 m long, which is used at the fishing and resort town of Huanchaco (Moche Valley) and at a few other places (Bawden 1996: Figs. 2.2, 2.3; Benson 1995a; Bourget 1994b; Buse 1981; Donnan 1978:102–106; Larco Hoyle 2001,I:328–333; Donna McClelland 1990; Schaedel 1988:43–45, 79–83). Also called a *tule* or *totora* raft or boat, the caballito is made of four tapering, cylindrical bundles of rushes or reeds tied together to make a pointed bow, a square stern, and a small, flat, stern cockpit where a single occupant kneels or sits, propelling the raft with a split-cane paddle. Sixty years ago John Gillin (1947:34–35) noted that the entire population of Huanchaco, including children, knew how to construct these rafts. The town has grown and developed other methodologies, but the rafts are still used as dinghies, for sport at the water's edge, and for line fishing, small-net fishing, or catching crabs near the shore. When not in use, they are stood up on the sandy shore to dry. Moche fishermen probably went out at midday and fished overnight, navigating by the stars, as modern fishermen have done.

Rafts were used for transit as well as for fishing. The Moche traveled to offshore islands and had contact with Ecuador and with peoples to the south. The spread of influence and the movement of goods indicate considerable traffic. Large or heavy cargo could usually be moved more expeditiously on a raft than by man or llama, although there was certainly land traffic as well.

Light balsa wood rafts are depicted on a few Moche bottles. Although ancient in southern Ecuador and still made there, balsa rafts are rare in Peru.

FISHERMEN

The best time for fishing off the coast from Huanchaco is between the evening rising of the Pleiades in November and their heliacal rising in June (Urton 1982:236). In this period fish normally run close to the surface, and fishermen work just offshore or farther out to sea. From July to October they fish along the coast to the south. Ethnohistoric and ethnographic sources report communities of fishermen and watercraft specialists, separate from farming and other communities, with fishermen in Chicama, for example, having a separate language or dialect (Bawden 1996:78–79; Gillin 1947:30; Ramírez 1995; Ramírez-Horton 1980:126; Schaedel 1988:42). This pattern seems to have held through much of North Coast prehistory and history, with many variations. Patricia Netherly (1977:54–57) found that modern Huanchaco fishermen say that their sisters marry men from the highlands, and she saw this as signifying an exchange process that is part of the socioeconomic structure. With the discovery of new sources, Netherly (2009) finds the situation more complicated. María Rostworowski (1977, 1981:84–100) determined that at the time of Spanish contact fishing-family women might marry fishermen from afar, but not local farmers. Given some interdependence, interests of farmers and fishermen were different. As Michael Moseley (1992:47) says, "Fishermen worry about sharks and turbulent seas, farmers about insects and droughts." Both worry about El Niño.

Fishermen today use nets that have Moche prototypes (Buse 1981; Gillin 1947:33; Rodríguez 2001). A circular dip net with a handle is shown on many bottles. A casting net was probably used as well. The modern two-man fishing net is similar to netting in Moche deer hunt scenes. If something like the present-day set line existed in Moche times, large rafts may not always have been necessary to catch big fish; good food fish, such as corvina, bonito, and bacalao, are now caught with this net extended into water perpendicular to the shore. The ceramics also provide examples of hook-and-line fishing. At Pacatnamu fishing gear has been found in graves, normally in male burials (Donnan 1995:150).

FISH

Techniques for drying and storing fish, especially anchovies and sardines, must have been known for a long time. Whether fresh, dried, or salted, fish was important for protein consumption and for trade. (A llama loaded with baskets of fish is shown on some Moche bottles.) Sardines (*Sardinops sagax*) and anchovies (*Engraulis ringens*) were of basic importance. The Moche surely used fish, especially the heads, for fertilizer.

Fish remains have been found as offerings and

in Phase V Moche burials and ruins (Donnan and McClelland 1997; Franco, Gálvez, and Vásquez 2001b; see also Alarco 1997:223–276; Vásquez and Rosales 2004, 2008; Vélez 1980). In the tomb of an official at Huaca de la Luna (Cárdenas, Rodríguez, and Aguirre 1997; Uceda 1997d:178–179), seven species were found, the most common being sardine, *jurel* (spiny mackerel, *Trachurus symmetricus*), *cachema* (also called *ayanque*, *Cynoscion analis*, a drum of the Sciaenidae, to which corvina belongs), and *life*, of the Trichomycteridae—small, parasitic South American catfishes that are plentiful in river mouths and canals. The last swim into the mouths of large fish or into urogenital openings of human bathers, where they lodge and feed on blood or tissue (Migdalski and Fichter 1983:166; Paxton and Eschmeyer 1995:110). In excavations in the residential area near Huaca de la Luna, Victor Vásquez, Teresa Rosales, and others (Vásquez and Rosales 1998, 2004, 2008; Vásquez et al. 2003) identified some 36 species of fish, many of which could have been caught from shore with a line and net; only 10 would have had to be caught from boats. The former included *cachema* and *bagre* (*Galeichthys peruvianus*, a sea catfish), as well as sharks (*tollo* [*Mustelus* sp.], and *angelote* [*Squatina armata* or *S. californica*]); guitarfish (a ray [*Rhinobatus planiceps*]); mullet (*Mugil cephalus*), which lives in salt and fresh water, lagoons and river estuaries; sole (*Paralychthys* sp.); *trambollo* (a blenny, *Labrisomus philippi*); *mojarilla* (*Stellifer minor*); and several drums and croakers. The six species that had to be caught from boats are *jurel*, cabrilla (*Paralabrax humeralis*), bonito (*Sarda sarda chiliensis*), a tuna (*Scomberomorus maculatus*), and quantities of merluza (*Merluccius gayi*), sardines, and bagre. Brian Billman (1999) also lists near-shore and pelagic fish encountered in archaeological sites in the Moche Valley.

Identification of fish in Moche art is controversial. Many cartilaginous fish—sharks and rays—swim off the coast. Rays are identifiable, at least as to family. Catfish can be identified by the whiskerlike barbels around the mouth, but there are hundreds of species, and it is often difficult to tell which is intended. Moreover, a stylized catfish head can be confused with the head of a snake with a bifurcated tongue.

The fish on which the Fish Monster (Figure 11.1) is based is problematic; the monster usually has large

FIGURE 11.1 The Snake-belt God with the Fish Monster on a line. *From the Chan Chan–Moche Valley Project. Drawing by Donna McClelland.*

dorsal and ventral fins, plus a pair of smaller fins near the rounded caudal fin (Kutscher 1983: Abbn. 234–240, 251–256). The prototype has been variously identified as angelote (angel shark or angelfish), bonito, and *borracho* (or *pez borracho*). The angelote defends itself with its teeth, looks rather like a ray, and is common on the north coast, where its roe is dried and sold for medicinal use (Alarco 1997:218; see also Migdalski and Fichter 1982:67; Schweigger 1964:221–222; Vásquez and Rosales 1998, 2004). The Fish Monster holds a human head and a knife; shark derivation would make symbolic sense, but the monster fin conformations do not resemble those of the angelote.

After discussion with local fishermen, Steve Bourget (1994b) concluded that the Fish Monster is a borracho (*Scartichthys gigas*), of the Blennidae (see also Alarco 1997:228; Schweigger 1964:287–288; Vásquez and Rosales 1998, 2004). This fish, however, stays in fairly shallow water, whereas the Fish Monster resembles a pelagic fish. Pictures of the borracho do not match the Fish Monster closely, although its caudal fin is similar, and the borracho has tentacles over its large eyes, like those of the monster. Bourget argues that psychoactive and central nervous system effects of a toxin in the borracho's head made it important for shamanic reasons, and that the fish was decapitated to obtain the substance. Borracho is used by curers to induce a state of somnolence or drunkenness (hence, its name). The trambollo, a relative of the borracho, more closely resembles the monster; its remains have been found at the Cerro Blanco Complex (Vásquez and Rosales 2004).

The bonito, or Pacific bonito (Figure 11.2), of the mackerel and tuna family, has been widely proposed as the Fish Monster prototype (de Bock 1988: Nos. 99–102; Donnan 1978:38; Makowski 1996:70; see also Alarco 1997:227–228; Schweigger 1964:227–273). Many nonmonster effigy bottles probably represent a bonito, as suggested by Rafael Larco Hoyle (2001, I: Fig. 104). The bonito bears some resemblance to the monster, but less than it might. The depictions can be more compact than the actual fish, and this was often a convention of Moche style. The bonito, too, is used medicinally, apparently with effects similar to those of the borracho in combating insomnia and acting as a "cerebral tonic."

Luis Jaime Castillo (1989:113), who has closely examined the Fish Monster, suggests that it is a hybrid derived from various species, and he may well be right. Michael Coe, who is as experienced a fisherman as he is an archaeologist, agrees: in a personal communication, he observes that the Fish Monster seems to combine elements of various pelagic fish. The shape of the monster's dorsal fin, for example, often resembles that of a sailfish.

FIGURE II.2 Phase III bottle in the form of a bonito. The body is shortened and the face somewhat humanized. *Courtesy Museo Arqueológico Rafael Larco Herrera, Lima.*

SHELLS

Many shells are encountered in Moche archaeological remains—some unworked, some worked by craftsmen, some used as inlay in a complex object. *Spondylus princeps, Strombus galeatus,* and *Conus fergusoni* were imported (perhaps by raft) from Ecuador. These shells, plus *Oliva* and *Thais* (which may have been used as a dye as well as a food), appear in offering caches and high-status burials (Alarco 1997:303–304, 355; Bourget 1994b, 1997a:87–88; Cárdenas, Rodríguez, and Aguirre 1997; *Spondylus* 1999; T. Topic 1982:273–274; Vásquez and Rosales 1998, 2004; Vásquez et al. 2003).

In earlier archaeological reports, objects are described as carved from pink shell, but until Walter Alva (1994, 2001:239; Alva and Donnan 1993: Fig. 57) encountered the Lord of Sipán, flanked on both sides by *Spondylus* and *Conus*, whole *Spondylus* had rarely been named in pre-Phase V offerings. *Spondylus* beads, pendants, or pieces have now been excavated at Dos Cabezas, Huaca

de la Luna, and San José de Moro. In the late Huaca Fortaleza, at Pampa Grande, cut and polished *Spondylus* pieces were interred as an offering in a subfloor pit. *Spondylus* appears in many contexts at Pampa Grande, where Izumi Shimada (1994a:213–216, 238–243) uncovered evidence for working the shell in small, dispersed workshops. No documented use of *Strombus* has yet been found at Pampa Grande, and *Conus* is rare there. *Spondylus* is depicted in Cupisnique art and in later Sicán and Chimu art, and is known to have been valued in Inca times, but it was never clearly represented in Moche art, although Alana Cordy-Collins (1990, 2001a) proposes possible Moche depictions of the shell, held by the Moon Goddess, and suggests that the goddess's moon/raft may be a *Spondylus* shell.

THE SHORE

On the rocky and sandy coast, the Moche gathered mussels, scallops, clams, and sea snails (Alarco 1997; Narváez 1994; Netherly 1977:57–58; Vásquez and Rosales 1998, 2004; Vásquez et al. 2003). In the urban area near Huaca de la Luna, a clam common on sandy north coast shores (*Donax obesulus*), particularly in times of El Niño, was found in every complex investigated. *Chloromytilus chorus* appeared in quantity in the Cerro Blanco Complex and at Cerro La Mina. *Pteria peruviana*, an inedible oyster, provided mother-of-pearl. *Pecten purpuratus* can be found in sand under moving water. The Moche undoubtedly caught crabs and saltwater shrimp on the coast, as fishermen do today; freshwater shrimp were taken from irrigation canals and lagoons. Effigy ceramics represent shellfish and ducks, and marsh scenes with waterbirds, fish, reeds, and waterlilies attest to the importance of the shore to the Moche (Kutscher 1983). Later local lords controlled marshes behind beaches, where freshwater fish and aquatic fowl were caught, and rushes cut for raft construction, mat making, and building (Ramírez-Horton 1982:126).

THE ISLANDS

Islands in the sea off the north coast of Peru provided rich resources (Benson 1995a; Murphy 1925:322–323,

1936,II; Netherly 1977:26, 45–53; Rostworowski 1977, 1981:79–83, 1997; Shimada 1987:135–136). The important islands were Guañape (off the Virú Valley), Macabí (off Chicama), and Lobos de Tierra and Lobos de Afuera (off Lambayeque). The Chincha Islands, off the south coast, were a reported source of Moche artifacts, but there seems to be no hard evidence for a Moche presence there (Kubler 1948; Shimada 1994a:91, 267 n.62). The northern islands must have been used by the Moche as stations for pelagic fishing. North Coast fisherman today still dry and salt fish on Lobos de Tierra. A Moche group, or groups, may have controlled fishing and guano mining on the islands. Offshore islands are apparently depicted on a few effigy bottles, including an Early Moche one with people, sea lions, boats, a structure, and a hill of guano (Berrin 1997: No. 48; see also Baessler 1902–3: Fig. 62; Schmidt 1929:158).

Island scenes depict activities different from those in raft scenes. Several modeled vessels may show activities related to the collecting of guano left by the huge flocks of birds that gather on the islands. In the nineteenth century, guano was a primary source of wealth for Peru, which supplied most of the world's fertilizer. Guano was also taken from the islands in Inca times, and it was likely used and traded by the Moche. In a climate with rainfall guano would be washed away, as it is in El Niño events, when birds are scarce because anchovies, their main food source, are driven to the bottom of the sea, forcing birds to abandon the area (Murphy 1936, II:903–904; B. Nelson 1980:108, 209). Normally, however, the arid climate created by the Humboldt Current allows for thousands of birds and tons of guano.

The Peruvian "guano trio" comprises three species of Pelecaniformes: the guanay cormorant (*Phalacrocorax bougainvillii*), in recent times the most important guano producer; the Peruvian pelican (*Pelecanus thagus*), closely related to the brown pelican (*P. occidentalis*); and the Peruvian booby, or *piquero* (*Sula variegata*) (Figure 11.3), once the greatest guano producer along with the blue-footed booby (*S. Nebouxii*). The guanay cormorant has been described as a "machine for converting fish into guano" (Murphy 1936, II:901; see also Alarco 1997:45–46; Benson 1995a; Harrison 1985; Murphy 1936, I:286–295, II:807–819; B. Nelson 1980; Schweigger 1964:339–367). Most cormorants

dive for bottom-feeding fish, but guanays feed in flocks on surface schools. These birds used to feed in dense masses but are now endangered. The guanay ranges from Lobos de Tierra south, and the Peruvian booby from Lobos de Afuera north.

The South American sea lion (*Otaria byronia*) (Figure 11.4) was once plentiful on islands off the north coast, which is now the northern limit of its range (Alarco 1997:115–116; Gillin 1947:124; J. King 1983; Murphy 1925:257–261; Schaedel 1988:49; Schweigger 1964:306–312; M. Shimada and Shimada 1981; Vásquez and Rosales 1998). Effigy bottles, sometimes found in burials, represent full-figure sea lions or their heads (Figure 11.5; see also Figures 4.5, 12.2), which can also be finials (Chapter 12; Alva 1994: Láms. 205–210; Alva and Donnan 1993: No. 218; Bourget 2001b:100–104; Donnan 1978:136–137, 1995:147; Franco, Gálvez, and Vásquez 2001a: Fig. 48A; Hecker and Hecker 1992b:45; Joralemon and Sharon 1993; Larco Hoyle 2001,I:325–328; Sharon and Donnan 1974:55). Otaries have been hunted for food, hide, and fat, and their whiskers could be used for brushes. Modern healers use the teeth and bones, which may also have been used by Moche curers. Sea lions take pebbles into their stomachs, and hunting scenes depict the animals being hit on the head with a club, perhaps to make them regurgitate the stones, as suggested by the

FIGURE 11.3 Pelicans on the island of Lobos de Tierra, off Lambayeque. *Photograph by the author.*

FIGURE 11.4 Sea lions on the beach and rocks of Hormigas de Afuera, off the central coast. *Photograph by the author.*

FIGURE 11.5 Effigy bottle with a sea lion emerging from the handle, and a painted scene on the body showing a sea lion hunt. *Courtesy Linden-Museum, Stuttgart, 119020.*

apparently spitting sea lion on the right in Figure 11.5. The stones are found in some Moche burial contexts and were probably thought to have special power. Ceramics show humanized sea lions and sea birds in the soft garb of priests, often holding a drum (Benson 1975: Figs. 17, 18).

In ceramic scenes with marine contexts, men fishing on rafts or hunting sea lions on shore usually wear a loincloth and headgear with thin, diagonally upward projections (usually two) that seems to be specific to marine activity. On human figures these are simple (see Figure 11.5), but when supernaturals wear this headdress, there may be a different number of spikes, and they may end in snake or animal heads (see Figure 11.1).

Sea lions inhabited the mainland coast; however, the sea-surrounded islands—where they would have been more plentiful—surely had higher symbolic significance for the people who viewed them. The island shores that can be crowded with sea lions or expanses of guano with thousands of nesting pelicans (Figures 11.3, 11.4) may be littered with skeletons of these creatures after a severe El Niño event. Sea lion populations have been decimated also by deliberate slaughters to protect the livelihood of fishermen. Sea lions have a bad reputation for breaking nets and stealing fish, especially in El Niño conditions, when fish are scarce, and man and sea lion are in competition for food. Sea lions are also threatened by killer whales, who attack young otary populations, and humans who kill them for their valuable skins.

Sea turtles (*Chelonia* and others) are reported on Lobos de Tierra and on the coast, and lizards are apparently abundant on the islands as well as on parts of the coast (Alarco 1997; Murphy 1936, I:280; Netherly 1977:48; Schweigger 1964:304–305). Bats, specifically vampire bats (*Desmodus rotundus*), are thought to inhabit coastal caves and more southerly islands, and were probably present on northern islands (Benson 1987a; Murphy 1925:203). Although significant in sacrificial and priestly iconography, bats do not figure in island scenes, as owls do. Owls have been observed on other islands and must have inhabited those near the north coast as well, for they appear with marine motifs and are portrayed on wooden objects found on guano islands (Kubler 1948). Ceramic effigy owls sometimes carry a shell on the back. Vultures (including condors)—transformers of the dead—are present in certain scenes and still live on the islands (Schaffer 1983).

Some painted-relief "collage" bottles combine relatively realistic figures—fish, sea lions, sea birds, owls, serpents, priests—with animated objects, anthropomorphized shell creatures, a condor head, and part of the lopsided, wrinkled face of a god with a snake ear ornament, presumably the Snake-belt God or his marine twin, who is here truly wrinkle-faced (see Figure 11.1; see also Figure 4.5; Donnan 1978: Fig. 157; Donnan and McClelland 1999: Figs. 4.12–4.14; Schmidt 1929:Abb. 166). The odd compositions, mixed up and overlapping like images seen under water, might express a ritual drug experience. According to Hocquenghem (1987:61), "collage" island scenes display disorder. Perhaps they represent the chaos that occurs when the god is under the sea, or El Niño is roiling the waters.

THE OTHER WORLD

White with guano, the islands rise from the sea as the snow-capped mountains rise from the land; the islands are cosmic models, miniature landscapes with the primal sea around them, symbolizing the fecundity, richness, and energy of the sea and its life, the guano fertilizer for the land, and the beaches crowded with sea lions or birds. Surely the islands were huacas, meaning that raft trips to visit them would have been, on one level, pilgrimages. The islands might have been thought of as transformed ancestors or gods, a concept proposed in Contact-period literature (Rostworowski 1992:36, 1997:33–36; Salomon, in Salomon and Urioste 1991). Part of the world of living, working people, they also mark entry to the underseas, which was perhaps the world of the dead.

Shells and fish placed in mainland graves evoke the sea and fecundity. *Spondylus* and *Conus* are found in elite tombs, and *Strombus* is depicted in burial scenes but has not been found in real graves. The women in the ceramic Burial Theme (Donnan and McClelland 1979) wear garments that seem to be made of net, a possible reference to fishing and the sea.

Ceramic scenes of sea lion hunts depict them as rites with priestly figures accompanying the hunters (Donnan and McClelland 1999: Fig. 4.87; Hocquenghem

1987: Figs. 120, 121). In the mid-nineteenth century, on certain islands, carved effigies, staffs, and other wooden objects of Phase IV iconography and style were dug from deep piles of guano then being removed for commercial use after a long hiatus in mining (Kubler 1948; see also Benson 1975, 1995a; Netherly 1977:52–53; Rostworowski 1997:36–37n.16; Shimada 1994a:267n.62). On Macabí, gold figures and masks were said to have been found (and taken by work crews), as well as quantities of cotton textiles and headless mummies (which were thrown overboard). On Guañape, vessels and sheets of silver and gold were encountered, and also tools, weaving implements, and textiles. Dating of the nonwooden objects is uncertain. Offerings were probably made at various times.

Among the wooden effigies are captives resembling ceramic sacrificial victims. At least one is a well-dressed captive with a rope around the neck and the shirt and headdress of the Plate-shirt God (Benson 1982b). Other wooden objects include supernatural owls with panpipes and a figure in a shelter, perhaps a king, ancestor, or god. The objects relate to ritual war and to offerings for fertility on both land and sea, and likely offerings for the gods or spirits of islands and sea. Although the islands lack Phase V remains, a Phase V bottle depicts an island (or shore) around which fish and sea lions swim while animated items of warrior's gear surround two seated captives, with ropes around their necks, and a priestly figure is sheltered in a simple house (Donnan and McClelland 1999: Fig. 5.74).

In Moche ceramic scenes both gods and mortals fish (Hocquenghem 1987:126–131; Kutscher 1983: Abbn. 254, 314–320; Donna McClelland 1990; McClelland, McClelland, and Donnan 2007). An ordinary man fishes from an ordinary reed raft, but sometimes, even for a human fisherman, the raft becomes a huge, supernatural fish or has at its ends the fox-snake head (Donnan 1978: Nos. 102–106, 159–164). The Snake-belt God or his marine twin fishes from a raft with animal-head ends, propelled by anthropomorphic cormorants (Kutscher 1983: Abb. 253). In Phase V, a radiance supernatural being, often called the Paddler, likely a version of the Snake-belt God or his twin, appears in a raft but does not fish (see Figure 1.7). In the "hold" of some rafts are jars (containing chicha, water, or blood?) tied at the neck; sometimes there is an equal number of captives and jars with a rope at the neck. These are equivalent, for both contain valuable liquid. The scale of the late rafts is greater than that on earlier ceramics, when most fishing rafts carry only one person. The largest rafts contain the Snake-belt God and two women, and occasionally a fourth person or a sea lion (Berrin 1997: No. 89; Hocquenghem 1987: Fig. 107). The size and cargo of the late rafts might suggest that fishermen were out long enough to require liquid, but other interpretations are more likely, for the images are supernatural, and jars symbolize ritual. The jars may equip a deity's journey through the night, the sun sinking into the underworld, or the moon traveling through the western sky.

The Moon Goddess goes to sea on many Phase V fine-line bottles, either in a raft or a crescent (see Figures 8.4, 13.3). Cordy-Collins (2001a) notes the presence of a diving weight on her clothing (see also Benson 1985, 1988b; de Bock 1988; Donnan and McClelland 1999; Kutscher 1988). North Coast peoples have observed relationships between the running of fish and phases of the moon, as well as the movements of the Pleiades (Urton 1982; see also Cobo 1990 [1653]:30). In her marine aspect, the Moon Goddess may have been, like the Inca goddess Urpay Huachac, a deity of sea life and shore birds.

Early Moche produced few sea or island scenes, but the southern region in Middle Moche (the time of the wooden offerings) provides many images of fishing from a raft. Donna McClelland (1990:76–77),

in her large sample of drawings of Phase V fine-line bottles (which seem to be mostly northern), pointed to a great increase in maritime subjects, but fishing rarely seems to be the object of the voyage. When the Moche were going to the islands for rites and leaving remains, sea scenes showed fishing. When the ceramics depict supernaturals on a voyage with captives, the destination may have been the other world.

There are many questions. What astronomical events figured in this iconography? Did sacrifice ceremonies relate to a ritual calendar, or to a Niño event and the resulting mass deaths of island and sea creatures, a kind of natural sacrifice on the islands? Could any—or all—of the water scenes depict a flood rather than the sea? Floods are a part of many creation myths in the Americas and elsewhere. El Niño flooding could have easily inspired a watery scene, giving rise to a myth about the creation of the sea. Later Lambayeque oral tradition tells of a "30-day deluge" with "catastrophic flooding" (Moseley 1990:19). Are the captives who are propelled by a deity due to be sacrificed, or are they already dead? On what occasion were captives taken to the islands—or simply out to sea?

Today highlanders work to collect guano on some of the islands, but it appears to be a task that coastal people do not favor. In the past, captives might well have been transported to do the work, but in scenes with deities in rafts, captives may be involved in a more serious rite, possibly being transported by gods to the world of the dead.

CHAPTER TWELVE   # Burial and the Afterlife

IN 1995 CHRISTOPHER DONNAN published an account of 326 Moche burials from 18 sites (most are in the Moche and Jequetepeque valleys), a summation of funerary chambers, burials, and grave goods excavated by archaeologists, including Donnan, before 1992. His report is the basis of this chapter, which also incorporates data from many more recent excavations.

CEMETERIES AND OTHER BURIAL PLACES

Donnan sees a Moche tendency to cluster interments. At Pacatnamu he found 84 burials in isolated clusters, with 67 in one cemetery (Donnan and McClelland 1997:17). High-status burials occurred in only one, severely looted cemetery. John Verano (1997:194), finding craniofacial differences in remains in different cemeteries, cites Cieza de León, who in 1547 noted that in Jequetepeque there was a cemetery for each lineage or group. Luis Jaime Castillo and the Proyecto Arqueológico San José de Moro are exploring a large cemetery with a long history of occupation; it has so far produced more than 60 Moche burials of varying rank and period, including 23 Middle Moche tombs in alignment (Castillo 2001, 2003; Castillo et al. 2008; Donnan and Castillo 1994; Nelson and Castillo 1997:144). In the Piura Valley, Loma Negra was the resting place of lords who had control there in the third century AD (Jones 1993; Kaulicke 2000:129–139; Schaffer 1985), and nearby Yécala has a large mortuary area (Kaulicke 2000:117, Fig. III.1). At Pampa Juárez, Krzysztof Makowski (1994b) excavated two large elite cemeteries; a more isolated cemetery nearby has royal burials.

Moche cemeteries are usually located on the edge of cultivated land or on the flanks of hills near ceremonial centers (Millaire 2002, 2004); centers and their huacas also contain graves, although, in Piura, architecture and graves are rarely associated (Jones 2001). People of high rank were usually interred in the center of the center, sometimes in burial platforms, as at Galindo, up in the Moche Valley (Bawden 1996:288–289; Shimada 1994a:240–242), and most notably at Huaca Rajada Sipán, which has yielded many rich graves, including the tomb of the Lord of Sipán (Tomb 1), with its wealth of dazzling jewelry and other objects (Figure 12.1; see also Figures 6.4, 6.5, 7.5, 7.6).

FIGURE 12.1 The tomb of the Lord of Sipán (Tomb 1) with replicas of the grave goods. *Photograph by the author.*

Walter Alva and his team have excavated more than 12 tombs in that funerary platform (Alva 1988, 1994, 2001; Alva and Donnan 1993), and Luis Chero has excavated another important burial (*El Comercio*, 2 September 2007a, 8 September 2007). The rich burial found by Steve Bourget in 2008 at Úcupe, in the Zaña Valley, had material very like that in graves at Huaca Rajada Sipán (Atwood 2010:21; *El Comercio*, 5 July 2008; 26 July 2008). Huaca Cao Viejo has yielded many burials (Franco 2009; Franco, Gálvez, and Vásquez 1999b, 2001a, 2003; Williams 2006).

Remains of many burials have been excavated in the Cerro Blanco Complex. Max Uhle found a looted Phase III cemetery on the slopes of Cerro Blanco, next to Huaca de la Luna, and in a platform in front of Luna, he excavated 37 graves with pottery from Phases II through IV (Menzel 1977; see also Pimentel and Álvarez 2000). The Chan Chan–Moche Valley Project excavated graves in and near Huaca del Sol, at the base of Luna, and in the urban area between the huacas, as well as at nearby Huanchaco (see Chapter 1). Santiago Uceda and the Proyecto Arqueológico Huacas de Moche team have found burials within Huaca de la Luna and close by (Bourget 2001a; Chapdelaine 2001; R. Tello, Armas, and Chapdelaine 2003; Tufinio 2001b; Uceda, Mujica, and Morales 1997, 1998, 2000, 2004, 2006, 2008a, 2008b). Many burials, high status and low, have been encountered, often in houses in the urban area between the huacas, by Claude Chapdelaine (1997, 1998, 2000, 2001) and others (Chapdelaine, Bernier, and Pimentel 2004; R. Tello 1998; Tello, Armas, and Chapdelaine 2003; various authors in Uceda, Mujica, and Morales 2000, 2004, 2008a, 2008b). In the ceramic workshop excavated by Uceda and José Armas (1998; Uceda, Armas, and Millones 2008), a man and woman, presumed to be potters, were interred with copper objects and pottery, some of high quality.

Burials can be found in fill, refuse, or sand, or under house floors. The tomb of the Warrior Priest in Huaca de la Cruz, one of the richer burials known, was placed in a crudely made shaft in a deposit of refuse (Strong and Evans 1952:151). Two of the tombs in Huaca Dos Cabezas were constructed in two large erosion channels in the major structure (Donnan 2007). Phase V burials at Galindo were put in above-floor benches in the chief domestic space (Bawden 2001:299).

Interments are not usually separated by age or sex, but Donnan has pointed out that a few cemeteries apparently were limited to special groups, such as the one for runners at the Cerro Blanco Complex; at Pacatnamu he found a cemetery with three child burials (Donnan and McClelland 1997:17). Bourget excavated three child burials near each other in Plaza 3A at Huaca de la Luna (Bourget 2001a; Bourget and Millaire 2000). Donnan (2001, 2003, 2007) located three burials in Platform II of Luna and found three graves close together at Dos Cabezas, suggesting that in both places interments occurred within a short time.

MOCHE MORTUARY PRACTICES

Single burials are usually simple. Those with a major personage and an accompanying person or entourage inform us that the important dead did not go to the otherworld alone. Multiple burials can also include mass graves, those that intrude into or disrupt older ones, reburials, and secondary burials of incomplete or disarticulated skeletons. Some burials may be building dedication offerings or other sacrifices.

High-status tombs are usually adobe chambers, rectangular and sometimes room-sized, often formed within a huaca by adding or removing bricks, depositing brick fill, or building a new structure. Tombs at Huaca de la Luna, Huaca Cao Viejo, and Dos Cabezas are embedded in sacred structures. The burial platform at Huaca Rajada Sipán was surely sacred space, altered to accommodate new interments (Alva 1988, 2001, 2004; *El Comercio*, 2 September 2007a). A tomb might be constructed by excavating a rectangular pit and lining the walls with adobes, or occasionally rocks, set in clay or mortarless. The Moche at Pacatnamu and San José de Moro produced boot-shaped tombs as well as chambers. In most sites important burials were placed inside architecture, but in Piura shaft-and-chamber tombs, unusual for the Moche, are rarely associated with a building.

Virtually all tombs appear to have been covered with roofing of cane, algarrobo trunks, or other wooden beams, or with adobes forming a false arch. Many high-status tomb chambers have niches, which may contain objects—sometimes skulls, sometimes pottery—or be left empty. Some tomb walls were painted (Franco, Gálvez, and Vásquez 1999b, 2001a: Fig. 29; Narváez 1994). Elite chamber tombs often had an antechamber. At Dos Cabezas three tombs, each containing a very tall man (1.8 m [nearly 6 ft]), had a connecting miniature compartment in which the burial was reproduced, approximately, with a small effigy figure and offerings of small or normal size (Donnan 2001, 2003, 2007; Jiménez 2000:77). Some tombs at Huaca Rajada Sipán, Huaca Cao Viejo, and Huaca de la Luna also had a separate compartment for offerings (Alva and Donnan 1993; Franco, Gálvez, and Vásquez 1998b; Uceda 1997b).

Coffins made of wooden planks were reserved for people of very high rank and are extremely rare (large pieces of wood were scarce). At Huaca Rajada Sipán, it is evident that two primary burials had plank coffins (Alva 1994:47–48, 150; Alva and Donnan 1993:56–60, 144–147), and remains found by Franco, Gálvez, and Vásquez (2001b:157) at Huaca Cao Viejo suggest a plank coffin there. Elite adult coffins were usually of cane. A cane frame could be crimped to be folded into four sections and then wrap-tied with rope (Donnan and Barreto 1997; Ubbelohde-Doering 1967:Pl. 64). Two unusual ones in Phase V tombs at San José de Moro each held the remains of a presumed priestess: copper arms, legs, and a mask, and one had a head-dress sewn onto the exterior of the coffin, remains of which were found in a room-sized burial chamber (see Chapter 8; Castillo 1996; Castillo and Donnan 1994b; Castillo and Uceda 2008; Castillo et al. 2008; Donnan and Castillo 1992, 1994).

Burials differed not only according to status, but also by period and place. In general, however, the Moche tended to be buried supine and fully extended, hands at the sides or over the pelvic area. Bodies were normally laid out on a north-south axis, with the head to the south, although some Phase IV burials in the south had the head to the west. Phase V burials at San José de Moro were usually placed east-west.

The Moche treated bodies and grave goods in various ways. Red mineral pigment can appear on the skeleton and/or on offerings, a custom that occurs in many places in the world, presumably because red is the color of blood and, so, of life. Where preservation is good, gourds are common, placed under the head or covering the face or other body parts, or used to hold food remains. Organic materials—textiles, cordage, basketry, hides, feathers, and wood and other plant material —are usually in poor condition. Plant remains are not common, but maize, beans, peanuts, avocado, and edible seaweed, as well as ulluchu fruit, coca, and cotton seeds, have been found (Donnan and McClelland 1997:33; Gumerman 1997; Jones 1993; Uceda 1997d:179; Vásquez and Rosales 2004). Spinning and weaving implements, usually encountered in women's graves, are often deteriorated.

Wrapping and tying were important in burial preparation. The corpse was usually enclosed in a plain cotton shroud and sewn up. The shroud might then be reinforced with wood or cane splints to keep the body rigid, or the shroud-wrapped body put inside a tube of tied canes or on a rigid cane frame; the whole was wrapped in a larger shroud and sewn. A high-status body could be wrapped in several shrouds and placed in a cane coffin. At Huaca Rajada Sipán, a plank coffin had been wrapped with a red cloth (Alva and Donnan 1993:148). Most corpses did not seem to be dressed, although cloth and garments were commonly placed in burials. The head or body might rest on a stack of textiles, or cloth or unspun cotton was put under the head like a pillow. In some burials, unspun cotton was placed over the eyes or face before cloth was tied over the body. Wool yarn or cotton strips of cloth were often used to tie or wrap coffins, bodies, body parts, and objects within a burial; at Pacatnamu, maize cobs were tied in wool yarn or cotton string (Donnan and McClelland 1997:33). Bourget (2006:89) proposes that small, tied rectangles depicted on fine-line vessels are wrapped bits of copper. The burial of a footless child in the urban complex near Huaca de la Luna contained a piece of copper wrapped in cloth and tied with string, resembling the object seen on bottles (Chapdelaine et al. 1997:78), and small copper plaques with disintegrated textile remains were found near llama bones at Huaca Rajada Sipán (Alva 1994:41). Few Loma Negra textiles have lasted, but corroded silvered-copper objects found there had textile remains and impressions on all sides (Schaffer 1985), and copper grave goods in a Huaca de la Luna burial were wrapped in cloth (Uceda 1997d; Chapdelaine et al. 1997:78), as was a stirrup-spout bottle in the form of a sea lion head excavated at Huaca Cao Viejo (Figure 12.2; Franco, Gálvez, and

FIGURE 12.2 Bottle in the form of a sea lion head, wrapped in cloth, from a burial in Huaca Cao Viejo. *Courtesy of Régulo Franco and Proyecto Arqueológico Complejo El Brujo.*

Vásquez 2001a). A bundle in a Dos Cabezas burial was "wrapped" with clay (Donnan 2007:72).

A chunk of copper or a folded or broken sheet piece, often wrapped in cloth, was commonly inserted into the mouths of the Moche dead; in higher-status graves there might be gilded-copper objects in the mouth, or even gold or silver (Alva 1994:84; Alva and Donnan 1993:55; Chapdelaine 2001:82; Donnan 2001:69, 2003:61; Donnan and Mackey 1978:154; Donnan and McClelland 1997:34; *El Comercio*, 2 September 2007; Tufinio 2000:28; Uceda 1997d:179). Eight gilded circular pendants with owl heads and a small gold plaque, all wrapped in cotton, came from the mouth of a woman at Huaca Cao Viejo (Franco, Gálvez, and Vásquez 1999b). The man buried in the richest tomb excavated in Dos Cabezas had five gold objects in his mouth, all folded or misshapen; one was in the form of an owl head (Donnan 2007:100).

Sometimes a copper piece was placed in a hand and/or elsewhere on the body.

While lower-status graves had only a few copper pieces, the great burials at Sipán and Loma Negra contained quantities of showy objects of gold, silver, or gilded or silvered copper (see Chapters 6 and 7), which were usually not deliberately damaged, as plain copper ones often were. Metal objects were often put next to the body part where they would have been worn or used. Metal placed over the face varies from a simple copper sheet to an elaborate mask of inlaid gold. Nose ornaments—of gold, silver, or copper—are often found in high-status graves, as are ear ornaments, bracelets, necklaces, and pectorals; copper disks are particularly common. In a recently excavated Sipán burial a nose ornament was found under a hand of the deceased (*El Comercio,* 8 September 2007).

Julie Jones (1993, 2001:213) has observed that "the greatest lords of the land were buried totally covered with metal objects." She argues that the placement of metal objects around the face and hands was a major part of burial rites, affording lords protection and status in the otherworld.

HUMAN ATTENDANTS AND BONE REUSE

Among the offerings in high-status Moche graves were humans (Alva 1994, 2001; Alva and Donnan 1993; Benson 1975, 1988b; Benson and Cook 2001; Bourget 2006; Donnan 2007; Hocquenghem 1980b; Millaire 2002, 2004). Strong and Evans (1952) found four peripheral burials at the tomb of the Warrior Priest: an adult male lay outside, two women were crammed between the cane coffin and the wall, and a boy lay extended in the coffin with the Warrior Priest. Verano (1995:196–697, 2001b:168–169) calls these "retainer burials," noting that the females "appear to have been forced into the corners"; Donnan (2007) calls such women "sacrifices." Although women have not appeared in remains of sacrifice rites, and women in Moche art are not depicted as sacrificial victims, virtually every elite burial contains remains of one or two women who may have been put in alive but were likely strangled with a cord, as was apparently true of a female face down in Tomb 2 at Huaca Rajada Sipán (Alva 1994; Alva and Donnan 1993) and a woman at

Huaca de la Cruz (Strong and Evans 1952). Remains of three women accompanied the Lord of Sipán, but their disarticulation suggests that these were secondary burials. The earlier Sipán Tomb 3 had one young female retainer. Two women were buried with the first priestess at San José de Moro, the first important female Moche burial excavated, while a single female accompanied the second priestess (Donnan and Castillo 1994); one young woman was with the Lady of Huaca Cao Viejo, and each of two other prominent women at the site were also so accompanied (*El Comercio*, 18 May 2006; Franco and Gálvez 2010; Franco, Gálvez, and Vásquez 1999b).

The burials of men who may be guardians or psychopomps appear outside of tombs. Huaca Rajada Sipán Tombs 1 and 2 each had a guardian above the tomb (Alva 1994; Alva and Donnan 1993:55, 143); this occurs also at Huaca Cao Viejo, the tomb of the Warrior Priest, and elsewhere.

In the Lord of Sipán's tomb, a woman and a powerfully built man with a war club were placed separately beside the main burial (Alva 1988, 1994, 2001; Alva and Donnan 1993); both lacked a left foot, and in excavations at both Huaca de la Luna and Huaca Rajada Sipán, a man with both feet cut off lay atop the coffin of a primary burial. At Sipán, a young man lying above the tomb of the lord wore a gilded-copper helmet and held a copper disk or shield; both feet were cut off, and in their place lay two pieces of a metal disk. Bipedal amputation may have been a way of ensuring that the guardian or psychopomp did not leave his post. A woman buried with the Lord of Úcupe had with her two owl-effigy bottles whose feet had been broken off (Steve Bourget, personal communication, March 2010). A guardian of the tomb of the Warrior Priest retained his feet, but his ankles and knees were tied, as were those of the Warrior Priest (Strong and Evans 1952; see also Franco, Gálvez, and Vásquez 2001a; Verano 2003).

Some burials were apparently delayed, because it is obvious that some bodies had been dead for a length of time before being placed in a grave (Millaire 2004; Nelson and Castillo 1997). Many accompanying bodies had been dead longer than the primary figure; these may have come from sacrificial rites.

Sacrifice and funerary rites are related. Bourget (2001b) observes that Huaca de la Luna Platform II was used for funerary rites and the nearby plaza for sacrifices, and tombs of likely sacrificer priests were located above the sacrificial area (see also Millaire 2004). Attendants or retainers who accompanied the important dead were probably not the primary sacrifices shown as captives in fine-line scenes, although some bodies or body parts may have come from such a rite. Sacrifices may have been held at the time of, or the anniversary of, a funerary rite. Some ceramics showing sacrifice come from mortuary contexts.

Dedicatory burials, secondary offerings of human remains, and the collection and curation of body parts from other burials are a part of this pattern (Cordy-Collins 2009; Kaulicke 1994:331–332; Millaire 2002, 2004; Tufinio 2001a, 2001b, 2002; Uceda 1997d:186). Some buried bodies were disturbed by earthquakes, El Niño flooding, or human or animal activity; other bodies were disarticulated, moved, and rearranged in "intentional manipulation, modification, or reposition of human remains," as noted by Verano (1995:199–203, 2001b:158). Gisela and Wolfgang Hecker (1992) describe bones from old burials as offerings in Moche interments in Pacatnamu, and Heinrich Ubbelohde-Doering (1983) found in a burial there a jawless skull wrapped in cloth. Uhle (Menzel 1977:60) observed that some Cerro Blanco Complex burials were accompanied by an extra skull. Evidence of disarticulation and bone reuse in burial contexts, especially of skulls and long bones, comes from many sites. Jean-François Millaire (2002, 2004) has focused on this subject, as has Alana Cordy-Collins (2009), looking especially at Dos Cabezas and San José de Moro (see also Alva and Donnan 1993:165; Chapdelaine 2001:76; Donnan and Mackey 1978; Franco, Gálvez, and Vásquez 1998b:12, 1999b, 2001a, 2003:163; Narváez 1994:66; Nelson and Castillo 1997; R. Tello 1998:121–122; Verano 1998). Cut-off arms and legs occur in fine-line sacrifice scenes, and effigy vessels can take the form of a forearm or lower leg, perhaps for use in a sacrifice rite or to commemorate or substitute for the rite.

Bones are missing from many interments (Bourget 1994a:74–75; Uceda 1997d; Verano 2001c:116), and some recent bone finds suggest movement from another place. In the Huaca de la Luna urban area, a burial had been opened, and the two clavicles and a large part of the skull had been taken out (Chapdelaine 2001:82–83). In Huaca Cao Viejo, Régulo Franco

(1998:105) excavated a skeleton without a head and without offerings except for textile remains.

A Phase III chamber tomb at Cao Viejo, with an adjacent chamber for grave goods, had been opened and the body of the principal personage removed; many bones of attendants were taken away and scattered, ceramic offerings were smashed and strewn, and parts of other offerings were removed. Of the principal's jewelry, only one ear ornament and half of a pectoral were left (Franco, Gálvez, and Vásquez 1998b, 2001a, 2001b). This significant chaos was seemingly achieved in a long and intricate rite, after which the tomb was resealed, and the empty chamber was covered with poles on which were placed bodies of sacrificial victims.

ANIMAL AND OTHER OFFERINGS

Whole and partial animal and object offerings were placed in tombs and moved from tomb to tomb. The most frequently identified animal remains in tombs are those of camelids, usually llamas, most often a headless body or a bodiless head, or simply body parts, perhaps wrapped in textile or cane. Llamas were commonly offered at Huaca Rajada Sipán, most decapitated, although sometimes only a head was found (Alva 1994, 2001:234–235, 239; Alva and Donnan 1993). At Dos Cabezas Tomb 2, a woman and a llama lay above the primary burial, and llama heads were found in this and other burials (Donnan 2001, 2003, 2007), as was true also at Huanchaco (Donnan and Mackey 1978). The cane-wrapped man on top of the tomb of the Warrior Priest rested on llama bones (Strong and Evans 1952). Llamas were excavated in 13 graves at Pacatnamu (Donnan and McClelland 1997:34), and they are common at San José de Moro, and interchangeable with human bones at the feet of some burials (Castillo and Donnan 1994b:119; Castillo and Uceda 2008; Donnan and Castillo 1992:38, 1994). Llama remains occur also in Huaca Cao Viejo (Franco, Gálvez, and Vásquez 1999b:51, 2001a:64) and the Cerro Blanco Complex (Chapdelaine 2001:82; Menzel 1977:60; Montoya 2000:43; Uceda 1997d:179; Vásquez and Rosales 1998:187). The llama, useful to the living, was likely regarded as being of service to the dead. Llama effigies also were put in tombs.

Dogs appear in burial lore and in graves throughout the Americas (Benson 1991; Schwartz 1997). At Huaca Rajada Sipán, a dog lay in the burial of the Lord of Sipán and in Tomb 2, and dog-faced jars appeared in the tomb of the Old Lord (Alva 1994:104, 180, Lám. 334; 2001; Alva and Donnan 1993:123. 159). Dog remains were also reported at Pacatnamu (Donnan 1995:147) and in the urban area near Huaca de la Luna (Esquerre et al. 2000). Dog (or fox) remains come from burials at the Cerro Blanco Complex (Cárdenas, Rodríguez, and Aguirre 1997) and Huaca Cao Viejo, and one grave at Cao Viejo had an dog effigy bottle at the feet of the deceased (Franco, Gálvez, and Vásquez 1999b:29, 2001b:151). Fox remains turned up at Huanchaco (Donnan and Mackey 1978) and Huaca de la Cruz (Strong and Evans 1952). Metal fox-head headdress ornaments are fairly common, and one was found in Tomb 3 at Sipán (Alva and Donnan 1993: Fig. 199; see also Donnan 1996). Guinea pig bones have been found in burials at the Cerro Blanco Complex (R. Tello et al. 2004; Vásquez and Rosales 2004; Vásquez et al. 2003) and Pacatnamu (Donnan and McClelland 1997:34).

Sea lion bones are reported from two burials at Pacatnamu (Donnan 1995:147), and a scapula was found at San José de Moro (Castillo and Donnan 1994b). The canine tooth of a sea lion pup was put on the sternum of a burial on Huaca de la Luna Platform II, and there were remains and a sea lion bottle in the nearby elite urban area (Esquerre et al. 2000:154; Vásquez and Rosales 1998; Vásquez et al. 2003). Bourget (1990, 2001b:100–104) points out that some gold faces from Sipán tombs are faces of sea lions. The first-known tomb at Huaca Rajada Sipán contained two copper sea lion masks, and the tomb of the Old Lord had a necklace of several of these (Alva 1988, 1994; Alva and Donnan 1993:200). A sea lion bottle accompanied a guardian of the tomb of the Warrior Priest (Strong and Evans 1952:151), and a sea lion head (Figure 12.2) and a florero painted with sea lions were found in a burial at Huaca Cao Viejo (Franco, Gálvez, and Vásquez 2001a: Figs. 48, 52). Two sea lion whistling bottles were excavated from tombs at Dos Cabezas (Donnan 2007). Otary remains and images are found also near sacrificial victims. Sea lions may have played, even more successfully, the dog's role of leading the dead across water to the underworld

(Arriaga 1968 [1621]:64; Benson 1995a:262; Kubler 1948:40 n.47).

Fish, mollusks, and crustaceans, including *Spondylus*, appear in burials (Alva and Donnan 1993; Castillo and Donnan 1994b; Donnan and McClelland 1997:34; Franco, Gálvez, and Vásquez 1999b: Fig. 49; T. Topic 1982:273; Uceda 1997d:181), suggesting the connection between the sea and the otherworld. Other treasured goods include flamingo feathers from a headdress found with the Lord of Sipán (Alva and Donnan 1993), and a macaw skeleton and two parrot skeletons placed in graves at Dos Cabezas (Donnan 2003, 2007). Objects of turquoise, chrysocolla, sodalite, and other stone (Castillo and Donnan 1994b; Franco, Gálvez, and Vásquez 1999a, 2001a), carvings from human or animal bone, and wooden maces and staffs were found in graves (Alva 2001; Bourget and Newman 1998; Franco, Gálvez, and Vásquez 1998b:12–13; Strong and Evans 1952).

While some graves contain no ceramic vessels, the burial of the Lord of Sipán yielded 1,137, mostly crude, "token" ceramics. Burials often have both simple and elaborate vessels. The presence of whistling vessels in graves has been discussed by Colin McEwan (1997); floreros are frequent in burial assemblages, often containing an offering. Earlier-style ceramic remains appear in burials at several sites. Miniature ceramics and other objects come from Dos Cabezas (Donnan 2001, 2003, 2007) and San José de Moro (Castillo and Donnan 1994b:125); the Lord of Sipán's coffin yielded miniature sheet-copper maces, shields, and copper spear points (Alva 2001; Alva and Donnan 1993:117).

Ceramics repeat the conventions of bone use; bone and ceramic fragments are often mixed, probably accidentally sometimes, but sometimes deliberately. Many archaeologists have observed the presence of both whole and deliberately broken and partial ceramics and other objects. The remarkable gilded copper and inlay figure from the tomb of the Old Lord of Sipán (see Figure 6.4) was found buried as separate pieces (Alva and Donnan 1994).

A BURIAL AT HUACA DE LA LUNA

Two of the first four tombs excavated by the Proyecto Arqueológico Huacas de Moche within Huaca de la Luna each contained the body of a male official or priest between the ages of 20 and 35; both lacked some bones (Uceda 1997d). The first tomb had been looted, but Tomb II offered the rare excitement of excavating an unlooted tomb. The other tombs contained reburials or offerings. The four burials may have been part of the same rite; all were placed in fill when the old building was sealed under new construction.

The man in Tomb II lay supine with his head to the south. Offerings at the sides of the coffin included ceramics and gourds with fish, mollusks, remains of a llama, maize, avocado, and coca seeds. Pieces of thick cloth with three gilded-copper platelets—one an animal head—had likely formed a headdress. A gourd covered the face; another lay under the head. In the hands and under the feet were pieces of copper, folded over and covered with cloth. Several pieces of copper lay in the pelvic area and on the thorax; the latter probably belonged to a garment. A copper spatula or stick rested on the right arm, and near the right hand lay a probable lime container of copper. Five ceramics were placed in the coffin. Two were of fine quality but fragmented: a florero and a stirrup-spout anthropomorphic duck effigy with a club and a shield in its hands. Outside the coffin were mostly stirrup-spout bottles with painted birds; one showed a crested animal. The only non-stirrup-spout vessel was a jar with a rope painted on it.

A BURIAL AT HUACA CAO VIEJO

Most of the tombs excavated at Huaca Rajada Sipán were spectacular, with remarkably fine gold and gilded-copper objects and quantities of ceramic vessels. A burial found recently at the huaca at Úcupe was quite similar (Atwood 2010:21; *El Comercio*, 5 July 2008; 26 July 2008), but the most dramatic recent excavation was that of the burial of the Lady of Huaca Cao Viejo, in a tomb in the pyramid at that site (*El Comercio*, 18 May 2006, 21 May 2006; Franco 2009; Franco, Gálvez, and Vásquez 2010; Franco and Gálvez 2010; Williams 2006).

In the floor of a space with richly painted walls (Figure 12.3), under a stone slab, a large bundle had been placed in Early Moche times, with ceramics arranged and a teenage girl lying beside it. The bundle was removed from the tomb by Régulo Franco and

FIGURE 12.3 The richly painted space where the Lady of Huaca Cao Viejo was found buried under the floor. *Photograph by the author.*

his team and taken with ceremony down the pyramid to the site laboratory. Over a year of careful work was required to unwrap the cloth bundle and remove the many fine objects within it that accompanied the body of the Lady of Huaca Cao Viejo, who was about 25 years old. Her body—with tattooed arms, hands, legs, and feet—had been sprinkled with red pigment and elaborately wrapped in 26 layers of cotton cloth that contained, among other things, 31 metal nose ornaments (more, I believe, than in any other known burial); gilded-copper crowns, collars, and diadems; a garment or cloth on which gilded-copper platelets were sewn in horizontal rows; 23 elaborate spear-throwers; and two tall maces of wood encased in gilded copper, surely symbols of her importance and authority.

The burial was extraordinary because of the quality and quantity of the objects in it, but especially because such a rich burial was that of a woman. In most earlier excavations women seem to have been sacrificed to accompany the principal burial's trip to the otherworld. The first important female entombments excavated were those of the two probable priestesses at San Jose de Moro, dressed in the

garments and accessories of the supposed Moon Goddess. A few female burials found in the Cerro Blanco Complex (Chapdelaine 2001) and at Huaca Cao Viejo suggest that they had a certain prominence, but the burial of the Lady of Huaca Cao Viejo reveals a personage of great importance. Presumably royal male burials at Loma Negra contained a quantity of nose ornaments, but other women do not have them—and most men do not. There are wooden clubs in some burials and caches, usually rather plain ones—the body of the Lord of Úcupe was laid out on clubs (Steve Bourget, personal communication, 2010)—but the nearly 2 m tall wooden staffs covered with gilded-copper sheathing found in the Lady of Huaca Cao Viejo's tomb are thus far unique in size and craftsmanship. She also had elaborate spear-throwers in her tomb. She was likely a ruler, possibly a great shaman, and perhaps both.

THE SIGNIFICANCE OF GRAVE GOODS

Offerings in rich burials surely had various purposes. Some must indicate offices held, deeds accomplished, or rites undertaken: special headgear, a lime container, a waterlily staff, a sacrificial knife, a mace, a shield, or a rattle. The Phase V priestess burials at San José de Moro exemplify a specific role. The war club as a symbol of office is demonstrated by the burial of the two with the Lady of Huaca Cao Viejo. A tomb excavated in 1995 at Dos Cabezas was that of an elderly man with gilded-copper jewelry (Cordy-Collins 2001b:29–33). His forearms were muscular; near his right hand lay a small, ceramic human head, broken off a face-neck jar; in his left hand was a copper knife, or *tumi*. He was probably a sacrificer. Huaca Rajada Sipán Tomb 8, a chamber with niches, contained a man with shields, war clubs, and spear points, a copper headdress, a nose ornament, a scepter, and two banners or large ornaments, one depicting the Fish Monster attacking a man (Alva 2001:235–240, Figs. 17–25). Another tomb at the same site contained war clubs and shamanic objects; rattles and sacrificial knives appeared in yet another.

Some grave goods seem to express general conventions rather than specific roles. Many reflect beliefs about the otherworld and the passage to it, and they appear to equip the deceased for status and, perhaps, generosity in the world of the ancestors. Food and chicha were likely provided for the journey; offerings may have been taken to the ancestors by the newly dead.

A recurring pattern is the presence of a quantity of one kind of object. Anne-Louise Schaffer (1985) points out a pattern of stacking similar objects at Loma Negra. Many interments had multiple ear ornaments, and nose ornaments were particularly common: the Lady of Huaca Cao Viejo had 32, and many were buried with a lord at Loma Negra (Jones 1993, 2001:212). A tomb at Dos Cabezas held 10 nose ornaments and 14 examples of a distinctive headdress of cane, cloth, and copper (Donnan 2001:71, 2003:55–56, 2007; Jiménez 2000:77). Steve Bourget (personal communication, 11 March 2010) found 11 gilded copper diadems and 7 crowns with the Señor de Úcupe, who was wearing two masks. Multiple pectorals were excavated in a Huaca Rajada Sipán tomb (Alva 1994, 2001:224–225, 242–243). Alva observes that earlier Huaca Rajada Sipán burials have multiple nose ornaments, whereas later burials have repeated ear ornaments or headgear; he notes also the presence of multiple necklaces or pectorals. A nose ornament transforms the face and masks it; ornaments peripheral to the face give it context. All of these refer to the status of the wearer, but it is not yet clear why there is concentration on one kind of object rather than another.

THE LIVING, THE DEAD, AND THE ANCESTORS

"Mortuary practices reflect the dynamic relationship between the living, the dead, and the supernatural in the Andean world," writes Verano (1995:189; see also R. Burger 1997:70; Kaulicke 1997, 2000; Millaire 2004; Salomon 1995, 1998b:10; Sharon 2000:8, 13; Uceda and Tufinio 2003:218). Powerful, sacred ancestors were central to burial rites. Thomas Dillehay (1995:16–17) sees ancestor cults as strengthening the cohesion of the community, for graves were centers of power from which rulers derived authority, largely through ritual (see also Bourget 2006). The relation between the living and the dead was critical for the functioning of the society and its world. Makowski (1996:84) holds that objects evoking certain rites were

deposited in an elite tomb so that the dead could occupy in the otherworld a position like that held in the heart of society. Anne Marie Hocquenghem (1987:84) writes that images on ceramics placed in graves allowed the dead to continue to function in the otherworld and ensured the survival of their descendants. The practice imposed on the living a dependence on the ancestors that reinforced the cult and maintained order, for each image, carrying an ideology, was an instrument of government. Offerings were made to the ancestors, who were believed to control people, their lives, sacred things, food, and the fertility of their fields. Andean ancestors were considered to be donors of continuing fertility for the living, and the Incas observed agrarian transitional times with appeals and offerings to the ancestors. Today the dead are believed to care for the growth of plants and ensure the harvest.

In the Andes death and burial belonged to a process parallel to the cycle of planting, germination, growth, fruition, death, and regeneration (Allen 1998:21, 23, citing Goss 1994 and Salomon 1998; see also Franco, Gálvez, and Vásquez 1999b:24; Rostworowski 1992:27; Salomon and Urioste 1991:16; Uceda 1997d:131–132). The Quechua word *mallqui*, known from the sixteenth century, conveys the idea of a dry thing that will have new life (Arriaga 1968 [1621]:27; see also Classen 1993:89–90, 104; Kaulicke 2001:26; Salomon 1995; Urton 1993:131–133). That bones were thought to be seedlike explains, in part, the archaeological evidence for their manipulation. Catherine Allen (1982) has observed that in the highlands in modern times, dried and shriveled seeds and tubers are likened to dead people. Hocquenghem (1977:169, 1987:136, 144, 171), too, notes that the equation of plant and corpse still exists, that the corpse prepared for the otherworld is viewed as a seed that will grow, and that movements of burial are those of planting. Bourget (2006:20) points out that today— and probably in the Moche past—the same stick is used for planting and digging graves.

Andean thought emphasizes transition from soft to hard, from living being to ancestor (R. Burger 1997:30; Frame 2001; McEwan 1997:178; Salomon 1995:325, 328). (The idea of turning to stone may relate to this concept.) Water for the living is believed to come from desiccation of the dead; water is the blood of ancestors. The body's immortality materialized in preserved bones; the dead had existence as long as any part of the body—or clothing or an effigy—was preserved (Salomon and Urioste 1991:130n, 693). Bones could serve as guides between the worlds of the living and the dead.

Uceda (1997d:184–186, 2001:62; Uceda and Tufinio 2003; Uceda et al. 1994:294–296), who has considered these subjects in depth, describes the ritual of sealing and burying a temple by enclosing it with a new temple (see also Franco, Gálvez, and Vásquez 1999b:121). Part of the rite was the interment, within the structure, of people important to temple activities, and the insertion into tombs of pieces of burials from other places. Uceda sees this process as crucial to the renewal and reconsecration of the structure and the power that it symbolized. The burial of priests and old bones in the rebuilding reinforced, relegitimized, and regenerated the power that came from ancestors via priests. The ancestors needed representatives to embody them in social acts and rituals. Buried priests became potent ancestors with power materializing in the world of the living.

At the time of Spanish contact, the dying and the recently deceased in the Andes were believed to form a single class; it took about a year for the corpse to make the transition to ancestorhood, to hardened, permanent being. Those dead less than a year were thought to move among the living. "Death was perceived as a state of transition," Peter Kaulicke (1997:7) writes—a process of mortuary stages, including relations with the living (see also Betanzos 1996 [1551]). The person being interred still had a social identity and feasted with the living in burial and mourning rites. Pablo José de Arriaga (1968 [1621]:64) wrote that Indians of the Colonial period were "persuaded that the dead feel, eat and drink" (see also Bourget 1994a:118; Frame 2001; Makowski 1994b:110; Netherly 1977:121–122; Uceda 1997d:177). The burial place was a passageway from the living world to that of the dead—to that of the ancestors. Community rites were held in cemeteries. Some time after burial the kin of the dead would invite the community to drink chicha and dance. Such beliefs may explain why figures in "dance of the dead" and other scenes are partially skeletal.

Describing a modern Day of the Dead at Mórrope, a town in the Lambayeque Valley where pottery is made by ancient methods and a church has a stepped altar and algarrobo roof supports, James Vreeland (1992a) notes feasting, drinking, and visiting by descendants who come to pay respects (see also Elera 1984; Netherly 1977:121–122; Shimada 1994a:197–201, 1994b). Skulls and long bones, signifying the presence of the dead, are placed in small chapels outside the cemetery. Graveside visitors share news and tales with dead family members. On the way to the cemetery, vendors sell food, drink, and offerings formed like fruit, animals, body parts, and objects.

The Moche likely also had funerary feasts, when survivors feasted with the dead, who needed food for the initial afterlife (Guaman Poma 1980:206–209, 211–213; Hocquenghem 1987:134–135; Larco Hoyle 2001, II:166–169; see also Ramírez-Horton 1980:124). Some grave goods had surely been used in funerary rites: musical instruments, vessels, food, clothing, and perhaps digging sticks like the elaborate ones found in Huaca de la Cruz.

CERAMIC SOURCES OF INFORMATION

Depictions of the Burial Theme on bottles in northern Phase V graves show a shaft tomb with a burial chamber (Figure 12.4), ropes being used to lower a coffin, and graveside attendants (Donnan and McClelland 1979; see also Castillo and Donnan 1994b; Donnan and McClelland 1999; Rostworowski 1992:61–68). *Strombus* shells are shown as offerings, perhaps intended to be interred after being played as trumpets, although none, as far as I know, has been found in a burial.

Of the bottles that feature effigy adobe houses, some display closed doors, while others include one or more solemn figures. One example with a step-roof house on its deck shows, drawn below: ceramics; two women; two priests in what looks like a prayer pose, gazing up with seeming reverence at the three-dimensional house; and two fine-line houses, one with a vulture hovering over club heads on its roof (Figure 12.5). These seeming mortuary scenes may depict a tomb as a cosmic house.

Effigy figures carrying a rolled mat and pottery imply a mortuary context. Two mats, braided from reeds, were found in a grave atop Huaca del Sol, one placed under the body, another covering the whole

FIGURE 12.4 A depiction of the Burial Theme. *Proyecto Arqueológico San José de Moro. Drawing by Donna McClelland.*

assemblage (Uceda et al. 1994; see also Conklin and Versteylen 1978). A body and its offerings in Huaca Rajada Sipán were wrapped in a sedge mat (Alva 1994), and remains of mats were discovered in graves at Huaca Cao Viejo (*El Comercio*, 18 May 2006; Franco, Gálvez, and Vásquez 2001a; Williams 2006; see also Bourget 1994a:116).

Ceramic priest images may have been put in graves to guide or guard the dead. Some distinguished-looking effigies play a flute; more simply clad, dis-eased, or skeletal ones play a drum, as do effigy, priest-dressed figures with bird or sea lion traits. Panpipers often appear in scenes with the dead (Benson 1975, 1982b:204; Classen 1993:19; Donnan 1982). Music relates to liminal rites—transitions between day and night, life and death—and is an agent of transformation in many cultures.

SKELETONS AND SEX

Music and dance as depicted on ceramics and in murals often appear to be part of funerary or sacrificial rites (Arsenault 1993; Benson 1972, 1975; Donnan 1982; Jiménez Borja 1950–1951, 1955; Larco Hoyle 2001, II:166–181). Fine-line military/priestly dance scenes might depict a funerary rite; nonskeletal dancers in some scenes hold cord or cloth possibly used for funerary tying. Scenes, usually in low relief, that show partially skeletal figures (often only the face is skeletal) are referred to as dances of the dead (Figure 12.6). They might picture the realm of the sacred ancestors or a rite

FIGURE 12.5 Effigy bottle with a house above a scene of priestly figures and architecture. *Private collection. Photograph by Christopher B. Donnan.*

in the transition to death. Often one figure is frontal and wears the two-disk headdress seen on some elite men and on a major figure in fine-line military/priestly scenes; other figures in the dance suggest his burial entourage. The priests may be psychopomps or guardians; some play instruments, usually panpipes. Women and children, not present in warrior-priest dances, are seen here and may refer to the practice of interring women and a child with an important adult. A man holds a staff with maize ears, which is appropriate, since the dead control fertility. In these scenes a dog can be present, ceramics are often shown, and floreros are prominent. Archaeological remains found in Huaca de la Luna Plaza 3C give evidence for postmortem

FIGURE 12.6 Bottle with a skeletal or diseased drummer as deck figure above a Dance of the Dead scene in relief. Figures with backflaps and two-disk headdresses hold hands and dance between small pipers. *Courtesy Linden-Museum, Stuttgart, M 30163. Photograph by Didoni.*

treatment of sacrificed skeletons; Bourget (2006:125–126), Uceda (2000a:211), and Verano (2008:209–210) propose that rearticulated skeletons of certain sacrificed, flayed figures might have actually been displayed or used like dancers during certain rituals, given that some body parts with rope tied on them suggest suspension and display. What seem to be dancers pictured on ceramics might represent such an activity.

Bottles shaped like figures in amorous poses occur in graves of men, women, and children (Figure 12.7; Benson 1972, 1975; Bergh 1993; Bourget 1994a, 2006; Larco Hoyle 1965b). Sometimes both males and females are partially skeletal, but often only the male. The women—one or two—may be those who accompany an elite male to the otherworld. Often one woman is alive, the other skeletal, which might indicate the condition in which they were put into a grave. The scenes likely come from the interim after death. Couples often look as if they are mourning rather than enjoying sex. They can be accompanied by ceramic vessels, presumably grave goods. Below some scenes a wave motif suggests the underworld sea; broad, horizontal lines may represent the steps of a burial place. Some scenes involving apparently live figures seem to belong to this genre.

Probably all captives and all male, partially skeletal figures have an erect penis. Genitalia did not die. The ceramics emphasize organs and erection, and depict sodomy, masturbation, and foreplay, but probably never actual vaginal coitus. Cieza de León (1959 [1550, 1553]:314) described "chiefs" and male temple attendants in female attire engaging in sodomy during religious feasts, and Hocquenghem (1987:140–141), on the basis of certain modern customs, has interpreted sodomy as a mourning rite that inverts usual activity because it does not lead to fertility (see also Bourget 2006:73). The otherworld is an inversion of this one, and funerary ritual is inverted.

Enrique Vergara (1990) points out that sexuality is a sacred theme in many cultures in the world because it concerns the secret of existence, fecundity, and the continuity of life.

A depiction of a live Moche figure seated on a throne can have a huge phallus. This is often described as humorous, but the enthroned men are extremely dignified and well dressed; one man in a stepped shirt has a portrait face. One implication is that a leader

FIGURE 12.7 Effigy of a woman holding the penis of a man with a skeletal face. Probable grave offerings are drawn in front of them. *National Museum of the American Indian, Smithsonian Institution, Washington, DC.*

must have an impressive phallus, denoting fertility of all kinds. In another image an older man with a priest's carrying cloth tied around his waist crouches in "prayer pose," his head topped by the glans of a penis. Susan Bergh (1993) sees a connection between male sexuality and plant growth through an analogy between semen and foamy, rushing, mountain water (see also Zighelboim 1995). Chicha in funerary jars belongs to this complex. Bergh notes parallels between spout/chicha and phallus/semen, observing ritual humor in funerary rites in the Americas and other places, and noting aspects to which humor and this kind of punning might apply at times of liminality.

One two-leveled, low-relief composition features a large, alive-looking man with a god's mouth and figure-8 ear ornaments (although no snake belt) being drawn into the underworld—or raised to the upper world (Figure 12.8) (Donnan 1982: Fig.23; Hocquenghem 1987: Fig. 133); a second version of this figure does not have godly attributes. On both levels, skeletal figures dance. The transitional figure is flanked on the upper level by two figures apparently throwing stones at him; a live couple performs sodomy, and near them a caped figure facing a flying bat blows into an instrument; on the other side of the central figure is a bird and four figures moving in pairs. Below, two panpipers stand near dancers, and a skeleton rides a llama. Pottery is shown below the dangling feet of the transitional figure, and an animal—llama or dog?—lies or floats at the side. Two chamber tombs have a single figure in each. The beliefs, myths, and rites of death and the afterlife are listed here in a kind of shorthand.

FIGURE 12.8 Two-level scene from a bottle with a relief surface. *Museo Amano, Lima. Drawing by Donna McClelland.*

CHAPTER THIRTEEN

The End of the Moche Worlds

IN AD 535 THE ISLAND OF JAVA was split by a severe volcanic eruption that created worldwide atmospheric disturbances of dust, water, sulphuric acid, and aerosols that blocked sunlight, destroyed crops, and altered weather for years. In the latter half of the sixth century, the Moche experienced a 30-year, famine-causing drought along with El Niño events, including a flood around AD 556, a disaster that would have destroyed irrigation systems and spread disease. Records from ice cap cores indicate frequent severe El Niño conditions toward the end of the sixth century and the first half of the seventh, with long periods of drought between, when rainfall in the highlands was 30 percent less than usual, soil was damaged, and food production drastically cut (Dillehay 2001:268–270; Moseley 1992:209–212; Sandweiss and Quilter 2008; Shimada 1994a:122–131; Shimada et al. 1991).

Evidence of drought and inundations, first of water and then of windblown sand, is seen in the archaeological record at many North Coast sites (Bawden 1996:263–268, 2001:291–294; Donnan 2007; Kaulicke 2000; Moseley, Donnan, and Keefer 2007; Shimada 1994a:247–254). The Cerro Blanco Complex experienced severe El Niño flooding during Phase IV, at some time before AD 600 (Morales 2000a; Uceda and Canziani 1993). Serious flood damage to the huacas was repaired, but sand swept in, burying much of the city; deep alluvial deposits between the huacas signify El Niño activity. The major pluvial event that struck the Cerro Blanco site is seen also in the stratigraphy of Huaca Cao Viejo, which had rain damage several times and was partially dismantled and abandoned during Phase IV (Franco 2001; Gálvez and Briceño 2001). More heavy rains followed.

Beset by drought, flood, and long periods of sand intrusion, people who had engaged in intensive agriculture abandoned once-cultivated land and moved inland to places that had some protection from offshore winds and enveloping sand. On upvalley gradients, scarce water could be managed more efficiently and diverted to arable land. Upvalley sites were also better placed for interaction with—or defense against incursions from—the highlands.

The Moche power structure that had prospered in and dominated the early stages of Phase IV could not stand up to the disasters that began in the mid-sixth century, nor to other emerging problems. Internal stresses were likely a factor, and the lower classes may have acted against the elite. Outside peoples with whom the Moche related may have rebelled against exploitative tribute or exchange, resource control, or other issues. Competition for water and food was strong. Thomas Dillehay (2001:262) has observed that many Phase V sites in the middle and lower sections of the Jequetepeque and Zaña valleys are walled or have hilltop fortifications above the site (see also Bawden 1996:264–275; Castillo 2003; Daggett 1985; J. Topic and Topic 1983; T. Topic 1991). The Moche seem to have abandoned or lost control of sites in valleys south of the Cerro Blanco Complex. Old strategies no longer worked. The introduction of the Rayed God, in late Phase IV, perhaps indicates an attempt to improve Moche fortunes. The sacrificial area of Huaca de la Luna (Platform 2 and Plazas 3A and 3C) was constructed during the late architectural phases (Bourget 2001b; Tufinio 2004a).

One method that the elite tried to use in coping with problems was to change iconography in mural programs at Huacas de la Luna and Cao Viejo. A twenty-first-century excavation at Huaca de la Luna Platform I revealed late painted reliefs displayed across the north facade after a severe El Niño event (Figure 13.1; Huaca de la Luna–Moche, Perú 2009; Tufinio 2008). Dancers hold hands in the lowest row. Above is a row of spiderlike motifs, and above them, in profile, wrinkle-faced gods hold an unusual staff with a probable rattle on it. The gods have a foot that is a monster head, a motif from Cupisnique/Chavín times. At the top, under the ramp (see Figure 5.3), a row of red dragons marches on a white ground, each bearing a human trophy head. Dissatisfaction with the

FIGURE 13.1 Huaca de la Luna murals on the North Facade. *Photograph by the author.*

former, repeated mural program and a need to return to ancient protagonists are reflected by archaic motifs; images from thriving Phase IV cities were no longer to be relied on. The Cerro Blanco people seem to have been calling to the ancestors for help. Phase IV ceramics are still found elsewhere until ca. AD 800, but no Phase V ceramics have been found at the site (Castillo and Uceda 2008:718). There are carbon 14 dates from the urban area later than those in Huaca de la Luna (Uceda, Chapdelaine, and Verano 2008).

At both Huaca de la Luna and Cao Viejo, the North Facade murals are interrupted at one end by a pavilion whose late, Complex Theme relief murals show people, animals, trees, boats, and objects (Franco, Gálvez, and Vásquez 1996, 1998a, 2001b:167; Gálvez and Briceño 2001:151–153). Much of this subject matter appears in Middle Moche ceramics, but not in murals. This mural use seemed unique to Huaca Cao Viejo until an almost identical mural program was uncovered at Huaca de la Luna in a similar location (Figure 13.2). A ritual calendar may be depicted, as proposed by Régulo Franco and Juan Vilela (2004), or a seasonal rite, or possibly a sky map (stars are among the images). The life of a powerful ancestor may be presented, perhaps the founder of a late-introduced dynasty. Wearing a headdress that resembles a European crown, the possible ancestor appears several times in these murals, more prominent than a normal human being but lacking obvious supernatural traits. The murals may combine several of these interpretations. They may relate to a new group of people fitting into an old setting, or to an old group introducing change.

THE HUARI QUESTION

The Middle Horizon is usually defined by the powerful influence through much of Peru of the city known as Huari, in the southern highlands near modern Ayacucho. Traces of Huari influence on North Coast peoples are found first in Phase IV and became stronger in V. Moche-Huari style ceramics—which are Moche in shape and subject, but Huari color and drawing—began to be produced, and objects of both styles occur together in burials (Figure 13.3). The Huari style may have been used by the Moche elite

FIGURE 13.2 Huaca de la Luna. A pavilion wall showing the Complex Theme, in front of the North Facade. *Photograph by the author.*

in the search for new power symbolism. Phase V is essentially a Middle Horizon style, and it appears with other Middle Horizon styles in Late Moche remains (Bawden 1983, 1996:263–308; Castillo 2001: Fig. 13, 320–325, 2003; Cook 2001; Donnan and McClelland 1999:154–161; Kaulicke 1994:127; Mackey and Hastings 1982; Donna McClelland 1990:94, 100; McClelland, McClelland, and Donnan 2007:Figs. 3.80–3.90; Menzel 1977:39–41, 59–60; Shimada 1994a; T. Topic 1991; Willey 1953:412).

Huari is often named as a factor in the decline of Moche culture. The possibility of Huari conquest of the North Coast has been much discussed and usually rejected. Huari-influenced pottery is found as far north as Piura, but not in heavy concentration. Huari grave goods occur at Huaca del Sol, which was surely a sacred place in the post-Moche period. Huaca de la Luna generally lacks Huari remains, although a vessel found there by Uhle combined Moche V and Huari styles (Menzel 1977, see above), and some murals in Luna may show Huari influence. The summit of Cerro Blanco was a shrine for offerings in the Middle Horizon, as it had been earlier (Bourget 1997b). In addition to Huari, influences on the Moche came from Cajamarca, the Callejón de Huaylas (in the highlands), and Pachacamac and other Central Coast sites.

FIGURE 13.3 The Moche Moon Goddess painted in Huari style. *Amano Collection, Lima. Photograph by Christopher B. Donnan.*

The decline of a civilization surely never has a single cause, but environmental stresses were major factors in the Moche demise. The highlands, suffering less from catastrophes, benefited from the distress of coastal peoples. At another time it would not have been propitious for Huari and other highland peoples to make their presence felt on the coast. The archaeological record shows this, but a detailed picture cannot yet be drawn.

To a large extent, Moche cities and regions had always gone their own ways, and so it was at the end. The civilization ended differently in different places, and at quite different times.

CERRO BLANCO, THE UPVALLEY CITIES, AND THE NORTHERN REGION

At the beginning of the Middle Horizon, many sites that had been important in Phase IV ceased construction and, often, active occupation. The Cerro Blanco Complex was not completely abandoned, as was thought before recent excavations, but the city was no longer at the center of power. Santiago Uceda and Elías Mujica indicate that the last construction phases of Huaca del Sol and Huaca de la Luna date to the late eighth century AD (Uceda and Mujica 1997:12; Uceda and Tufino 2003:215; Morales 2003). In the last phase Huaca del Sol became more important than Huaca de la Luna. Plaza I and the sacred precincts of Luna were sealed off, and Platform III of Luna was built to the east, and higher on the flank of Cerro Blanco, after the ravaging of Platforms I and II by El Niño rains. With its "animated objects" and fox-warrior murals, Platform III became the new ritual center. In the seventh and eighth centuries (early Middle Horizon), some people were still living in residential areas at the Cerro Blanco site, but access was more limited. Claude Chapdelaine notes an "almost complete absence of Moche V ceramic vessels in domestic or funerary contexts" there (Chapdelaine 2001:71; Chapdelaine et al. 1997:91).

As the Cerro Blanco site was winding down, some other Moche sites were expanding. The Moche Valley seat of power in Phase V was Galindo, near the neck of the valley, but within view of Cerro Blanco (Bawden 1983, 1996, 2001; see also Moore 1996:58–64,

180; Reindel 1993:232–237; J. Topic and Topic 1987). Galindo architecture, much less grand than that of the Cerro Blanco Complex, was placed in space confined by foothills. It comprised rectangular complexes with small platforms and mounds within high adobe walls, a little like walls at Huari sites or later Chimu ones. A mound of moderate size faces a steep hill across a plaza; mound, plaza, and a small, elite residential sector are surrounded by an access-limiting wall. Galindo architecture suggests that grand ritual was eschewed, and populations were more egalitarian. Stone is available in the upper valley, and residential architecture was built with cobblestone foundations and cane superstructures. Garth Bawden, who began excavating at Galindo during the Chan Chan–Moche Valley Project, describes the structures as expressing a centralized, secular government, with walls to impose social control. Another wall, possibly defensive, runs along the flank of the hill opposite the site, enclosing it further. (Having examined this architecture, Bawden [2001] points out the need to study architectural innovation in terms of internal organization and external threat.)

One can imagine a group of people moving upvalley from Cerro Blanco and building Galindo in a new way, while diehards stayed at Cerro Blanco, keeping Phase IV ceramics and adding a new ritual building interment, and new structures and murals, in a desperate effort to hold on to the glory of that site. According to Bawden (1996:288–291), people at Galindo rejected the ideas of the Middle Moche power holders and adopted an ideology associated with broader Andean concepts. Galindo burials have few grave goods except for pieces of copper. New ceramic forms and wares appear in the official complex, in the most elaborate residential structures, and in richer burials—and only in these places. The ceramics are described as having a fairly thick temper, principally of sandy material, fired in a partially reduced atmosphere, smoothed, and highly polished; wares were generally black or brown. One type of molded decoration presented a single figure that takes up most of the surface. Another, more common type has small, repeated, geometric motifs covering most of the surface; often these are variant step motifs, with a snake or ray head. Elaborate double-chamber vessels were usually found near higher-status buildings and sacked tombs.

The significance of Galindo notwithstanding, the late-period center of power clearly shifted from the Moche Valley to Pampa Grande (Figure 13.4), Lambayeque, upvalley from Sipán and 55 km from the coast, a site excavated mostly by Izumi Shimada (1994a, 1997, 2001; see also Anders 1981; Bawden 1996:291–296; Moore 1996:57–59, 113, 180; Reindel 1993:314–326). The city covers some 6 km² with essentially traditional Moche architecture, although it has innovative features. Residential areas had an estimated 10,000 to 15,000 inhabitants. Dry gullies were modified to become streets, and some of the wider ones might have allowed llama caravans to pass through. The major structure, Huaca Fortaleza (also called Huaca Grande, Huaca La Capilla, and Huaca Iglesia), is placed close to the first range of foothills. This huaca was nearly as large as Huaca del Sol (180 × 275 × 38 m) and much larger than any building at Galindo. It would have been a highly visible structure, to which access was tightly controlled by a gigantic enclosure. It may have been a ceremonial center, or a residence of the ruling elite, or both. Although architecture at Pampa Grande was more like that at Cerro Blanco than that at Galindo, there were walled residential complexes, and movement was controlled.

Shimada's inventory of Pampa Grande ceramics includes jars of varying shapes with press-mold decoration, various bowl forms, plates, and high quality, fine-line stirrup-spout bottles, as well as double-spout-and-bridge bottles. Ceramic drums, storage and serving vessels, and food remains were also found. Both Gallinazo and Moche V styles are represented. Shimada describes a city divided into northern and southern sectors, with Moche remains in the north and Gallinazo in the south, with restricted passage between the two. Fine Moche pottery comes from the northern sector; utilitarian wares and face-neck jars were found in the southern sector. Neither Galindo nor Pampa Grande ceramic collections have yet yielded evidence for a Huari presence.

Both sites had small populations in Phase IV. During Phase V they may have been "symbiotic or paired," as William Conklin (1990:53–54) has suggested, or there may have been rivalry between them (see Bawden 1996:305–307; Shimada 1994a:127, 1997; T. Topic 1991). Galindo seems to have been a focus for the weakened southern valleys, and Pampa Grande a

FIGURE 13.4 The Huaca Fortaleza at Pampa Grande, at the foothills of the mountains. *Photograph by the author.*

focus for the stronger north. Both cities lasted about 150 years. An increase in urbanism may be indicated by prominent storage facilities at both. Bawden (2001:294) reported "a large area of storage terraces" at Galindo, and both Shimada (1994a:216–224) and Martha Anders (1981) found large-scale storage facilities at Pampa Grande. Chapdelaine (2001:75) has discovered a surprising quantity of such facilities in the urban area at the Cerro Blanco Complex.

In the Jequetepeque Valley, sites near the sea remained significant. San José de Moro, on the northern edge of the valley, was on the coastal route (the Pan-American Highway now cuts through it) and near a route into the mountains where Early Horizon ruins are found on the way to Cajamarca. With an occupation from Middle Moche through Chimu, San José was, according to Luis Jaime Castillo (2001:309), "essentially a cemetery and ceremonial center continuously occupied for more than a thousand years." Pampa Grande and Galindo, in contrast, were more residential, less mortuary, and of short duration (Castillo 2000b, 2003; Castillo et al. 2008; Castillo and Donnan 1994b; Disselhoff 1958; Donnan and Castillo 1994; Rucabado and Castillo

2003). Late Moche at San José lasted until ca. AD 800, when a transition to Lambayeque/Sicán began. Apparently the most important Late Moche center of its kind, San José had a large concentration of burials surrounded by sacred spaces for rites, for which people came from all over the Jequetepeque Valley and beyond. Obsidian and other materials and objects significant to other peoples—to the Huari, for example, but not to earlier Moche—were found at San José. Evidence of large-scale chicha making suggests that a major activity there was the production of maize beer for ritual use. A large chicha storage jug often marked the mouth of a boot-shaped tomb. In one building, three rooms contained many types of chicha-making pottery, and broken fine-line ceramics were strewn about. These rooms had been ritually sealed, as a tomb might be.

The San José excavations have yielded fine-line ceramics with new versions of Moche themes, as well as imported objects, local copies of imports, and artifacts produced locally in a mixed style. One notable piece is a goblet with a human-headed club repeated around it, found in the tomb of one of the priestesses interred there (see Chapter 12 and Figure 4.2). A good deal of Cajamarca pottery has been found, as well as ceramics of Nievería (Central Coast), Huari, and combined Huari/Moche V styles.

San José had connections with the peoples of the Central Coast both along the coast and through Cajamarca, where Huari presence was strong (Castillo 2001:324–325; Castillo et al. 2008; Donnan and Castillo 1992; T. Topic 1991). Foreign ceramics made up a small percentage of the total number of objects at San José de Moro, however, and although Huari and Huari-derived vessels were excavated in elite Late Moche tombs, there were no Huari or other foreign tombs. A large quantity of Phase V Moche fine-line pottery comes from San José. After a near total absence of fine-line bottles in Jequetepeque in Phase IV, a sudden burst of its production occurred in an adaptation of the southern pictorial style. Castillo has considered the possibility that ceramists might have migrated to Jequetepeque from the south, and suggests that most typical Phase V fine-line ceramics may have come from San José (see Figures 4.2, 12.4; Castillo 2001:317–318; Castillo et al. 2008; Donnan and McClelland 1999:22).

Sites that thrived in the Jequetepeque Valley at this time include Pacatnamu, where Donnan and Cock (Donnan 1997b) found a long-lasting Moche occupation, strongest in Phases II/III and V, but lasting until ca. AD 900. Pacatnamu was surely more of a political power center than San José; it may also have been a sacred center, and possibly a pilgrimage place. Its site above the sea is spectacular, and its funerary assemblages were grand. Excavations there reflect Huari ceramic influence at the end of Moche occupation, but such influence is not evident in textiles or funerary practices. (Huari burials are usually seated.)

MIXED MOTIFS AND OTHER MATTERS OF ICONOGRAPHY

Late Phase IV and Phase V Moche ceramics show an iconography of desperation, often with drastic splittings and regroupings of subject matter, reflecting outside influence, internal instability, and change in meaning. The examples should be used with care in considering the relationships of core Moche iconography, but they are a rich source for interpreting Late Moche. As the realism of Phase IV disappeared, a style with a *horror vacui* evolved, and little evidence remains of elite individualism. New themes were added and old ones dropped. Portrait heads and effigies of priests vanished or are poorly made, fine-line human figures are uncommon, and effigy animals and vegetables are missing.

Continuing complexes and motifs, now in crowded scenes (Figure 13.5), include the Runner, Deer Hunt, and Waterlily rites; a god battling a monster; dancing warriors and priests; beans and bean-warriors; the Conch Monster; and the anthropomorphic crab. Scenes of warfare are rare, probably because the Moche were no longer powerful warriors; the Presentation Theme and owl imagery, long major motifs, are even rarer. Formerly single themes are often grouped and sometimes merged in barely decipherable visual narrative. Motifs are mingled in the Complex Scene murals at Huacas de la Luna and Cao Viejo, and a confusion of themes in the "animated objects" mural in Huaca de la Luna Platform III includes "foreign" star maces, a bag, and odd garments from the Coca Complex, along with goblets and bowls, and a priest

FIGURE 13.5 Bottle with complex, crowded collection of subject matter. *Private collection. Photograph by Christopher B. Donnan.*

from the Libation Rite. Earlier these would not likely have been combined. The Coca Complex, as such—which had been strong since Early Moche—disappears completely in Phase V.

Although the Rayed God changed or faded away in Phase V (there is an occasional radiant figure), the Snake-belt God, now probably always with a wrinkled face, made a comeback, appearing, often with Iguana, in the Burial Theme, which is new (Donnan and McClelland 1979; McClelland, McClelland, and Donnan 2007:96–113), as well as other scenes. Sometimes the Snake-belt God takes on attributes of the Rayed God, or the two are conflated; a new god, or a new aspect of the Snake-belt God, may appear fleetingly in V. A male god in a raft is depicted with a snake belt and often an animal head on his headdress. As before, he goes to sea as the god or his marine twin, but now a radiance (of clubs or weapons bundles) floats around him (see Figure 1.7).

On one florero a large, splayed figure reminiscent of the god face in murals at Huacas de la Luna and Cao Viejo has eight large snake projections; he holds

a sacrificial knife and points to a smiling-face sun or star (Donnan and McClelland 1999: Fig. 5.17). This is another return to an early form, a version of the Decapitator, the X Sacrificer, the Spider God. A profile Snake-belt God with wrinkled face and knife stands at his side, gazing at him. Radiant suns or stars appear throughout the composition.

Marine subjects are found on more than half of Phase V fine-line bottles, according to Donna McClelland (1990), who pointed out many of the changes between the iconography of Phases IV and V (see also Benson 1975:138; Cordy-Collins and McClelland 1983; McClelland, McClelland, and Donnan 2007). A new sea motif, identified by McClelland as an animated wave, is a human figure, often with an aura of club heads, holding what looks like a splash or stream of water (Figure 13.6). Sometimes the stream is straight; sometimes the splash curves, and the figure is upside down, as if tumbled by a wave. It is not clear if this is a known god as a wave or as the sea, or if it personifies the sea or the threat of a wave, but it appears as a new opponent to the Snake-belt God.

The other late-arrival opponent of the god (it seems to come in late in Phase IV, before the wave appears) is the Circular Creature, who may also be sea-related (see figure second from left, Figure 13.6). Its round body, and sometimes its headgear, usually has a pattern of small circles that occasionally float away from the figure like bubbles. The knife-carrying Circular Creature plucks at the Snake-belt God, and the god tweaks the edge of the creature's circular form, actions that should give a clue to its identity (Castillo 1989:55–63; Kutscher 1983:Abb. 263A; Lieske 2001:189–191; McClelland, McClelland, and Donnan 2007: Figs. 3.49–3.56; Shimada 1994a:7.35c). Bourget's (1994a) proposal that this is a puff fish—a highly toxic species that swells up at approaching danger—is, I think, the best identification that has been suggested. The fish that most resembles this monster is the oscillated freshwater stingray (*Potamotrygon motoro*), which has a venomous spine and round markings all over its round body (Paxton and Eschmeyer 1995:69), and is said to be feared more than piranhas; however, it was not likely known on the coast. The Circular Creature does not always appear in watery contexts, but this may not be critical to its identity since creatures with fins appear on land in these scenes. The earlier

FIGURE 13.6 The Snake-belt God with the Circular Creature and Wave Creature. *Fowler Museum of Cultural History, University of California, Los Angeles. Drawing by Donna McClelland.*

monsters who faced the god have strange heads and lack headgear; the two late ones have faces and head-dresses. The Circular Creature seems to start out with a semicircular headdress with two projections and later wears a sort of helmet.

On other bottles, the rafting Moon Goddess, some-times drawn sloppily or in abbreviated form, is more common than the male raft god (see Figures 13.3, 1.7, 8.4; McClelland, McClelland, and Donnan 2007). First featured in the Presentation Theme, she takes on increased importance as the Rayed God loses his iden-tity and the Plate-shirt God virtually disappears. (Raft scenes can appear in Huari painting style and colors.)

In the Burial Theme (see Figure 12.4; see also Don-nan and McClelland 1979), the eyes of the splayed figure—and sometimes the entombed figure—usually show one simple eye, with no pupil, and one styl-ized eye tapering to a point on the outside, a form common on Lambayeque/Sicán gold masks, a style that was beginning to develop by Phase IV. This eye is unusual for a Moche portrayal, but the remark-able, early, inlaid-metal figure from Tomb 3 at Huaca Rajada Sipán—a frontal male with a skyband and clawed hands and feet—has eyes of the same elon-gated type (see Figure 6.4; Alva 1994; Alva and Don-nan 1993: Figs. 204, 215). This eye and other non-matching eyes on objects found in Tomb 3 may be persistent, if uncommon, northern traits. A gold face from Sipán Tomb 3 that looks rather like the Snake-belt God has one pink *Spondylus* eye and one white-shell eye, both with the tapered shape (Alva 1994:Lám. 195), and another object was buried with an eye inlay missing. On Phase IV ceramics priestly figures are often blind in one eye.

The Burial Theme and late raft scenes may have been produced only in the Jequetepeque Valley, and possibly only at San José de Moro. The importance of the moon and the Moon Goddess increased in response to changing circumstances, perhaps an El Niño event that affected fishing. In Phase IV, sacrifi-cial blood became increasingly important, and women became more prominent in ceramic scenes, with a role in sacrifice rites. Steve Bourget (1994a:62, 2006:138) sees the connection between menstrual blood and sacrificial blood, and between the menstrual cycle and the lunar cycle. At the time of Spanish contact a House of the Moon, dedicated to the Moon Goddess, was located near San José de Moro. Antonio de la Calancha (1974–1982 [1638], IV:1239) wrote that ritual activity took place there at solar and lunar eclipses (see also J. Rowe 1948:50), and this region had a long tra-dition of moon veneration.

MATERIAL CULTURE CHANGES

Many archaeologists have pointed out the decline, in late Phase IV, in the technical and artistic qualities of Moche ceramics. They had previously indicated shifts in socio-politico-religious situations, and techniques had changed, but there had never before been such a loss in quality. Some new forms and techniques were introduced, but stirrup-spout bottles continued to be produced in the North Coast region until the time of the Conquest, as did marine iconography. Monkeys and other ornaments might appear on Phase V stirrup-spout bottles, as they often do on later ceramics. Floreros are common in Phase V, sometimes with geometrized, textile-like designs. The double-spout-and-bridge bottle, a Huari form, appears with Moche motifs.

Castillo (2001; Castillo et al. 2008: Figs. 53, 54) notes that Huari style objects were likely introduced as the Moche attempted to stabilize power. He feels that the elite were weakened rather than overthrown, and considers it likely that the "end of Moche" was the end of the elite. From evidence at San José de Moro, Castillo observes that Moche decline was marked by changes in funerary patterns and ceramic styles, with boot-shaped tombs and fine-line ceramics vanishing at the same time. He observes also that as Moche culture waned, metal technology declined, and metal appears in very limited quantities in funerary contexts, suggesting that weakened power of the elite resulted in reduced production from metal workshops.

MOCHE SUCCESSORS

As Huari influence subsided, the Lambayeque/Sicán culture of the Late Intermediate arose. A new elite class appeared, with basic Moche populations probably remaining. Material in preparation suggests that the mtDNA of the Lambayeque/Sicán elite was not close to that of the Moche, indicating that they came from elsewhere (Shimada et al. 2008). An Ecuadorian source is possible. Legends reported by Miguel Cabello Balboa in the sixteenth century tell of the arrival by sea, in a balsa raft, of a founder, Naymlap (Cordy-Collins 1990; Donnan 1990; Moore 1996:177–179; Netherly 1990; J. Rowe 1948). New ceramic forms appeared, as well as a new mask shape for the Lambayeque/Sicán face, which may depict the legendary Naymlap and represent a new religious/political complex. But if outside people came in at the end of Moche V, it is curious that certain Lambayeque/Sipán traits appeared earlier. Perhaps the new people came

in gradually, and the takeover was more complex than the simple story of the "founder" arriving in a raft.

As the Moche had built on the remains of earlier structures, later peoples built on Moche sites, which in a final version of a Moche world were held in special veneration and often used for burials. Lambayeque/Sicán burials have been excavated at Huaca Cao Viejo and San José de Moro (Castillo 2001:326–327; Castillo et al. 2008; Franco, Gálvez, and Vásquez 1996; Gálvez and Briceño 2001:155; Rucabado and Castillo 2003). Pacatnamu had an important Lambayeque/Sicán occupation, beginning ca. AD 1050, after a probably El Niño–caused break in occupation (Donnan 1997b:13; Donnan and Cock 1985; Shimada 1995). The Lambayeque/Sicán presence there damaged some Moche construction. Indeed, many Moche sites were at least partially covered by later occupations. Batán Grande (Lambayeque Valley) is an example; Pacatnamu is another.

In the pre-Inca period, across the valley from Cerro Blanco, the Chimu people, who had conquered Lambayeque/Sicán, dominated the kingdom of Chimor from their enormous "capital" at Chan Chan. Just as the Moche were likely descendants of the Cupisnique people, so the Chimu were surely descended from the Moche. The association was recognized as early as 1913, when Uhle called Moche "Proto-Chimu," and a little later when Kroeber (in 1930) used "Early Chimu." Some scholars argue that Chimu principles of statecraft were inherited from the great period of the Moche, and others have posited the development of Chimu architecture out of that of Galindo (Bawden 1996:289; Cordy-Collins and McClelland 1983:199; T. Topic 1982:280–284). But the North Coast world was differently focused in Chimu times than in the Moche period, with Chimu architecture almost an inversion of Moche concepts. Instead of great platforms rising in the landscape, there were high-walled enclosures. Nevertheless, metallurgy and weaving traditions continued, and the stirrup-spout bottle remained the major ceramic form. Many Moche themes were depicted, but Chimu ceramic craftsmanship was less inventive, more mass-produced.

Chimu tombs and offerings have been found on top of—or inside—Moche buildings and burials—places of the sacred ancestors. At the Cerro Blanco Complex, graves and other remains have been uncovered in Huaca de la Luna (Armas et al. 2004; Tufinio 2008), around Huaca del Sol, in the urban area, and on the summit of Cerro Blanco, where most sherds are Chimu (Bourget 1997b; Castillo 2000c: Fig. 51; Chapdelaine, Bernier, and Pimentel 2004:189; Donnan and Mackey 1978; Morales 2000b:236–237, 2004). Two miniature, three-dimensional wooden scenes with figures came from burial excavations in Huaca de la Luna (Uceda 1997a). Theresa Topic (1982) notes that the high status of Chimu burials there speaks of Chimu respect for the site. Max Uhle climbed to the summit of Cerro Blanco in 1899 and discovered walls of a Chimu temple with red-and-white murals (Menzel 1977:26–28, 40–41; see also Bourget 1997b). He excavated graves of young people buried with textiles, feathers, and wooden statuettes, and concluded that they were sacrificial victims. *Spondylus* and *Conus* shells were strewn about, and evidence points to two shell workshops, one Chimu, one Moche. Current excavations are finding evidence of Chimu occupation at the north end of the Central Plaza. The Chimu were putting their mark on this Moche huaca, and Chimu remains have been also found at San José de Moro and at Huaca Cao Viejo, where there are also remains of a Colonial convent (Franco and Vilela 2004:20–21; Gálvez and Briceño 2001:156).

The Chimu were conquered by the empire-building Incas, and many of its craftsmen were taken to Cuzco to work. The Incas were conquered by empire-building Spaniards some 800 years after the end of Moche

civilization. Inca burials have been found in Huaca del Sol, but not yet in Huaca de la Luna (Morales 2003). Surely one reason for the early Spanish founding of the city of Trujillo was the importance of that valley to the local people and the presence of the Cerro Blanco Complex, Chan Chan, and a number of other sites from the impressive prehistory of the valley.

Some Colonial texts refer to Huaca del Sol as "Pachacamac" (Netherly 1988; Rostworowski 1992:73; see also Salomon, in Salomon and Urioste 1991:16). The name may reflect a comparison with the prominent Central Coast city, long important in its own right but also much affected by Huari and a likely source of Huari influence in the Moche region. The use of the name may have referred to the similarity of the two great ghost cities in the desert in Colonial times, as if *pachacamac* were the word for such a place. It may also be a reference to the eponymous Inca god, who energized everything. The once-splendid structures at the base of Cerro Blanco still evoke a sense of awe, as does Cerro Blanco itself, that powerful huaca, where precious offerings have been given through a long history.

This history is being given new life today with the extraordinary discoveries of intensive archaeological investigations and with new museums and publications making the discoveries available to scholars and others interested in the Moche. The multifaceted worlds of the Moche are being rediscovered and enlivened in a new and complex reality.

REFERENCES AND

FURTHER READING

Acosta, Joseph de. 1970 [1590]. *The Natural and Moral History of the Indies*. Trans. Edward Grimston. New York: Burt Franklin.

Alarco de Zadra, Adriana. 1997. *Nuestra Fauna: Comentarios acerca de 521 ejemplares*. Lima: Sociedad Geográfica de Lima.

Alarcón, Francisco X. 1992. *Snake Poems: An Aztec Invocation*. San Francisco: Chronicle Books.

Allen, Catherine J. 1988. *The Hold Life Has: Coca and Cultural Identity in an Andean Community*. Washington, DC: Smithsonian Institution Press.

———. 1998. "When Utensils Revolt: Mind, Matter, and Modes of Being in the Pre-Columbian Andes." *res* 33:18–27.

Alva, Walter. 1986a. *Cerámica temprana en el Valle de Jequetepeque, Norte del Perú*. Materialen zur allgemeinen und vergleichenden Archäologie, vol. 32. Bonn: KAVA.

———. 1986b. *Las Salinas de Chao: Asentamiento Temprano en el Norte del Perú*. Materialen zur allgemeinen und vergleichenden Archäologie, vol. 34. Bonn: KAVA.

———. 1988. "Discovering the New World's Richest Unlooted Tomb." *National Geographic* 174 (4):510–549.

———. 1994. *Sipán*. Lima: Cervecería Backus and Johnston, S.A.

———. 2001. "The Royal Tombs at Sipán: Art and Power in Moche Society." In Pillsbury, ed., 223–245.

Alva, Walter, and Ignacio Alva Meneses. 2008. "Ventarrón." *Lundero*, 2nd edición especial (Compendio de Arqueología Nor Peruana), *La Industria de Chiclayo*, 34–35.

Alva, Walter, and Christopher B. Donnan. 1993. *Royal Tombs of Sipan*. Los Angeles: University of California, Fowler Museum of Cultural History.

Amaro, Iván. 1994. "Reconstruyendo de identidad de un pueblo." In Makowski et al., 23–81.

Anders, Martha. 1981 "Investigation of State Storage Facilities in Pampa Grande, Peru." *Journal of Field Archaeology* 8 (4):391–404.

Arguedas, José María. 1978. *Deep Rivers*. Trans. Frances Horning Barraclough. Austin: University of Texas Press.

Armas, José, Javier Aguilar, Raúl Bellodas, Jorge Gamboa, Olga Haro, and Delicia Regalado. 2004. "Excavaciones en la Plaza I y el Frontis Norte de la Plataforma I de la Huaca de la Luna (1998–1999)." In Uceda, Mujica, and Morales, eds., 55–98.

Arriaga, Father Pablo Joseph de. 1968 [1621]. *The Extirpation of Idolatry in Peru*. Trans. L. Clark Keating. Lexington: University of Kentucky Press.

Arsenault, Daniel. 1993. "El personaje del pie amputado en la cultura mochica del Peru: Un ensayo sobre la arqueología del poder." *Latin American Antiquity* 4 (3):225–245.

———. 1995a. "Balance de los estudios moche (Mochicas) 1970–1994, Primera parte: Análisis iconográfico." *Revista Andina* 13 (1):237–270. Cusco.

———. 1995b. "Balance de los estudios moche (Mochicas) 1970–1994, Segunda parte: Trabajos arqueológicos." *Revista Andina* 13 (2):443–480. Cusco.

Asmat, Miguel, and Arabel Fernández. 2002. "Atuendo ceremonial." In Uceda and Mujica, eds., 249–263.

Asmat, Miguel, Ricardo Morales, and Arabel Fernández. 2004. "Atuendo litúrgico Moche en Huaca

de la Luna: Conservación y aporte para su interpretación." In Uceda, Mujica, and Morales, eds.,
457–464.

Atwood, Roger. 2010. "Lord of Úcupe." *Archaeology*
63 (1):21.

Ayasta Vallejo, David Martín. 2006. *Los Cupisniques:
Antecesores de los Mochicas en la costa norte del Perú.*
Chiclayo: Kon.

Baessler, Adolf. 1902–1903. *Ancient Peruvian Art.*
Trans. A. H. Keene. New York: Dodd, Mead and
Co.; Berlin: A. Asher.

Bankes, George. 1980. *Moche Pottery from Peru.* London: British Museum Publications.

Bastien, Joseph. 1978. *Mountain of the Condor:
Metaphor and Ritual in an Andean Ayllu.* American
Anthropological Society Monograph 64. St. Paul,
MN: West Publishing.

———. 1987. *Healers of the Andes: Kallawaya Herbal-
ists and Their Medicinal Plants.* Salt Lake City: University of Utah Press.

Bawden, Garth. 1982. "Community Organization
Reflected by the Household: A Study of Pre-
Columbian Social Dynamics." *Journal of Field
Archaeology* 9:165–181.

———. 1983. "Cultural Reconstitution in the Late
Moche Period: A Case Study in Multidimensional
Stylistic Analysis." In Leventhal and Kolata, 211–235.

———. 1996. *The Moche.* Cambridge, MA, and
Oxford: Blackwell.

———. 2001. "The Symbols of Late Moche Social
Transformation." In Pillsbury, ed., 285–305.

Bennett, Wendell C. 1939. *Archaeology of the North
Coast of Peru: An Account of Exploration and Excavation in Viru and Lambayeque Valleys.* Anthropological Papers of the American Museum of Natural History 37 (1). New York.

———. 1944. "The Highlands of Peru: Excavations in
the Callejón de Huaylas and of Chavín de Huántar." *Anthropological Papers of the American Museum
of Natural History* 39 (1):5–116.

———. 1950. *The Gallinazo Group, Virú Valley, Peru.*
Yale University Publications in Anthropology no.
43. New Haven.

Bennett, Wendell C., ed. 1948. *A Reappraisal of Peruvian Archaeology.* Society for American Archaeology,
Memoir 4. Menasha, WI.

Benson, Elizabeth P. 1972. *The Mochica: A Culture of*
Peru. New York and London: Praeger Publishers
and Thames and Hudson.

———. 1974. *A Man and a Feline in Mochica Art.*
Studies in Pre-Columbian Art and Archaeology 14.
Washington, DC: Dumbarton Oaks.

———. 1975 "Death-associated Figures on Mochica
Pottery." In E. P. Benson, ed., *Death and the Afterlife
in Pre-Columbian America*, 105–144. Washington,
DC: Dumbarton Oaks.

———. 1976a. "Ritual Cloth and Palenque Kings." In
Merle Greene Robertson, ed., *The Art, Iconography
and Dynastic History of Palenque*, part 3, 45–58. Peb-
ble Beach, CA: Robert Louis Stevenson School.

———. 1976b. "'Salesmen' and 'Sleeping' Warriors in
Mochica Art." 41 Congreso Internacional de Ameri-
canistas (Mexico, 1974), vol. 2:27–32.

———. 1978. "The Bag with the Ruffled Top: Some
Problems of Identification in Moche Art." *Journal of
Latin American Lore* 4 (1):29–47.

———. 1979. "Garments as Symbolic Language in
Mochica Art." Actes du XLII Congrès International
des Américanistes (1976), vol. 7:291–299. Paris.

———. 1982a. "The Man with the V on His Headdress: A Figure in Moche III-IV Iconography." *Indiana* 7 (2):201–215.

———. 1982b. "The Well-dressed Captives: Some
Observations on Moche Iconography." *Baessler-
Archiv* 30:181–222. Berlin.

———. 1983. "Moche and Vicús." In Lois Katz,
ed., *Art of the Andes: Pre-Columbian Sculpted and
Painted Ceramics from the Arthur M. Sackler Collections*, 69–77. Washington, DC: The Arthur M.
Sackler Foundation and the AMS Foundation for
the Arts, Sciences and Humanities.

———. 1984a. "A Moche 'Spatula'." *Metropolitan
Museum Journal* 18:39–52.

———. 1984b. "The Men Who Have Bags in Their
Mouths." *Indiana* 9 (1):367–381.

———. 1985. "The Moche Moon." In Kvietok and
Sandweiss, eds., 121–135.

———. 1987a. "Bats in South American Iconography."
Andean Past 1: 165–190.

———. 1987b. "The Owl as a Symbol in the Mortuary Iconography of the Moche." In *Arte Funerario:
Coloquio Internacional de Historia del Arte*, ed. Beatriz de la Fuente and Louise Noelle, 75–82. Mexico:
Universidad Nacional Autónoma de México.

————. 1988a. "New World Deer-Hunt Rituals." In *Simpatías y diferencias, relaciones del arte mexicano con el de América Latina: X Coloquio Internacional de Historia del Arte del Instituto de Investigaciones Estéticas*, 45–59. Mexico City: Universidad Nacional Autónoma de México.

————. 1988b. "Women in Mochica Art." In *The Role of Gender in Pre-Columbian Art and Architecture*, ed. Virginia E. Miller, 63–74. Lanham, MD: University Press of America.

————. 1989. "In Love and War: Hummingbird Lore." In *"In Love and War: Hummingbird Lore" and Other Selected Papers from LAILA/ALILA's 1988 Symposium*, ed. Mary H. Preuss, 3–8. Culver City, CA: Labyrinthos.

————. 1991. "The Chthonic Canine." *Latin American Indian Literatures Journal* 7 (1):95–107.

————. 1993. "Moche Myth, Rite, and Grave Goods: What Might the Sipán Grave Goods Tell Us?" Paper presented at the Northeast Conference on Andean Archaeology and Ethnohistory, Carnegie Museum of Natural History, Pittsburgh.

————. 1995a. "Art, Agriculture, Warfare, and the Guano Islands." In *Andean Art: Visual Expression and Its Relation to Andean Beliefs and Values*, ed. Penny Dransart, 245–264. *Worldwide Archaeology Series* 13. Avebury Aldershot, England.

————. 1995b. "The Fox in the Andes: South American Myth and the Use of Fox Skins." *Journal of the Institute of Maya Studies* 1 (1):1–15. Miami.

————. 1997a. *Birds and Beasts of Ancient Latin America*. Gainesville: University Press of Florida.

————. 1997b. "Moche Art: Myth, History, and Rite." In Berrin, ed., 41–49, and various catalogue entries.

————. 1998. "The Lord, the ruler: Jaguar Symbolism in the Americas." In Saunders, ed., pp. 53–76.

————. 2001. "Why Sacrifice?" In Benson and Cook, eds., 1–20. Austin: University of Texas Press.

————. 2003. "Cambios de temas y motivos en la cerámica moche." In Uceda and Mujica, eds., I:477–495.

————. 2004. "Los Mayas y los Mochicas: Expresiones en el arte." In *Acercarse y mirar: Homenaje a Beatriz de la Fuente*, ed. María Teresa Uriarte y Leticia Staines Cicero, 283–297. Mexico City: Universidad Nacional Autónoma de México, Instituto de Investigaciones Estéticas.

————. 2008. "Archaeology Meets Iconography." In Bourget and Jones, eds., 1–31.

————. 2010. "Maya Political Structure as a Possible Model for the Moche." In Quilter and Castillo, eds., 17–46.

————, ed. 1971. *Dumbarton Oaks Conference on Chavín*. Washington, DC: Dumbarton Oaks.

————. 1979. *Pre-Columbian Metallurgy of South America*. Washington, DC: Dumbarton Oaks.

Benson, Elizabeth P., and Anita G. Cook, eds. 2001. *Ritual Sacrifice in Ancient Peru*. Austin: University of Texas Press.

Berezkin, Yuri. 1980. "An Identification of Anthropomorphic Mythological Personages in Moche Representations." *Ñawpa Pacha* 18:1–26.

Bergh, Susan E. 1993. "Death and Renewal in Moche Phallic-spouted Vessels." *Res* 24 (Autumn 1993):78–94.

Berrin, Kathleen, ed. 1997. *The Spirit of Ancient Peru: Treasures from the Museo Arqueológico Rafael Larco Herrera*. San Francisco and New York: Fine Arts Museums of San Francisco, and Thames and Hudson.

Betanzos, Juan de. 1996 [1551]. *Narrative of the Incas*. Trans. and ed. Roland Hamilton and Dana Buchanan. Austin: University of Texas Press.

Billman, Brian R. 1999. "Reconstructing Prehistoric Economies and Cycles of Political Power in the Moche Valley, Peru." In Brian R. Billman and Gary M. Feinman, eds., *Settlement Pattern Studies in the Americas*, 131–159. Washington, DC, and London: Smithsonian Institution Press.

Bird, Junius. 1948. "Preceramic Cultures in Chicama and Virú." In Bennett, ed., 21–28.

Bird, Junius B., John Hyslop, and Milica Dimitrijevic Skinner. 1985. *The Preceramic Excavations at the Huaca Prieta, Chicama Valley, Peru*. Anthropological Papers of the American Museum of Natural History 62 (1). New York.

Bischof, Henning. 1997. "Cerro Blanco, valle de Nepeña, Peru." In Bonnier and Bischof, 202–234.

Bonavia, Duccio. 1961. "A Mochica Painting at Pañamarca, Perú." *American Antiquity* 26 (4):540–543.

————. 1985. *Mural Paintings in Ancient Peru*. Trans. Patricia J. Lyon. Bloomington: Indiana University Press.

Bonavia, Duccio, and Cristóbal Makowski. 1999. "Las pinturas murales de Pañamarca." *Iconos* 2:40–54.

Bonnier, Elisabeth, and Henning Bischof, eds. 1997. *Arquitectura y civilización en los Andes prehispánicos / Prehistoric Architecture and Civilization in the Andes.* Archaeológica Peruana 2. Mannheim: Reiss-Museum.

Boone, Elizabeth Hill, ed. 1996. *Andean Art at Dumbarton Oaks.* Washington, DC: Dumbarton Oaks.

Bourget, Steve. 1990. "Caracoles sagrados en la iconografía moche." *Gaceta Arqueológica Andina* V (20):45–58. Lima.

———. 1994a. *Bestiaire sacré et flore magique: Ecologie rituelle de l'iconographie de la culture Mochica, côte nord du Pérou.* Ph.D. dissertation, Université de Montréal. Ann Arbor: UMI, 1997.

———. 1994b. "El mar y la muerte en la iconografía Moche." In Uceda and Mujica, 425–447.

———. 1995. "Los sacerdotes a la sombra del Cerro Blanco y del Arco Bicéfalo." *Revista del Museo de Arqueología, Antropología, e Historia* 5:81–126.

———. 1997a. "La colère des ancêstres." *Les Cahiers d'anthropologie* 1:83–99. Montreal: Université de Montréal.

———. 1997b. "Excavaciones en el Cerro Blanco." In Uceda, Mujica, and Morales, 109–123.

———. 1997c. "Las excavaciones en la plaza 3A." In Uceda, Mujica, and Morales, 51–59.

———. 1998. "Excavaciones en la Plaza 3A y en la Plataforma II de la Huaca de la Luna durante 1996." In Uceda, Mujica, and Morales, eds., 43–64.

———. 2001a. "Children and Ancestors: Ritual Practices at the Moche Site of Huaca de la Luna, North Coast of Peru." In Benson and Cook, eds., 93–118.

———. 2001b. "Rituals of Sacrifice: Its Practice at Huaca de la Luna and Its Representation in Moche Iconography." In Pillsbury, ed., 89–109.

———. 2003. "Somos diferentes: Dinámica ocupacional del sitio Castillo de Huancaco, valle de Virú." In Uceda and Mujica, eds., vol. 1, 245–267.

———. 2006. *Sex, Death, and Sacrifice in Moche Religion and Visual Culture.* Austin: University of Texas Press.

———. 2010. "Cultural Assignations during the Early Intermediate Period: The Case of Huancaco, Virú Valley." In Quilter and Castillo, eds., 201–222.

Bourget, Steve, and Jean-François Millaire. 2000. "Excavaciones en la Plaza 3a y Plataforma II de la Huaca de la Luna." In Uceda, Mujica, and Morales, 47–84.

Bourget, Steve, and Margaret E. Newman. 1998. "A Toast to the Ancestors: Ritual Warfare and Sacrificial Blood in Moche Culture." *Baessler-Archiv*, Neue Folge, Band XLVI, Heft 1, 85–106. Berlin.

Bourget, Steve, and Kimberly L. Jones, eds. 2008. *The Art and Archaeology of the Moche: An Ancient Andean Society of the Peruvian North Coast.* Austin: University of Texas Press.

Brennan, Curtis T. 1980. "Cerro Arena: Early Cultural Complexity and Nucleation in North Coastal Peru." *Journal of Field Archaeology* 7 (1):1–22. Cambridge.

Briceño Rosario, Jesús G. 1999a. "Quebrada Santa María: Las puntas en cola de pescado y la antigüedad del hombre en Sudamérica." In Kaulicke, ed., 19–39.

———. 1999b. "Los restos humanos más tempranos del norte del Perú." In Kaulicke, ed., 55–67.

Browman, David L., and Ronald A. Schwarz, eds. 1979. *Spirits, Shamans, and Stars: Perspectives from South America.* The Hague: Mouton Publishers.

Bruhns, Karen Olsen. 1976. "The Moon Animal in Northern Peruvian Art and Culture." *Ñawpa Pacha* 14:21–39.

———. 1994. *Ancient South America.* Cambridge and New York: Cambridge University Press.

Burger, Richard L. 1992. *Chavín and the Origins of Andean Civilization.* London: Thames and Hudson.

———. 1996. "Chavín." In Boone, ed., 45–86.

———. 1997. "Life and Afterlife in Prehispanic Peru." In Berrin, ed., 21–32.

———. 2008. "Chavín de Huántar and Its Sphere of Influence." In Silverman and Isbell, eds., 681-703.

Burger, Richard, and Lucy Salazar-Burger. 1993. "The Place of Dual Organization in Early Andean Ceremonialism: A Comparative Review." In Millones and Onuki, 97–116.

Buse, Hermann. 1981. *Actividad Pesquera.* Lima: Documenta.

Cabello Balboa, Miguel. 1951 [1586]. *Miscelanea antarctica.* Lima: Universidad Nacional Mayor de San Marcos.

Cabieses, Fernando. 1974. *Dioses y enfermedades (La medicina en el antiguo Perú) / Gods and Disease*

(Medicine in Ancient Peru). Lima: Ediciones y Impresiones Artegraf.

Calancha, Antonio de la. 1974–1982 [1638]. *Corónica moralizada del Orden de San Augustín en el Perú.* Ignacio Prado Pastor, ed. 4 vols. Lima. Universidad Nacional Mayor de San Marco.

Campana, Cristóbal. 1983. *La vivienda mochica.* Trujillo: n.p.

————. 1994. *La cultura mochica.* Lima: Consejo Nacional de Ciencia y Tecnología, CONCYTEC.

————. 1995. *Arte Chavín: Análisis estructural de formas e imágenes.* Lima: Universidad Nacional Federico Villarreal.

————. 1999. *Vicús y la alfarería norandina.* Lima: Universidad Nacional Federico Villarreal.

————. 2000. *Tecnologías constructivas de tierra en la costa norte prehispánica.* Trujillo: Instituto Nacional de Cultura—La Libertad.

Campana, Cristóbal, and Ricardo Morales. 1997. *Historia de una deidad mochica.* Lima: A&B S.A.

Canziani Amico, José. 2010. "City Planning and Architecture in the Analysis of Moche Social Formation." In Quilter and Castillo, eds., 159–180.

Carcedo de Mufarech, Paloma. 2000. "Silver in Precolumbian Peru." In H. King, ed., 24–29.

Carcedo Muro, Paloma. 1998. *Cobre del Antiguo Perú / The Copper of Ancient Peru.* Lima: AFP Integra.

Cárdenas, Juan, Julio Rodríguez, and Luis Aguirre. 1997. "El material orgánico en Huaca de la Luna." In Uceda, Mujica, and Morales, eds., 129–149.

Carlson, John B. 1993. "Venus-Regulated Warfare and Ritual Sacrifice in Mesoamerica." In *Astronomies and Cultures,* ed. Clive L. N. Ruggles and Nicholas J. Saunders, 202–252. Niwot: University Press of Colorado.

Castillo, Luis Jaime. 1989. *Personajes míticos, escenas y narraciones en la iconografía mochica.* Lima: Pontificia Universidad Católica del Perú, Fondo Editorial.

————. 1996. *La tumba de la sacerdotisa de San José de Moro.* Lima: Centro Cultural Pontificia Universidad Católica del Perú.

————. 2000a. "La ceremonia del sacrificio: Batallas y muerte en el arte mochica." In *La Ceremonia del Sacrificio,* 14–29.

————. 2000b. "The Evolution of Complex Societies in Ancient Peru." In H. King, ed., 6–23.

————. 2000c. "*El templo mochica: Rituales y ceremonias.*" In Makowski et al., 91–135.

————. 2001. "The Last of the Mochicas: A View from the Jequetepeque Valley." In Pillsbury, ed., 307–332.

————. 2003. "Los últimos mochicas en Jequetepeque." In Uceda and Mujica, eds., vol. 2, 65–123.

Castillo, Luis Jaime, and Christopher B. Donnan. 1994a. "Los Mochica del Norte y los Mochica del Sur." In Makowski et al., 143–178.

————. 1994b. "La ocupación moche de San José de Moro." In Uceda and Mujica, 93–146.

Castillo, Luis Jaime, Andrew Nelson, and Chris Nelson. 1998. "'Maquetas' mochicas San José de Moro." *Arkinka* 2 (20):120–128.

Castillo B., Luis Jaime, Julio Rucabado Y., Martín del Carpio P., Katiusha Bernuy Q., Karim Ruiz R., Carlos Rengifo Ch., Gabriel Prieto B., and Carole Fraresso. 2008. "Ideología y poder en la consolidación, colapso y reconstitución del Estado Mochica del Jequetepeque: El Proyecto Arqueológico San José de Moro (1991–2006)." *Ñawpa Pacha* 29:1–86.

Castillo Butters, Luis Jaime, and Santiago Uceda Castillo. 2008. "The Mochicas." In Silverman and Isbell, eds., 707–729.

La ceremonia del sacrificio: Batallas y muerte en el arte mochica. 2000. Lima: Museo Arqueológico Rafael Larco Herrera and INTEGRA/AFP.

Chapdelaine, Claude. 1997. "Le tissu urbain du site Moche." *Les cahiers d'anthropologie,* 11–81. Montreal.

————. 1998. "Excavaciones en la zona urbana de Moche durante 1996." In Uceda, Mujica, and Morales, eds., 85–115.

————. 2000. "Investigaciones en los conjuntos arquitectónicos del centro urbano Moche." In Uceda, Mujica, and Morales, eds., 66–84.

————. 2001. "The Growing Power of a Moche Urban Class." In Pillsbury, ed., 69–87.

————. 2003. "La ciudad de Moche: Urbanismo y estado." In Uceda and Mujica, eds., vol. 2, 247–285.

————. 2008. "Moche Art Style in the Santa Valley." In Bourget and Jones, eds., 129–152.

————. 2010. "Moche Political Organization in the Santa Valley." In Quilter and Castillo, eds., 252–279.

Chapdelaine, Claude, Helene Bernier, and Victor Pimentel. 2004. "Investigaciones en la Zona Urbana

Moche, temporados 1998 y 1999." In Uceda, Mujica, and Morales, eds., 123–201.

Chapdelaine, Claude, Greg Kennedy, and Santiago Uceda. 1995. "Activación neutrónica en el estudio de la producción local de la cerámica ritual en el sitio Moche, Perú." *Boletín del Instituto Francés de Estudios Andinos* 24 (2):183–212.

Chapdelaine, Claude, María Isabel Paredes, Florencia Bracamonte, and Victor Pimentel. 1998. "Un tipo particular de entierro en la zona urbana del sitio Moche, costa norte del Perú." *Bulletin de l'Institut Français d'Etudes Andines* 27 (2):241–264. Lima.

Chapdelaine, Claude, and Victor Pimentel. 2003. "Un tejido único moche III del sitio Castillo de Santa: Una escena de cosecha de yuca." *Bulletin de l'Institut français des études andines* 32 (1):23–50. Lima.

Chapdelaine, Claude, Santiago Uceda, M. Moya, C. Jauregui, and Ch. Uceda. 1997. "Los complejos arquitectónicos urbanos de Moche." In Uceda, Mujica, and Morales, eds., 71–92.

Chauchat, Claude, César Gálvez, Jesús Briceño, and Santiago Uceda. 1998. *Sitios arqueológicos de la zona de Cupisnique y margen derecha del valle de Chicama.* Trujillo and Lima: Instituto Nacional de Cultura La Libertad and Instituto Francés de Estudios Andinos.

Chauchat, Claude, Jean Guffroy, and Thomas Pozorski. 2006. "Excavations at Huaca Herederos Chica, Moche Valley, Peru." *Journal of Field Archaeology* 31 (3):233–250.

Chauchat, Claude, and Belkys Gutiérrez. 2008. "Excavaciones en la Plataforma Uhle, temporada 2002." In Uceda, Mujica, and Morales, 2008b:53–91.

Cieza de León, Pedro de. 1959 [1550, 1553]. *The Incas.* Trans. Harriet de Onis, ed. Victor Wolfgang von Hagen. Norman: University of Oklahoma Press.

Classen, Constance. 1993. *Inca Cosmology and the Human Body.* Salt Lake City: University of Utah Press.

Cobo, Bernabé. 1979 [1653]. *History of the Inca Empire.* Austin: University of Texas Press.

———. 1990 [1653]. *Inca Religion and Customs.* Austin: University of Texas Press.

Coe, Michael D., and Justin Kerr. 1998. *The Art of the Maya Scribe.* New York: Harry N. Abrams.

Coe, Sophie D. 1994. *America's First Cuisines.* Austin: University of Texas Press.

Collier, Donald. 1955. *Cultural Chronology and Change as Reflected in the Ceramics of the Virú Valley, Peru.* Fieldiana Anthropology 43. Chicago: Chicago Natural History Museum.

El Comercio. 18 May 2006. "El mausoleo de la gobernante," a12–13 [Martín Huancas Chinga].

———. 21 May 2006. "El mundo mágico de la Señora de Cao," a23 [Martín Huancas Chinga].

———. 2 September 2007a. "El personaje hallado en Huaca Rajada complía rol religioso y administrativo," a8 [Wilfredo Sandoval].

———. 2 September 2007b. "Hallan hornos donde se fundieron ornamentos," a9.

———. 8 September 2007. "Narigueras confirmarían presencia de personaje de élite en Huaca Rajada" [Wilfredo Sandoval].

———. 11 November 2007. "Descubren templo y mural de unos 4.000 años de antigüedad," a8.

———. 5 July 2008. "Hallan tumba similar a la del Señor de Sipán," a1.

———. 5 July 2008. "Restos de gobernante mochica tienen 1.700 años de antigüedad," a2 [Wilfredo Sandoval].

———. 26 July 2008. "Presentan las joyas halladas en la tumba del Señor de Úcupe," a24 [Wilfredo Sandoval Bayona].

Conklin, William J. 1979. "Moche Textile Structures." In *The Junius B. Bird Pre-Columbian Textile Conference,* ed. Ann Pollard Rowe, Elizabeth P. Benson, and Anne-Louise Schaffer, 165–184. Washington, DC: The Textile Museum and Dumbarton Oaks, Trustees for Harvard University.

———. 1985. "The Architecture of Huaca de los Reyes." In Donnan, ed., 139–164.

———. 1990. "Architecture of the Chimu: Memory, Function, and Image." In Moseley and Cordy-Collins, eds., 43–74.

———. 1996. "Structure as Meaning in Ancient Andean Textiles." In Boone, ed., 321–328.

———. 2008. "The Culture of Chavín Textiles." In Conklin and Quilter, eds., 261–278.

Conklin, William J, and Jeffrey Quilter, eds. 2008. *Chavín: Art, Architecture, and Culture.* Monograph 61. Los Angeles: Cotsen Institute of Archaeology, University of California.

Conklin, William J, Ann Pollard Rowe, Anita G. Cook, and Mary Frame. 1996. "Nasca/Huari and Other South Coast Textile." In Boone, ed., 413–423.

Conklin, William J, and Eduardo Versteylen. 1978. "Textiles from a Pyramid of the Sun Burial." In Donnan and Mackey, 185–198.

Cordy-Collins, Alana. 1990. "Fonga Sigde, Shell Purveyor to the Chimu King." In Moseley and Cordy-Collins, eds., 393–417.

———. 1992. "Archaism or Tradition? The Decapitation Theme in Cupisnique and Moche Iconography." *Latin American Antiquity* 3 (3):206–220.

———. 1994. "An Unshaggy Dog Story." *Natural History* 103 (2):34–41.

———. 1997. "The Offering Room Group." In Donnan and Cock, eds., 283–292.

———. 1998. "The Jaguar of the Backward Glance." In Saunders, ed., 155–170.

———. 2001a. "Blood and the Moon Priestesses: Spondylus Shells in Moche Ceremony." In Benson and Cook, eds., 35–53.

———. 2001b. "Decapitation in Cupisnique and Early Moche Societies." In Benson and Cook, eds., 21–33.

———. 2001c. "Labretted Ladies: Foreign Women in Northern Moche and Lambayeque Art." In Pillsbury, ed., 247–257.

———. 2009. "Curated Corpses and Scattered Skeletons: New Data and New Questions Concerning the Moche Dead." In Marcus and Williams, eds., 181–194.

———, ed. 1982. *Pre-Columbian Art History: Selected Readings*. Palo Alto: Peek Publications.

Cordy-Collins, Alana, and Donna McClelland. 1983. "Upstreaming Along the Peruvian North Coast." In *Text and Image in Pre-Columbian Art: Essays on the Interrelationship of the Verbal and Visual Arts*, ed. Janet C. Berlo, 197–209. Oxford: BAR International Series 180.

Craig, Alan K. 1992. "Archaeological Occurrences of Andean Land Snails." *Andean Past* 3:127–135.

Daggett, Richard E. 1985. "The Early Horizon—Early Intermediate Period Transition: A View from the Nepeña and Virú Valleys." In Kvietok and Sandweiss, eds., 41–65.

de Bock, Edward. 1988. *Moche: Gods, Warriors, Priests*. Leiden: Spruyt, Van Mantgem & De Does.

———. 1998. "The Waterlily Ritual: An Andean Political and Religious Ceremony of the Moche Culture." *Journal of the Steward Anthropological Society* 26 (1 and 2):1–18.

Diez-Canseco, Magdelena. 1994. "La sabiduría de los ofebres." In Makowski et al., 183–209.

Dillehay, Thomas D. 1995. "Introduction." In Dillehay, ed., 1–26.

———. 1999. "Exploring South America." *Archaeology* 52 (1):62–67.

———. 2000. *The Settlement of the Americas*. New York: Basic Books.

———. 2001. "Town and Country in Late Moche Times: A View from Two Northern Valleys." In Pillsbury, ed., 259–283.

———, ed. 1995. *Tombs for the Living: Andean Mortuary Practices*. Washington, DC: Dumbarton Oaks.

Dillehay, Tom D., and Patricia J. Netherly. 1983. "Exploring the Upper Zaña Valley in Peru." *Archaeology* 36 (4):22–30.

Dillehay, Tom D., Jack Rossen, Thomas C. Andres, and David E. Williams. 2007. "Preceramic Adoption of Peanut, Squash, and Cotton in Northern Peru." *Science* 316 (5833):1890–1894.

Disselhoff, Hans Dietrich. 1958. "Tumbas de San José de Moro (Prov. Pacasmayo)." *Proceedings of the 32nd International Congress of Americanists* (Copenhagen, 1956), 364–367.

———. 1971. *Vicus: "Eine neu Entdeckte alperuanische Kultur."* Monumenta Americana 8, Biblioteca Ibero-Americana. Berlin: Gebr. Mann.

Donnan, Christopher B. 1965. "Moche ceramic technology." *Ñawpa Pacha* 3:115–138.

———. 1972. "Moche-Huari Murals from Northern Peru." *Archaeology* 25 (2):85–95. New York.

———. 1973a. *Moche Occupation of the Santa Valley, Peru*. University of California Publications in Anthropology, vol. 8. Berkeley, Los Angeles, and London.

———. 1973b. "A Pre-Columbian Smelter from northern Peru." *Archaeology* 26 (4):289–297.

———. 1978. *Moche Art of Peru*. Los Angeles: Museum of Cultural History, University of California.

———. 1982. "Dance in Moche Art." *Ñawpa Pacha* 20:97–120.

———. 1990. "An Assessment of the Validity of the Naymlap Dynasty." In Moseley and Cordy-Collins, eds., 243–274.

———. 1995. "Moche Funerary Practice." In Dillehay, 111–159.

———. 1996. "Moche." In Boone, ed., 123–162.

———. 1997a. "Deer Hunting and Combat: Parallel Activities in the Moche World." In Berrin, ed., 51–59.

———. 1997b. "Introduction." In Donnan and Cock, eds., 9–16.

———. 2001. "Moche Burials Uncovered." *National Geographic* 199 (3):58–73.

———. 2003. "Tumbas con entierros en miniatura: Un nuevo tipo funeraria moche." In Uceda and Mujica, eds., vol. 1, 43–78.

———. 2004. *Moche Portraits from Ancient Peru.* Austin: University of Texas Press.

———. 2007. *Moche Tombs at Dos Cabezas.* Monograph 59. Los Angeles: Cotsen Institute of Archaeology, University of California, Los Angeles.

———. 2009a. "The Gallinazo Illusion." In Millaire with Molion, 17–32.

———. 2009b. "The Moche Use of Numbers and Number Sets." In Marcus and Williams, 165–180.

———, ed. 1985. *Early Ceremonial Architecture in the Andes.* Washington, DC: Dumbarton Oaks.

Donnan, Christopher B., and Daisy Barreto C. 1997. "A Moche Cane Coffin from Pacatnamu." In Donnan and Cock, eds., 255–364.

Donnan, Christopher B., and Luis Jaime Castillo. 1992. "Finding the Tomb of a Moche Priestess." *Archaeology* 45 (6):38–42. New York: Archaeological Institute of America.

———. 1994. "Excavaciones de Tumbas de Sacerdotisas Moche en San José de Moro." In Uceda and Mujica, 415–424.

Donnan, Christopher B., and Guillermo A. Cock, eds. 1986. *The Pacatnamu Papers*, vol. 1. Los Angeles: University of California, Museum of Cultural History.

———. 1997. *The Pacatnamu Papers*, vol. 2: *The Moche Occupation.* Los Angeles: University of California, Fowler Museum of Cultural History.

Donnan, Christopher B., and Sharon G. Donnan. 1997. "Moche Textiles from Pacatnamu." In Donnan and Cock, 215–242.

Donnan, Christopher B., and Carol J. Mackey. 1978. *Ancient Burial Patterns of the Moche Valley, Peru.* Austin and London: University of Texas Press.

Donnan, Christopher B., and Donna McClelland. 1979. "The Burial Theme in Moche Iconography."

Studies in Pre-Columbian Art and Archaeology no. 21. Washington, DC: Dumbarton Oaks, Trustees for Harvard University.

———. 1997. "Moche Burials at Pacatnamu." In Donnan and Cock, 17–187.

———. 1999. *Moche Fineline Painting: Its Evolution and Its Artists.* Los Angeles: Fowler Museum of Cultural History, University of California.

Eisenberg, John F., and Kent H. Redford. 1999. *Mammals of the Neotropics*, vol. 3: The Central Neotropics. Chicago and London: University of Chicago Press.

Elera, Carlos G. 1983. "Morro de Etén, Valle de Lambayeque." *Boletín del Museo Nacional de Antropología y Arqueología* 8:25–26.

———. 1984. "El día de los muertos en Eten: Festividad religiosa en un pueblo traditional de la costa norte." *Boletin de Lima*, no. 36, 6:49–55. Lima.

———. 1993. "El Complejo Cultural Cupisnique: Antecedentes y desarrollo de la ideología religiosa." In Millones and Onuki, eds., 229–257.

Elera, Carlos, and José Pinilla. 1990. "Research Summary of the Projecto Puémape (1987–1989)." *Willay* 34:2–4. Cambridge, MA.

Esquerre, Francisco, María Guerrero, Rosario Peltroche, María Espinoza, and Gonzalo Rivera. 2000. "Investigaciones en el Conjunto Arquitectónico 18, Centro Urbano Moche." In Uceda, Mujica, and Morales, eds., 131–158.

Fernández López, Arabel. 2001. "Tejidos del periodo inicial en El Brujo." *Revista Arqueológica Sian* año 6 (10):15–19.

Ford, James, and Gordon R. Willey. 1949. "Surface Survey of the Viru Valley, Peru." *Anthropological Papers of the American Museum of Natural History* 43 (1). New York.

Frame, Mary. 2001. "Blood, Fertility, and Transformation: Interwoven Themes in the Paracas Necropolis Embroideries." In Benson and Cook, 55–92.

Franco Jordán, Régulo. 1998. "Arquitectura monumental Moche." *Arkinka* año 3, no. 27:100–110. Lima.

———. 2001. *El Brujo: Tradición y poder religioso.* Trujillo: Editorial Computer Age.

———. 2009. *Mochica: Los secretos de Huaca Cao Viejo.* Lima: Fundación Wiese.

Franco Jordán, Régulo, and César Gálvez Mora. 2003.

"Un ídolo de madera en un edificio mochica temprano, de la Huaca Cao Viejo, Complejo El Brujo." *Arkinka* año 8, no. 93:94–105.

———. 2009. "Gallinazo-Style Ceramics in Early Moche Contexts at the El Brujo Complex, Chicama Valley." In Millaire with Molion, eds., 91–104.

———. 2010. "Muerte, iconografía e identificación de roles de personajes de la elite Mochica en Huaca Cao Viejo, Complejo El Brujo." In Luis Valle Álvarez, ed., *Arqueología y Desarrollo: Experiencias y posibilidades en el Perú*, 79–102. Trujillo: Ediciones SIAN.

Franco, Régulo, César Gálvez, and Segundo Vásquez. 1994. "Arquitectura y decoración mochica en la Huaca Cao Viejo, Complejo El Brujo: resultados preliminares." In Uceda and Mujica, 147–180.

———. 1996. "Los descubrimientos arqueológicos en la Huaca Cao Viejo, Complejo 'El Brujo.'" *Arkinka* 1 (5):82–94. Lima.

———. 1998a. "Un cielorraso moche polícromo." *1/2C: Medio de construcción* no. 144:37–42.

———. 1998b. "Desentierro ritual de una tumba moche: Huaca Cao Viejo." *Revista Arqueológica Sian* año 3 (6).

———. 1999a. "Porras mochicas del Complejo El Brujo." *Revista Arqueológica Sian* año 4 (7):16–23.

———. 1999b. *Tumbas de cámara Moche en la Plataforma Superior de la Huaca Cao Viejo, Complejo El Brujo.* Programa Arqueológico Complejo "El Brujo," *Boletín* no. 1.

———. 2001a. "Desentierro y reenterramiento de una tumba de elite mochica en el Complejo El Brujo." Programa Arqueológico Complejo "El Brujo," *Boletín* no. 2.

———. 2001b. "La Huaca Cao Viejo en El Complejo El Brujo: Una contribución al estudio de los mochicas en el valle de Chicama." *Arqueológicas* 25:123–173. Lima, Museo Nacional de Arqueología, Antropología e Historia del Perú.

———. 2003. "Modelos, función y cronología de la Huaca Cao Viejo, Complejo El Brujo." In Uceda and Mujica, eds., vol. 2, 125–177.

———. 2005. *El Brujo: Pasado milenario.* Trujillo: Fundación Augusto N. Wiese, Instituto Nacional de Cultura—La Libertad, Universidad Nacional de Trujillo.

———. 2010. "Moche Power and Ideology at the El Brujo Complex and in the Chicama Valley." In Quilter and Castillo, eds., 110–131.

Franco Jordán, Régulo, and Antonio Murga Cruz. 1998. "Un modelo arquitectónico de piedra." *1/2 C: Medio de construcción* no. 138:16–22.

———. 2001. "Una representación arquitectónica en piedra en el Complejo Arqueológico El Brujo." *Arkinka* año 70:92–99. Lima.

Franco Jordán, Régulo, and Juan Vilela Puelles. 2005. *El Brujo: El mundo mágico religioso mochica y el calendario ceremonial.* Trujillo: MINKA.

Freidel, David, Linda Schele, and Joy Parker. 1993. *Maya Cosmos: Three Thousand Years on the Shaman's Path.* New York: William Morrow.

Fuentes, Carlos. 1989. *Christopher Unborn.* New York: Farrar, Straus, Giroux.

Furst, Peter T. 1968. "The Were-Jaguar Motif in the Light of Ethnographic Reality." In Elizabeth P. Benson, ed., Dumbarton Conference on the Olmec, 143–174. Washington, DC: Dumbarton Oaks.

Gálvez Mora, Cesar, and Jesús Briceño Rosario. 2001. "The Moche in the Chicama Valley." In Pillsbury, ed., 141–157.

Gálvez Mora, César A., J. Juan Castañeda Murga, and Rosario H. Becerra Urteaga. 1993. "Caracoles terrestres: 11,000 años de tradición alimentaria en la costa norte del Perú." In Rosario Olivas, ed., *Cultura, Identidad y Cocina en el Perú*, 55–76. Lima: San Martín de Porras.

Gálvez Mora, César, Antonio Murga Cruz, Denis Vargas Salvador, and Hugo Ríos Cisneros. 2003. "Sequencia y cambios en los materiales y técnicas constructivas de la Huaca Cao Viejo, Complejo El Brujo, Valle de Chicama." In Uceda and Mujica, eds., I, 79–118.

Garcilaso de la Vega. 1987 [1609]. *Royal Commentaries of the Incas and General History of Peru.* Trans. Harold V. Livermore. Austin: University of Texas Press.

Gillin, John. 1947. *Moche, a Peruvian Coastal Community.* Institute of Social Anthropology, Publication no. 5. Washington, DC: Smithsonian Institution.

Glantz, Michael H.. 2001. *Currents of Change: Impacts of El Niño and La Niña on Climate and Society.* 2nd ed. Cambridge: Cambridge University Press.

Glass-Coffin, Bonnie Kay. 1992. *The Gift of Life: Female Healing and Experience in Northern Peru.*

Ph.D. dissertation, University of California, Los Angeles. Ann Arbor: UMI, 1996.

Glass-Coffin, Bonnie, and Rafael Vásquez-Guerrero. 1991. "La brujería en la costa norte del Perú del siglo XVIII: El caso de María de la O." *Journal of Latin American Lore* 17 (1 & 2):103–130.

Golte, Jürgen. 1985. "Los recolectores de caracoles en la cultura Moche (Peru)." *Indiana* 10:355–369.

———. 1993. *Los dioses de Sipán: Las aventuras del dios Quismique y su ayudante Murrup.* Lima: IEP Ediciones.

———. 1994a. *Iconos y narraciones: La reconstrucción de una secuencia de imágenes Moche.* Lima: Instituto de Estudios Peruanos.

———. 1994b. *Los dioses de Sipán: La rebelión contra el Dios Sol.* Lima: IEP Ediciones.

———. 2009. *Moche: Cosmología y sociedad.* Lima and Cuzco: Instituto de Estudios Peruanos and Centro Bartolomé de las Casas.

Gose, Peter. 1994. *Deathly Waters and Hungry Mountains: Agrarian Ritual and Class Formation in an Andean Town.* Toronto: University of Toronto Press.

Grieder, Terence. 1978. *The Art and Archaeology of Pashash.* Austin and London: University of Texas Press.

Guaman Poma de Ayala, Felipe. 1980 [1614–1615]. *Nueva corónica y buen gobierno.* 3 vols. John V. Murra and Rolena Adorno, eds. Mexico City: Siglo Veintiuno.

Guffroy, Jean, Peter Kaulicke, and Krzysztof Makowski. 1989. "La prehistoria en el Departamento de Piura: Estado de los conocimientos y problemática." *Bulletin de l'Institut Francais d'Etudes Andines* 18 (2):117–142. Lima.

Gumerman, George, IV. 1997. "Botanical Offerings in Moche Burials at Pacatnamu." In Donnan and Cock, eds., 243–249.

Gwin, Peter, and Ira Block. 2004. "Peruvian Temple of Doom." *National Geographic*, vol. 206 (1):102–117.

Haas, Jonathan, Shelia Pozorski, and Thomas Pozorski, eds. 1987. *The Origins and Development of the Andean State.* Cambridge: Cambridge University Press.

Harrison, Peter. 1985. *Sea Birds.* Rev. ed. Boston: Houghton Mifflin.

Hastings, Charles Mansfield, and Michael E. Moseley.

1975. "The Adobes of Huaca del Sol and Huaca de la Luna." *American Antiquity* 40 (2):196–203.

Hecker, Giesela, and Wolfgang Hecker. 1985. *Pacatnamu y sus construcciones.* Frankfurt-am-Main: Verlag Klaus Dieter Vervuert.

———. 1992. "Huesos humanos como ofrendas mortuorias y uso repetido de vasijas." *Baessler-Archiv* n.s. 40 (1):171–195.

Helms, Mary, W. 1993. *Craft and the Kingly Ideal: Art, Trade, and Power.* Austin: University of Texas Press.

Henderson, John S., and Patricia J. Netherly, eds. 1993. *Configurations of Power: Holistic Anthropology in Theory and Practice.* Ithaca and London: Cornell University Press.

Hocquenghem, Anne Marie. 1977. "Quelques projections sur l'iconographie des Mochicas: Une image de leur monde d'après leurs images du monde." *Baessler-Archiv* n.s. 6 (2):163–191.

———. 1980a. "Forme, décor et fonction: Les vases à sonnaille des collections mochicas du Museum für Völkerkunde de Berlin." *Baessler-Archiv* Band 28, 181–202. Berlin.

———. 1980b. "Les offrandes d'enfants, Essai d'interprétation d'une scène de l'iconographie mochica." *Indiana* 6 (1).

———. 1981. "Les vases mochicas: Formes et sujets." *Ñawpa Paccha* 19:71–78.

———. 1987. *Iconografía mochica.* Lima: Pontificia Universidad Católica del Péru.

———. 1993. "Rutas de entrada del *mullu* en el extremo norte del Perú." *Bulletin de l'Institut Français d'Etudes Andines* 22 (3):701–719.

———. 1995. "Estudio de una colección de cerámica de Yacila, extremo norte del Perú." *Bulletin de l'Institut Français d'Études Andines.*

Hocquenghem, Anne Marie, and Patricia J. Lyon. 1980. "A Class of Anthropomorphic Supernatural Females in Moche Iconograpy." *Ñawpa Pacha* 18:27–48.

Holmberg, Allan R. 1957. *Lizard Hunts on the North Coast of Peru.* Fieldiana 36 (9).

Holmquist, Ulla. 1992. "El personaje mítico femenino de la iconografía mochica." Thesis, Facultad de Letras y Ciencias Humanas, Pontifícia Universidad Católica del Perú.

Horkheimer, Hans. 1965. "Vicús: Manifestiones de una cultura nebulosa." *Exposición auspiciada por la*

Universidad Técnica de Piura. Lima: Ediciones del Instituto de Arte Contemporaneo de Lima.

Huaca de la Luna, Moche, Perú. 2009. "Guía para el visitante: Visitor's Guide." Trujillo: Patronato Huacas del Valle de Moche. Lima: Fundación Backus.

Ídolo Moche: Complejo Arqueológico El Brujo. 2001. Trujillo: Banco Wiese.

Inca—Perú.: 3000 Ans d'Histoire. 1990. Brussels: Musées royaux d'Art et d'Histoire.

Isbell, William H. 1997. *Mummies and Mortuary Monuments: A Postprocessual Prehistory of Central Andean Social Organization.* Austin: University of Texas Press.

Jackson, Margaret A. 2008. *Moche Art and Visual Culture in Ancient Peru.* Albuquerque: University of New Mexico.

Jiménez, María Jesús. 2000. "Los tejidos Moche de Dos Cabezas (Valle de Jequetepeque) hacia una definición del estilo textil mochica." In *Actas de la I Jornada Internacional sobre Textiles Precolombinos,* ed. Victoria Solanilla Demestre, 76–96. Barcelona: Universitat Autònoma de Barcelona, Departament d'Art.

Jiménez Borja, Arturo. 1938. *Moche.* Lima: Editorial Lumen.

———. 1950–1951. "Instrumentos musicales peruanos." *Revista del Museo Nacional* 19–20:37–189. Lima.

———. 1955. "La danza en el antiguo Perú." *Revista del Museo Nacional* 24:111–136. Lima.

Jones, Julie. 1979. "Moche Works of Art in Metal: A Review." In Benson, ed., 53–104.

———. 1993. *Loma Negra: A Peruvian Lord's Tomb.* Exhibition pamphlet. New York: Metropolitan Museum of Art.

———. 2001. "Innovation and Resplendence: Metalwork for Moche Lords." In Pillsbury, ed., 207–221.

Joralemon, Donald, and Douglas Sharon. 1993. *Sorcery and Shamanism: Curanderos and Clients in Northern Peru.* Salt Lake City: University of Utah Press.

Kato, Yasutake. 1993. "Resultados de las excavaciones en Kuntur Wasi, Cajamarca." In Millones and Onuki, eds., 203–228.

Kaulicke, Peter. 1976. *El Formativo de Pacopampa.* Lima: Universidad Nacional Mayor San Marcos, Seminario de Historia Rural Andina.

———. 1991. "El Período Intermedio Temprano en el Alto Piura: Avances del Proyecto Arqueológico 'Alto Piura' (1987–1990)." *Boletín del Instituto Francés de Estudios Andinas* 20:381–422. Lima.

———. 1992. "Moche, Vicus Moche y el Mochica temprano." *Bulletin de l'Institut Francais d'Etudes Andines* 21 (3):853–903.

———. 1994. "La presencia mochica en el Alto Piura: Problemática y propuestas." In Uceda and Mujica, eds., 327–358.

———. 1997. "La muerte en el antiguo Perú." In Kaulicke, ed., 7–54.

———. 2000. *Memoria y muerte en el Perú antiguo.* Lima: Pontifícia Universidad Católica del Perú.

———, ed. 1997. La muerte en el Antiguo Perú: Contextos y conceptos funerarios. *Boletín de Arqueología PUCP* vol. 1. Lima: Pontificia Universidad Católica del Perú.

———. 1999. El período arcaíco en el Perú. *Boletín de Arqueología PUCP* no. 3.

Keatinge, Richard W. 1981. "The Nature and Role of Religious Diffusion in the Early Stages of State Formation: An Example from Peruvian Prehistory." In Grant D. Jones and Robert R. Kautz, eds., *The Transition to Statehood in the New World*, 172–187. Cambridge: Cambridge University Press.

Kembel, Silvia Rodríguez. 2008. "The Architecture at the Monumental Center of Chavín de Huántar: Sequence, Transformations, and Chronology." In Conklin and Quilter, eds., 35–81.

Kembel, Silvia Rodríguez, and John W. Rick. 2004. "Building Authority at Chavín de Huántar: Models of Social Organization and Development in the Initial Period and Early Horizon." In Silverman, 51–76.

Kerr, Justin. 1989. *The Maya Vase Book*, vol. 1. New York: Kerr Associates.

King, Heidi, ed. 2000. *Rain of the Moon: Silver in Ancient Peru.* New York: Metropolitan Museum of Art.

King, Judith E. 1983. *Seals of the World.* 2nd ed. Ithaca, NY: Comstock Publishing Associates, Cornell University Press.

Kosok, Paul. 1965. *Life, Land and Water in Ancient Peru.* New York: Long Island University Press.

Krickeberg, Walter. 1928. "Mexikanisch-Peruanische Parallelen: Ein Ueberblick und eine Ergänzung." Festschrift / Publication d'hommage offerte au P. W. Schmidt, 378–393. Vienna: Mechitharisten-Congregations-Buchdruckerei.

Kroeber, Alfred L. 1925. "The Uhle Pottery Collections from Moche." *University of California Publications in American Archaeology and Ethnology* 21 (5):191–234. Berkeley.

———. 1926. *Archaeological Explorations in Peru, Part I: Ancient Pottery from Peru.* Field Museum of Natural History, Anthropology Memoirs 2 (1). Chicago.

———. 1930. *Archaeological Explorations in Peru, Part II: The Northern Coast.* Field Museum of Natural History, Anthropology Memoirs 2 (2). Chicago.

———. 1944. *Peruvian Archaeology in 1942.* Viking Fund Publications in Anthropology 4. New York: Wenner-Gren Foundation.

Kubler, George. 1948. "Towards Absolute Time: Guano Archaeology." In Bennett, ed., 4:29–50.

Kutscher, Gerdt. 1950. *Chimu.* Berlin: Verlag Gebr. Mann.

———. 1951. "Ritual Races Among the Early Chimu." In *The Civilizations of Ancient America*, ed. Sol Tax, 244–251. Chicago: University of Chicago Press.

———. 1954. *Nordperuanische Keramik.* Berlin: Verlag Gebr. Mann.

———. 1976. "Ceremonial 'Badminton' in the Ancient Culture of Moche (North Peru)." In B. Setton Smith, ed., *The Games of the Americas*, 422–432. New York: Arno Press.

———. 1983. *Nordperuanische Gefässmalereien des Moche-Stils*, ed. Ulf Bankmann. Munich: Verlag C. H. Beck.

Kvietok, D. Peter, and Daniel H. Sandweiss, eds. 1985. *Recent Studies in Andean Prehistory and Protohistory: Papers from the Second Annual Northeast Conference on Andean Archaeology and Ethnohistory.* Ithaca, NY: Cornell University, Latin American Studies Program.

Lapiner, Alan. 1976. *Pre-Columbian Art of South America.* New York: Harry N. Abrams.

Larco, Laura. 2008. *Más allá de los encantos: Documentos sobre extirpación de idolatrías en Trujillo (siglos XVIII-XX).* Lima: Fondo Editorial UNMSM and Instituto Francés de Estudios Andinos.

Larco Hoyle, Rafael. 1938. *Los Mochicas*, vol 1. Lima: Casa Editora La Crónica y Variedades, S.A.

———. 1939. *Los Mochicas*, vol. 2. Lima: Impresa editoral Rimac S.A.

———. 1941. *Los cupisniques.* Lima: La Crónica y Variadades.

———. 1942. "La escritura mochica sobre Pallares." *Revista Geográfica Americana* año 9, vol. 18:93–103. Buenos Aires.

———. 1944. *La cultura Salinar.* Trujillo: n.p.

———. 1945a. *La cultura Virú.* Trujillo: n.p.

———. 1945b. *Los Mochicas (Pre-Chimu de Uhle y Early Chimu de Kroeber).* Buenos Aires: Sociedad Geografica Americana.

———. 1946. "A Cultural Sequence for the North Coast of Peru." In *Handbook of South American Indians*, vol. 2, ed. J. Steward, 149–175. Bureau of American Ethnology Bulletin 143. Washington, DC: Smithsonian Institution.

———. 1948. *Cronologia arqueologica del norte del Perú.* Buenos Aires: Sociedad Geográfica Americana.

———. 1962. *La cultura Santa.* Lima: n.p.

———. 1963. *Las épocas peruanas.* Lima: n.p.

———. 1965a. *La cerámica de Vicús.* Lima: Santiago Valverde.

———. 1965b. *Checan: Essay on Erotic Elements in Peruvian Art.* Geneva: Nagel Publishers.

———. 1966. *Peru.* Barcelona: Editorial Juventud.

———. 1967. *Vicús 2: La cerámica de Vicús y sus nexos con las demás culturas.* Lima: Santiago Valverde.

———. 2001. *Los mochicas.* 2 vols. 2nd ed. Lima: Museo Arqueológico Rafael Larco Herrera.

Lau, George F. 2000. "Espacio ceremonial Recuay." In Makowski et al., 179–197.

———. 2002–2004. "The Recuay Culture of Peru's North-Central Highlands: A Reappraisal of Chronology and Its Implications." *Journal of Field Archaeology* 29 (1 & 2):177–202.

———. 2004. "Object of Contention: An Examination of Recuay-Moche Combat Imagery." *Cambridge Archaeological Journal* 14 (2).

Lavalle, José Antonio de, ed. 1989. *Moche.* 2nd ed. Lima: Banco de Crédito en el Perú en la Cultura.

Lavalle, José Antonio de, and José Alejandro González García. 1991. *The Textile Art of Peru.* Piura: Industría Textil Piura, S.A.

Lechtman, Heather. 1976. "A Metallurgical Site Survey in the Peruvian Andes." *Journal of Field Archaeology* 3.

———. 1979. "Issues in Andean Metallurgy." In Benson, ed., 1–40.

———. 1980. "The Central Andes: Metallurgy Without Iron." In *The Coming of the Age of Iron*, ed.

Theodore A. Wertime and James D. Muhly, 267–334. New Haven: Yale University Press.

———. 1984a. "Andean Value Systems and the Development of Prehistoric Metallurgy." *Technology and Culture* 25 (1):1–36.

———. 1984b. "Pre-Columbian Surface Metallurgy." *Scientific American* 250 (6):56–63.

———. 1993. "Technologies of Power: The Andean Case." In Henderson and Netherly, eds., 244–280.

———. 1996. "Cloth and Metal: The Culture of Technology." In Boone, ed., 33–43.

Lechtman, Heather, Antonieta Erlij, and Edward J. Barry Jr. 1982. "New Perspectives on Moche Metallurgy: Techniques of Gilding Copper at Loma Negra, Northern Peru." *American Antiquity* 47:3–30.

Leventhal, Richard M., and Alan L. Kolata, eds. 1983. *Civilization in the Ancient Americas: Essays in Honor of Gordon R. Willey*. Albuquerque and Cambridge, MA: University of New Mexico Press and Peabody Museum of Archaeology and Ethnology, Harvard University.

Lieske, Bärbel. 2001. *Göttergestalten der altperuanische Moche-Kultur*, vol. 1. Berlin: Freie Universität.

Lizarraga, Fray Reginaldo de. 1968 [before 1615]. *Descripción breve de toda la tierra del Perú, Tucumán, Río de la Plata y Chile*. Biblioteca de Autores Españoles vol. 36. Madrid.

Lothrop, Samuel K. 1941. "Gold Ornaments of Chavín Style from Chongoyape, Peru." *American Antiquity* 6 (3):250–261.

———. 1951. "Gold Artifacts of Chavín." *American Antiquity* 16 (3): 226–240.

Lumbreras, Luis Guillermo. 1974. *The Peoples and Cultures of Ancient Peru*. Trans. Betty J. Meggers. Washington, DC: Smithsonian Institution Press.

———. 1979. *El arte y la vida Vicús: Colección del Banco Popular del Perú*. Lima: Banco Popular del Perú.

———. 1993. Chavín de Huántar: Excavaciones en la Galería de las Ofrendas. *Materialien zur Allgemeinen und Vergleichenden Archäologie* Band 51. Mainz-am-Rein: Verlag Philipp von Zabern.

Lyon, Patricia J. 1989. "Archaeology and Mythology II: A Re-consideration of the Animated Objects Theme in Moche Art." In Diana Clair Tkaczuk and Brian C. Vivian, eds., *Cultures in Conflict: Current Archaeological Perspectives*, 62–68. Proceedings of the Twentieth Annual Chacmool Conference. Calgary: Archaeological Association of the University of Calgary.

MacCormack, Sabine. 1991. *Religion in the Andes: Vision and Imagination in Early Colonial Peru*. Princeton, NJ: Princeton University Press.

Mackey, Carol J., and Charles M. Hastings. 1982. "Moche Murals from the Huaca de la Luna." In Cordy-Collins, ed., 293–312.

Mackey, Carol J., and Melissa Vogel. 2003. "La luna sobre los Andes: Una revisión del animal lunar." In Uceda and Mujica, eds., vol. 1, 325–342.

Makowski, Krzysztof. 1994a. "La figura del 'officiante' en la iconografía mochica: ¿Shamán o sacerdote?" In Luis Millones and Moisés Lemig, eds., *Al final del camino*, 52–101. Lima: Sidea Fondo Editorial.

———. 1994b. "Los señores de Loma Negra." In Makowski et al., 83–141.

———. 1996. "Los seres radiantes, el Aguila y el Buho: La imagen de la divinidad en la cultura mochica." In *Imágenes y mitos: Ensayos sobre las artes figurativos en los Andes prehispánicos*, ed. Krzysztof Makowski, Iván Amaro, and Max Hernández, 13–114. Lima: Australis, S.A., Casa Editorial, Fondo Editorial SIDEA.

———. 2000. "Las divinidades en la iconografía mochica." In Makowski et al., 137–175.

Makowski, Krzysztof, Iván Amaro, and Otto Eléspuru. 1994. "Historia de una conquesta." In Makowski et al., 211–281.

Makowski, Krzysztof, Richard L. Burger, Helaine Silverman, Santiago Uceda, Luis Jaime Castillo, Marco Curatola, Lucy Salazar, George F. Lau, and Julio C. Rucabado. 2000. *Los dioses del antiguo Perú*, vol. 1. Lima: Banco de Crédito del Perú.

Makowski, Krzysztof, Christopher B. Donnan, Iván Amaro, Luis Jaime Castillo, Magdalena Diez Canseco, Otto Eléspuru, Juan Antonio Murro. 1994. *Vicús*. Lima: Banco de Crédito del Perú.

Makowski, Krzysztof, and Julio Rucabado Young. 2000. "Hombres y deidades en la iconografía Recuay." In Makowski et al., 199–235.

Marcus, Joyce, and Patrick Ryan Williams, eds. 2009. *Andean Civilization: A Tribute to Michael E. Moseley*. Monograph 63. Los Angeles: UCLA Cotsen Institute of Archaeology Press.

Martin, Simon, and Nicolai Grube. 2000. *Chronicle of*

the *Maya Kings and Queens*. London and New York: Thames and Hudson.

Martínez Compañon y Bujanda, Baltasar Jaime. 1978, 1985, 1994. *Trujillo del Perú, al fines del S. XVIII, dibujos y acuarelas que mandó hacer el Obispo don Baltazar J. Martínez Compañón*. 9 vols., 3 appendices. Madrid: Cultura Préhispanica.

Matos Mendieta, Ramiro. 1965–1966. "Algunas consideraciones sobre el estilo de Vicus." *Revista del Museo Nacional* 34:95–130. Lima.

McClelland, Donald H. 1986. "Brick Seriation at Pacatnamu." In Donnan and Cock, 27–46.

McClelland, Donna. 1990. "A Maritime Passage from Moche to Chimu." In Moseley and Cordy-Collins, eds., 75–106.

———. 1997 "Moche Fineline Ceramics at Pacatnamu." In Donnan and Cock, eds., 265–282.

———. 2008. "*Ulluchu*: An Elusive Fruit." In Bourget and Jones, eds., 43–65.

McClelland, Donna, Donald McClelland, and Christopher B. Donnan. 2007. *Moche Fineline Painting from San José de Moro*. Los Angeles: Cotsen Institute of Archaeology at UCLA.

McEwan, Colin. 1997. "Whistling Vessels from Pre-Hispanic Peru." In *Pottery in the Making: World Ceramic Traditions*, ed. Ian Freestone and David Gaimster, 176–181. London: British Museum Press.

Means, Philip Ainsworth. 1931. *Ancient Civilizations of the Andes*. New York: Charles Scribner Sons.

Meggers, Betty J., Clifford Evans, and Emilio Estrada. 1965. *Early Formative Period of Coastal Ecuador*. Contributions to Anthropology vol. l. Washington, DC: Smithsonian Institution.

Meneses, Susana, and Luis Chero. 1994. "La arquitectura." In Alva, 248–257.

Menzel, Dorothy. 1977. *The Archaeology of Ancient Peru and the Work of Max Uhle*. Berkeley: University of California, R. H. Lowie Museum of Anthropology.

Migdalski, Edward C., and George S. Fichter. 1983. *The Fresh and Salt Water Fishes of the World*. New York: Greenwich House.

Millaire, Jean-François. 2002. *Moche Burial Patterns: An Investigation into Prehispanic Social Structure*. BAR International Series 1066.

———. 2004. "The Manipulation of Human Remains in Moche Society." *Latin American Antiquity* 15 (4):371–388.

———. 2008. "Moche Textile Production on the Peruvian North Coast." In Bourget and Jones, eds., 220–245.

———. 2010. "Moche Political Expansion as Viewed from Virú." In Quilter and Castillo, 223–251.

Millaire, Jean-François, with Magali Morlion, eds. 2009. *Gallinazo: An Early Cultural Tradition on the Peruvian North Coast*. Los Angeles: UCLA Cotsen Institute of Archaeology Press.

Millones, Luis. 1982. "Brujería de la costa, brujería de la sierra: Estudio comparativo de dos complejos religiosos en el area andina." In Millones and Tomoeda, eds., 229–274.

Millones, Luis, and Yoshio Onuki, eds. 1993. *El mundo ceremonial andino*. Senri Ethnological Studies no. 37. Osaka: Museo Nacional de Etnología.

Millones, Luis, and Hiroyasu Tomoeda, eds. 1982. *El hombre y su ambiente en los Andes Centrales*. Senri Ethnological Studies no. 10. Osaka: National Museum of Ethnology.

Molina, Cristóbal de. 1989 [1575]. *Fábulas y mitos de los Incas*. Madrid: Vierna.

Montoya, María. 1997. "Excavaciones en la Plaza 3B de la Huaca de la Luna." In Uceda, Mujica, and Morales, eds., 61–66.

———. 2004. "Textiles Moche en Huaca de la Luna: Testigo No. 6 de la Tumba 18." In Valle Alvarez, ed., vol. 1, 189–206.

Moore, Jerry D. 1996. *Architecture and Power in the Ancient Andes: The Archaeology of Public Buildings*. Cambridge: University of Cambridge Press.

Morales Chocana, Daniel. 2008. "The Importance of Pacopampa: Architecture in the Central Andean Formative." In Conklin and Quilter, 143–160.

Morales Gamarra, Ricardo. 1994. "La conservación de relieves de barro polícromos en la costa norte del Perú." In Uceda and Mujica, eds., 477–492.

———. 1995. "Murales en La Luna." *Arkinka* año 1 (1):54–61.

———. 2000a. "Fenómeno El Niño (1997–1998): Prevención y conservación de emergencia." In Uceda, Mujica, y Morales, eds., 291–302.

———. 2000b. "Max Uhle: Murales y materiales pictóricos en las Huacas de Moche (1899–1900)." In Uceda, Mujica, y Morales, eds., 235–266.

———. 2003. "Iconografía litúrgica y contexto arquitectónico en Huaca de la Luna, Valle de Moche." In
Uceda and Mujica, eds., vol. 1, 425–476.

———. 2004. "Atuendo ritual Moche en Huaca de la
Luna: Apuntes para una interpretación iconográfico
en contexto." In Uceda, Mujica, and Morales, eds.,
377–387.

Morales Gamarra, Ricardo, Miguel Asmat Valverde,
and Arabel Fernández López. 2000. "Atuendo ceremonial moche: Excepcional hallazgo en la Huaca
de la Luna." *Iconos* no. 3:49–53.

Morales Gamarra, Ricardo, Jorge Solórzano Solano,
and Manuel Asmat Sánchez. 1998. "Superficies
arquitectónicas: Tipología, tecnología y materiales."
In Uceda, Mujica, and Morales, eds., 211–219.

Morales, Ricardo, and Neil Torres Velásquez.
2000. "Estructuras y superficies arquitectónicas:
Tratamiento conservador." In Uceda, Mujica, and
Morales, eds., 269–290.

Moseley, Michael E. 1975a. *The Maritime Foundations
of Andean Civilization*. Menlo Park, CA: Cummings
Publishing.

———. 1975b. "Prehistoric Principles of Labor Organization in the Moche Valley, Peru." *American
Antiquity* 40 (2):191–196. Washington, DC: Society
for American Archaeology.

———. 1975c. "Secrets of Peru's Ancient Walls." *Natural History* 74:34–41.

———. 1982. "Introduction: Human Exploitation and
Organization on the North Coast." In Moseley and
Day, 1–24.

———. 1990. "Structure and History in the Dynamic
Lore of Chimor." In Moseley and Cordy-Collins,
eds., 1–41.

———. 1992. *The Incas and Their Ancestors: The
Archaeology of Peru*. London: Thames and Hudson.

Moseley, Michael E., and Alana Cordy-Collins, eds.
1990. *The Northern Dynasties: Kingship and Statecraft
in Chimor*. Washington, DC: Dumbarton Oaks.

Moseley, Michael E., and Kent C. Day, eds. 1982.
Chan Chan: Andean Desert City. Albuquerque: Uni-
versity of New Mexico Press. A School of American
Research book.

Moseley, Michael E., and Eric C. Deeds. 1982. "The
Land in Front of Chan Chan." In Moseley and Day,
25–53.

Moseley, Michael E., Christopher B. Donnan, and
David K. Keefer. 2008. "Convergent Catastrophe
and the Demise of Dos Cabezas: Environmental
Change and Regime Change in Ancient Peru." In
Bourget and Jones, eds., 81–91.

Moseley, Michael E., and Carol J. Mackey. 1972.
"Peruvian Settlement Pattern Studies and Small Site
Methodology." *American Antiquity* 37:67–81.

Moseley, M. Edward,, and Luis Watanabe. 1974. "The
Adobe Sculpture of Huaca de los Reyes." *Archaeology* 27 (3):154–161.

Muelle, Jorge C. 1936. "Chalchalcha (Un análisis de
los dibujos muchik)." *Revista del Museo Nacional* 5
(1):65–88. Lima.

Mujica, Elias. 1984. "Cerro Arena—Layzon: Relaciones costa-sierra en el norte del Perú." *Gaceta Arqueológica Andina* no. 10:12–15. Lima.

Murphy, Robert Cushman. 1925. *Bird Islands of Peru.*
New York and London: G. P. Putnam's Sons.

———. 1936. *Oceanic Birds of South America*. 2 vols.
New York: Macmillan and the American Museum
of Natural History.

Murra, John V. 1962. "Cloth and Its Functions in the
Inca State." *American Anthropologist* 64:710–728.

Murro, Juan Antonio. 1994. "Arqueología y Huaqueros." In Makowski et al., 3–21.

Narváez Vargas, Alfredo. 1994. "La Mina: Una tumba
Moche I en el valle de Jequetepeque." In Uceda and
Mujica, eds., 59–81.

———. 2001. *Dioses encantos y gentiles*. Lambayeque:
Museo del Sitio Túcume.

Nelson, Andrew, and Luis Jaime Castillo. 1997. "Huesos a la deriva: Tafonomía y tratamiento funerario
en entierros Mochica Tardío de San José de Moro."
In Kaulicke, ed., 137–163.

Nelson, Bryan. 1980. *Seabirds: Their Biology and Ecology*. London and New York: Hamlyn.

Netherly, Patricia J. 1977. *Local Level Lords on the
North Coast of Peru*. Doctoral thesis, Department of
Anthropology, Cornell University, Ithaca, NY. Ann
Arbor: UMI, 1984.

———. 1984. "The Management of Late Andean Irrigation Systems on the North Coast of Peru." *American Antiquity* 49 (2):227–234.

———. 1988. "From Event to Process: The Recovery of
Late Andean Organizational Structure by Means of
Spanish Colonial Written Records." In *Peruvian Pre-
history: An Overview of Pre-Inca and Inca society*, ed.

Richard Keatinge, 257–275. Cambridge: Cambridge University Press.

———. 1990. "Out of Many, One: The Organization of Rule in North Coast Politics." In Moseley and Cordy-Collins, eds., 461–487.

———. 1993. "The Nature of the Andean State." In Henderson and Netherly, eds., 11–35.

———. 2009. "Landscapes as Metaphor: Resources, Language, and Myths of Dynastic Origin on the Pacific Coast from the Santa Valley (Peru) to Manabí (Ecuador)." In *Landscapes of Origins in the Americas*, ed. Jessica Joyce Christie, 122–152. Tuscaloosa: University of Alabama Press.

Netherly, Patricia J., and Tom D. Dillehay. 1986. "Duality in Public Architecture in the Upper Zaña Valley, Northern Peru." In *Perspectives on Andean Prehistory and Protohistory*, ed. Daniel H. Sandweiss and D. Peter Kvietok, 85–114. Ithaca, NY: Latin American Studies Program, Cornell University.

Nicholson, H. B., and Alana Cordy-Collins. 1979. *Pre-Columbian Art from the Land Collection*. San Francisco: California Academy of Sciences.

Olsen, Dale. 1992. "Implications of Musical Technologies in the Pre-Columbian Andes." In *Musical Repercussions of 1492: Encounters in Text and Performance*, ed. Carol E. Robertson, 65–88. Washington, DC, and London: Smithsonian Institution Press.

Onuki, Yoshio. 1997. "Ocho tumbas especiales de Kuntur Wasi." In Kaulicke, ed., 79–114.

Orbegoso, Clorinda. 1998. "Excavaciones en el sector sureste de la Plaza 3C." In Uceda, Mujica, and Morales, eds., 67–73.

Paxton, John R., and William N. Eschmeyer, eds. 1995. *Encyclopedia of Fishes*. San Diego: Academic Press.

Pennington, T. D., C. Reynal, and A. Daza. 2004. *Illustrated Guide to the Trees of Peru*. Sherborne, England: David Hunt.

Pillsbury, Joanne, ed. 2001. *Moche Art and Archaeology in Ancient Peru*. Washington, DC: Dumbarton Oaks.

———. 2008. *Guide to Documentary Sources for Andean Studies, 1530–1900*. Norman: University of Oklahoma Press.

Pillsbury, Joanne, and Lisa Trever. 2008. "The King, the Bishop, and the Creation of an American Antiquity." *Ñawpa Pacha* 29:191–219.

Pimentel, Victor, and Gonzalo Álvarez. 2000.

"Relieves polícromos en la plataforma funeraria Uhle." In Uceda, Mujica, and Morales, eds., 181–203.

Plowman, Timothy. 1984. "The Origin, Evolution, and Diffusion of Coca, *Erythroxylum* spp., in South and Central America." In *Pre-Columbian Plant Migration*, ed. Doris Stone, 125–163. Harvard University Papers of the Peabody Museum of Archaeology and Ethnology 76.

Pozorski, Shelia G. 1976. *Prehistoric Subsistence Patterns and Site Economics in the Moche Valley, Peru*. Ph.D. dissertation, University of Texas at Austin. Ann Arbor: UMI, 1984.

———. 1979a. "Late Prehistoric Llama Remains from the Moche Valley, Peru." *Annals of the Carnegie Museum of Natural History* 48:139–170.

———. 1979b. "Prehistoric Diet and Subsistence of the Moche Valley, Peru." *World Archaeology* 11 (2):163–184.

———. 1987. "Theocracy vs. militarism: The significance of the Casma Valley in Understanding Early State Formation." In Haas, Pozorski, and Pozorski, 15–30.

Pozorski, Shelia, and Thomas Pozorski. 1979. "Alto Salaverry: A Peruvian Coastal Cotton Preceramic Site." *Annals of the Carnegie Museum* 49:337–375.

———. 1987. *Early Settlement and Subsistence in the Casma Valley*. Iowa City: University of Iowa Press.

———. 2003. "Arquitectura residencial y subsistencia de los habitantes del sitio de Moche: Evidencia recuperada por el Proyecto Chan Chan–Valle de Moche." In Uceda and Mujica, eds., vol. 1, 119–150.

Pozorski, Thomas. 1980. "The Early Horizon Site of Huaca de los Reyes: Societal Implications." *American Anthropologist* 45:100–110.

———. 1982. "Early Social Stratification and Subsistence Systems: The Caballo Muerto Complex." In Moseley and Day, eds., 225–253.

Pozorski, Thomas, and Shelia Pozorski. 1993. "Early Complex Society and Ceremonialism on the Peruvian North Coast." In Millones and Onuki, eds., 45–68.

Preston-Mafham, Rod. 1991. *The Book of Spiders and Scorpions*. New York: Crescent Books.

Proulx, Donald Allen. 1982. "Territoriality in the Early Intermediate Period: The Case of Moche and Recuay." *Ñawpa Pacha* 20:83–96.

————. 1985. *An Analysis of the Early Cultural Sequence of the Nepeña Valley*. Research Report 25. Amherst: University of Massachusetts, Department of Anthropology.

Prümers, Heiko. 2000. "Apuntes sobre los tejidos de la tumba del 'Señor de Sipán,' Peru." In *Actas de la I Jornada Internacional sobre Textiles Precolombinos*, ed. Victoria Solanilla Demestre, 97–109. Barcelona: Universitad Autònoma de Barcelona, Departament d'Art.

Quilter, Jeffrey. 1990. "The Moche Revolt of the Objects." *Latin American Antiquity* 1 (1):31–65.

————. 1996. "Continuity and Disjunction in Pre-Columbian Art and Culture." *res* 20/30:303–317.

————. 1997. "The Narrative Approach to Moche Iconography." *Latin American Antiquity* 8 (2):113–133.

————. 2001. "Moche Mimesis: Continuity and Change in Public Art in Early Peru." In Pillsbury, ed., 21–45.

————. 2002. "Moche Politics, Religion, and Warfare." *Journal of World Prehistory* 16 (2):145–195.

————. 2010. *The Moche of Ancient Peru: Media and Messages*. Cambridge, MA: Peabody Museum Press.

Quilter, Jeffrey, and Luis Jaime Castillo B., eds. 2010. *New Perspectives on Moche Political Organization*. Washington, DC: Dumbarton Oaks.

Ramírez, Susan E. 1995. "An Oral History of the Valley of Chicama, Circa 1524–1565." *Journal of the Steward Anthropological Society* 23 (1 & 2):299–343.

Ramírez-Gamonal, Carlos, and Bertha M. Herrera Mejía. 1994. "Summary of Investigaciones Arqueológicas en la Huaca del Sol (Valle de Moche), Costa Norte del Peru." *Willay* 41:15–21.

Ramírez-Horton, Susan. 1982. "Retainers of the Lords or Merchants: A Case of Mistaken Identity?" In Millones and Tomoeda, eds., 123–136.

"Recuperación de excepcionales Porras precolombinas." 2000. *íconos* no. 3:54–55.

Reents-Budet, Dorie. 1994. *Painting the Maya Universe: Royal Ceramics of the Classic Period*. Durham, NC, and London: Duke University Press.

Reichel-Dolmatoff, Gerardo. 1965. "Excavaciones arqueológicas en Puerto Hormiga (Departamento de Bolívar)." *Antropológica* no. 2. Bogotá: Universidad de los Andes, Departamento de Antropología.

————. 1985. *Monsú: Un sitio arqueológico*. Bogotá: Biblioteca Banco Popular Textos Universitarios.

Reichert, Raphael X. 1982. "Moche Iconography—The Highland Connection." In Cordy-Collins, ed., 279–291.

Reindel, Markus. 1993. *Monumentale Lehmarchitektur an der Nordküste Perus*. Bonner Amerikanistische Studien 22. Bonn.

Reinhard, Johan. 1996. "Peru's Ice Maidens." *National Geographic* 189 (6):62–81.

————. 1999. "Frozen in Time." *National Geographic* 196 (5):36–55.

Richardson, James B., III. 1994. *People of the Andes*. Montreal and Washington, DC: St. Remy Press and Smithsonian Books.

Richardson, James B., III, Mark A. McConaughy, Allison Heaps de Peña, and Elena B. Décima Zamecnik. 1990. "The Northern Frontier of the Kingdom of Chimor: The Piura, Chira, and Tumbez Valleys." In Moseley and Cordy-Collins, eds., 419–445.

Rick, John W. 2008. "Context, Construction, and Ritual in the Development of Authority at Chavín de Huántar." In Conklin and Quilter, eds., 3–34.

Rivero, Mariano Eduardo, and Johann J. von Tschudi. 1855. *Peruvian Antiquities*. Trans. F. L. Hawks. New York: A. S. Barnes.

Rodríguez Suy Suy, Victor Antonio. 2001. "Los pueblos pescadores muchik de ayer y siempre." *Revista Arqueológica Sian* año 6 (10):11–14. Trujillo.

Roe, Peter G. 1982. "Cupisnique Pottery: A Cache from Tembladera." In Cordy-Collins, ed., 231–253.

————. 1998. "Paragon or Peril: The Jaguar in Amazonian Indian Society." In Saunders, ed., 171–202.

Roosevelt, Anna Curtenius. 1991. *Moundbuilders of the Amazon: Geophysical Archaeology on Marajo Island, Brazil*. San Diego: Academic Press.

Rostworowski de Diez Canseco, María. 1977. "Coastal Fishermen, Merchants, and Artisans in Pre-Hispanic Peru." In *The Sea in the Pre-Columbian World*, ed. Elizabeth P. Benson, 167–186. Washington, DC: Dumbarton Oaks.

————. 1981. *Recursos naturales renovables y pesca: Siglos XVI y XVII*. Lima: Instituto de Estudios Peruanos.

————. 1989. *Costa peruana prehispánica*. 2nd ed. Lima: Instituto de Estudios Peruanos.

————. 1990. "Ethnohistorical Considerations about the Chimor." In Moseley and Cordy-Collins, eds., 447–460.

————. 1992. *Pachacamac y el Señor de los Milagros.* Lima: Instituto de Estudios Peruanos.

————. 1996. *Estructuras andinas del poder: Ideología religiosa y política.* 4th ed. Lima: Instituto de Estudios Peruanos.

————. 1997. "The Coastal Islands of Peru." In Berrin, ed., 33–39.

————. 1999. *History of the Inca Realm.* Trans. Harry B. Iceland. Cambridge: Cambridge University Press.

Rowe, Ann Pollard. 1984. *Costumes and Featherwork of the Lords of Chimor: Textiles from Peru's North Coast.* Washington, DC: The Textile Museum.

Rowe, John Howland. 1946. "Inca Culture at the Time of the Spanish Conquest." In *Handbook of South American Indians,* Bureau of American Ethnology Bulletin 143 (2):183–330. Washington, DC: Smithsonian Institution.

————. 1948. "The Kingdom of Chimor." *Acta Americana* 6:26–59.

————. 1954. *Max Uhle, 1856–1944: A Memoir of the Father of Peruvian Archaeology.* University of California Publications in American Archaeology and Ethnology 46 (1). Berkeley.

————. 1962. *Chavin Art: An Inquiry into Its Form and Meaning.* New York: Museum of Primitive Art.

————. 1971. "The Influence of Chavín Art on Later Styles." In Benson, ed., 101–124.

Rucabado Yong, Julio, and Luis Jaime Castillo. 2003. "El período transicional en San José de Moro." In Uceda and Mujica, eds., I, 15–42.

Russell, Glenn S., and Margaret Jackson. 2001. "Political Economy and Patronage at Cerro Mayal, Peru." In Pillsbury, ed., 159–175.

Russell, Glenn S., Banks L. Leonard, and Jesús Briceño R. 1994. "Cerro Mayal: Nuevos datos sobre producción de cerámica Moche en el valle de Chicama." In Uceda and Mujica, eds., 181–206.

————. 1998. "The Cerro Mayal Workshop: Addressing Issues of Craft Specialization in Moche Society." In Shimada, ed., 63–89.

Salas, José Antonio. 2002. *Diccionario Mochica–Castellano / Castellano-Mochica.* Lima: Universidad de San Martín de Porres.

Salazar, Lucy, and Richard L. Burger. 2000. "Las divinidades del universo religioso Cupisnique y Chavín." In Makowski et al., 29–68.

Salazar-Burger, Lucy, and Richard L. Burger. 1982. "La araña en la iconografía del Horizonte Temprano en la Costa Norte del Perú." *Beitrage zur allgemeinen und vergleichenden Archäologie* Band 4:213–253. Bonn: Archäologische Institut.

————. 1996. "Cupisnique." In Boone, ed., 87–100.

Salomon, Frank. 1995. "'The Beautiful Grandparents': Andean Ancestor Shrines and Mortuary Ritual as Seen Through Colonial Records." In Dillehay, ed., 315–353.

————. 1998. "How the *Huacas* Were: The Language of Substance and Transformation in the Huarochirí Quechua Manuscript." *res* 33:7–17.

Salomon, Frank, and George L. Urioste. 1991 [1608?]. *The Huarochirí Manuscript.* Austin: University of Texas Press.

Samaniego, Lorenzo, Enrique Vergara, and Henning Bischof. 1985. "New Evidence on Cerro Sechin, Casma Valley, Peru." In Donnan, ed., 165–190.

Sandweiss, Daniel H. 2009. "Early Fishing and Inland Monuments." In Marcus and Williams, eds., 39–54.

Sandweiss, Daniel H., and Jeffrey Quilter, eds. 2008. *El Niño, Catastrophism, and Cultural Change in Ancient America.* Washington, DC: Dumbarton Oaks.

Saunders, Nicholas J. 1998. "Architecture of Symbolism: The Feline Image." In Saunders, ed., 12–52.

————. 1999. "Biographies of Brilliance: Pearls, Transformations of Matter and Being, c. A.D. 1492." *World Archaeology* 31 (2):243–257.

————, ed. 1998. *Icons of Power: Feline Symbolism in the Americas.* London and New York: Routledge.

Sawyer, Alan R. 1966. *Ancient Peruvian Ceramics: The Nathan Cummings Collection.* New York: Metropolitan Museum of Art.

Schaedel, Richard P. 1948. "Stone Sculpture in the Callejón de Huaylas." In Bennett, ed., 66–79.

————. 1951. "Mochica Murals at Panamarca." *Archaeology* 4 (3):145–154. Cambridge. Reprinted 1967 in John Howland Rowe and Dorothy Menzel, eds., *Peruvian Archaeology: Selected Readings,* 104–114. Palo Alto, CA: Peek Publications.

————. 1988. *La etnografía Muchik en las fotografías de H. Brüning, 1886–1925.* Lima: Ediciones Cofide.

Schaffer, Anne-Louise. 1981. "A Monster-headed Complex of Mythical Creatures in the Loma Negra Metalwork." Paper presented at the 25th

Annual Meeting of the Institute of Andean Studies, Berkeley.

———. 1983. "Cathartidae in Moche Art and Culture." In *Flora and Fauna Imagery in Precolumbian Cultures: Iconography and Function*, ed. Jeanette F. Peterson. BAR International Series 171. Oxford.

———. 1985. "Impressions in Metal: Reconstructing Burial Context at Loma Negra, Peru." In Kvietok and Sandweiss, eds., 95–119.

Schele, Linda, and Peter Mathews. 1998. *The Code of Kings: The Language of Seven Sacred Maya Temples and Tombs.* New York: Scribner.

Schmidt, Max. 1929. *Kunst und Kultur von Peru.* Berlin: Propyläen-Verlag.

Schultes, Richard Evans, and Albert Hofmann. 1979. *Plants of the Gods.* New York: McGraw-Hill.

Schwartz, Marion. 1997. *A History of Dogs in the Early Americas.* New Haven: Yale University Press.

Schweigger, Erwin. 1964. *El litoral peruano.* 2nd ed. Lima: Universidad Nacional "Federico Villarreal."

Seler, Eduard. 1915. "Archäologische Reise in Süd- und Mittelamerika. 1910/1911." In *Gesammelte Abhanglungen zur Amerikanischen Sprach- und Altertumskunde*, vol. 5, 115–151. Berlin.

———. 1923. "Viaje arqueológico en Perú y Bolivia." *Inca*, vol. 1, no. 2:355–74. Lima.

Shady, Ruth, and Carlos Leyva, eds. 2003. *La ciudad sagrada de Caral-Supe.* Lima: Instituto Nacional de Cultura, Proyecto Especial Arqueológico Caral-Supe.

Sharon, Douglas. 1972. "Eduardo the Healer." *Natural History* 81 (9):32–47.

———. 1978. *Wizard of the Four Winds.* New York: Free Press.

———. 2000. *Shamanism and the Sacred Cactus: Ethnoarchaeological Evidence for San Pedro Use in Northern Peru.* San Diego Museum Papers 37.

Sharon, Douglas, and Christopher B. Donnan. 1974. "Shamanism in Moche Iconography." In *Ethnoarchaeology*, ed. Christopher B. Donnan and C. William Clewlow, Jr. Monograph IV. Los Angeles: Institute of Archaeology, University of California.

Shimada, Izumi. 1987. "Horizontal and Vertical Dimensions of Prehistoric States in North Peru." In Haas, Pozorski, and Pozorski, eds., 130–144.

———. 1994a. *Pampa Grande and the Mochica Culture.* Austin: University of Texas Press.

———. 1994b. "La producción de cerámica en Morrope, Peru." In Shimada, ed., 295–319.

———. 1995. *Cultura Sicán.* Lima: Edubanco.

———. 1997. "Organizational Significance of Marked Bricks and Associated Construction Features on the North Peruvian Coast." In Bonnier and Bischof, eds., vol. 2, 63–89.

———. 2001. "Late Moche Urban Craft Production: A First Approximation." In Pillsbury, ed., 177–205.

———, ed. 1994. *Tecnología y organización de la producción cerámica prehispánica en los Andes.* Lima: Pontificia Universidad Católica del Perú.

———. 1998. *Andean Ceramics: Technology, Organization, and Approaches.* MASCA Research Papers in Science and Archaeology Supplement to vol. 15. Philadelphia: University of Pennsylvania Museum of Archaeology and Anthropology, Museum Applied Science Center for Archaeology.

Shimada, Izumi, and Adriana Maguiña. 1994. "Nueva visión sobre la cultura Gallinazo y su relación con la cultura Moche." In Uceda and Mujica, 31–58.

Shimada, Izumi, and John F. Merkel. 1991. "Copper-Alloy Metallurgy in Ancient Peru." *Scientific American* 265 (1):80–86.

Shimada, Izumi, Crystal Barker Schaaf, Lonnie G. Thompson, and Ellen Mosley-Thompson. 1991. "Cultural Impacts of Severe Droughts in the Prehistoric Andes: Application of a 1,500-year Ice Core Precipitation Record." *World Archaeology* 22:247–270.

Shimada, Izumi, et al. 1998. "Formative Ceramic Kilns and Production in Batán Grande, North Coast of Peru." In Shimada, ed., 23–61.

Shimada, Izumi, Ken-Ichi Shinoda, Walter Alva, Steve Bourget, Claude Chapdelaine, and Santiago Uceda. 2008. "The Moche People: Genetic Perspective on Their Sociopolitcal Composition and Organization." In Bourget and Jones, eds., 179–193.

Shimada, Melody J., and Izumi Shimada. 1981. "Explotación y manejo de los recursos naturales en Pampa Grande, sitio Moche V: Significado del análisis orgánico." *Revista del Museo Nacional* 45:19–73. Lima.

———. 1985. "Prehistoric Llama Breeding and Herding on the North Coast of Peru." *American Antiquity* 50 (1):3–26.

Silverman, Helaine, ed. 2004. *Andean Archaeology.* Malden, MA: Blackwell.

Silverman, Helaine, and William H. Isbell, eds. 2008. *Handbook of South American Archaeology.* New York: Springer.

Silverman, Helaine, and Donald A. Proulx. 2002. *The Nasca.* Malden, MA, and Oxford: Blackwell Publishers.

Spondylus: Ofrenda sagrada y símbolo de paz. 1999. Lima: Museo Arqueológica Rafael Larco Herrera and Fundación Telefónica.

Squier, Ephraim George. 1877. *Peru: Incidents of Travel and Exploration in the Land of the Incas.* New York: Harper and Brothers.

Sreenivasan, Aparna. 2002. "Keeping Up With the Cones." *Natural History* 111 (1):41–47.

Stevenson, Robert. 1968. *Music in Aztec and Inca Territory.* Berkeley and Los Angeles: University of California Press.

Strong, William Duncan, and Clifford Evans Jr. 1952. *Cultural Stratigraphy in the Virú Valley, Northern Peru: The Formative and Florescent Epochs.* Columbia Studies in Archaeology and Ethnology 4. New York: Columbia University Press.

Sunquist, Mel, and Fiona Sunquist. 2002. *Wild Cats of the World.* Chicago and London: University of Chicago Press.

Suplee, Curt. 1999. "El Niño / La Niña." *National Geographic* 195 (3):72–95.

Tedlock, Dennis, trans. 1996. *Popol Vuh: The Definitive Edition of the Mayan Book of the Dawn of Life and the Glories of Gods and Kings.* Rev. ed. New York: Simon and Schuster.

Tellenbach, Michael. 1986. *Die Ausgrabungen in der formativzeitlichen Siedlung Montegrande, Jequetepeque-Tal, Nord-Peru/ Las excavaciones en el asentiamiento formativo de Montegrande, Valle de Jequetepeque en el norte del Perú.* Munich: C. H. Beck.

———. 1998. *Chavín: Investigaciones acerca del desarrollo cultural Centro-Andino en las épocas Ofrendas y Chavín-Tardío.* 2 vols. Andes: Boletín de la Misión Arqueológica Andina. University of Warsaw.

Tello, Julio C. 1923. "Wira Kocha." *Inca* vol. 1 (1):93–320, (3):583–606. Lima.

———. 1938. "Arte antiguo: Album fotográfico de las principales especies arqueológicas de cerámica muchik existentes en los museos de Lima, Parte primera: Tecnología y morfología." *Inca,* vol. 2. Lima.

———. 1956. *Arqueología del valle de Casma: Culturas Chavín, Santa o Huaylas, Yunga y Sub-Chimú.* Publicaciones Arqueolicas del Archivo "Julio C. Tello." Lima: Universidad Nacional Mayor de San Marcos.

———. 1960. *Chavín: Cultura matriz de la civilización andina.* Publicación Antropológica del "Archivo Julio C. Tello" 2. Lima: Universidad Nacional Mayor de San Marcos.

Tello, Ricardo. 1998. "Los conjunctos arquitectónicos 8, 17, 18 y 19 del centro urbano Moche." In Uceda, Mujica, and Morales, eds., 117–135.

Tello, Ricardo, José Armas, and Claude Chapdelaine. 2003. "Prácticas funerarias Moche en el complejo arqueológico Huacas del Sol y de la Luna." In Uceda and Mujica, eds., 151–187.

Tello, Ricardo M., Carlos Jordán, Carlos Zevallos, María Nuñez, Alicia Ponce, María Chiroque, Carola Madueño, and Vanessa Monge. 2004. "Investigaciones en el conjuncto arquitectónico 25, Área Urbano Moche." In Uceda, Mujica, and Morales, eds., 231–260.

Tierney, Patrick. 1989. *The Highest Altar: The Story of Human Sacrifice.* New York: Viking.

Topic, John R., and Theresa Lange Topic. 1983. "Coast-Highland Relations in Northern Peru: Some Observations on Routes, Networks, and Scales of Interaction." In Leventhal and Kolata, 237–259.

———. 1987. "The Archaeological Investigation of Andean Militarism: Some Cautionary Observations." In Haas, Pozorski, and Pozorski, eds., 47–55.

———. 1997. "Hacia una comprensión conceptual de la guerra andina." In *Arqueología, Antropología e Historia en los Andes: Homenaje a María Rostworowski,* by Rafael Varón Gabai and Javier Flores Espinosa, 567–590. Lima: Instituto de Estudios Peruanos and Banco Central de Reserva del Perú.

Topic, Theresa Lange. 1977. "Excavations at Moche." Ph.D. dissertation, Harvard University.

———. 1982. "The Early Intermediate Period and Its Legacy." In Moseley and Day, 255–284.

———. 1991. "The Middle Horizon in Northern Peru." In *Huari Administrative Structure: Prehistoric Monumental Architecture and State Government,* ed. William H. Isbell and Gordan F. McEwan, 233–246. Washington, DC: Dumbarton Oaks.

Towle, Margaret A. 1961. *The Ethnobotany of Pre-Columbian Peru.* Viking Fund Publications in Anthropology no. 30. New York.

Tufinio C., Moisés. 2000. "Excavaciones en la Unidad 5 (Amplicación Norte), Plataforma 1 de la Huaca de la Luna." In Uceda, Mujica, and Morales, eds., 17–31.

———. 2001a. "Excavaciones en la Plaza 2B." In Uceda and Morales, eds., 21–34.

———. 2001b. "Excavaciones en la Unidad 15 de la Plataforma I." In Uceda and Morales, eds., 11–20.

———. 2001c. "Plaza 3C." In Uceda and Morales, eds., 35–53.

———. 2004a. "Excavaciones en la Plaza 3C de la Huaca de la Luna (1998–1999)." In Uceda, Mujica, and Morales, eds., 99–120.

———. 2004b. "Excavaciones en la Unidad 12A (amplicación norte), Plataforma 1, Huaca de la Luna." In Uceda, Mujica, and Morales, eds., 21–39.

———. 2008. "Excavaciones en el Frontis Norte y Plaza 1 de Huaca de la Luna, temporada 2002." In Uceda, Mujica, and Morales, eds., 2008b, 18–31.

Ubbelohde-Doering, Heinrich. 1967. *On the Royal Highways of the Inca.* New York and Washington, DC: Frederick A. Praeger.

———. 1983. *Vorspanische Gräber von Pacatnamú, Nordperu.* Materialien zur Allgemeinen und Vergleichenden Archäologie Band 26. Munich: Verlag C. H. Beck.

Uceda Castillo, Santiago. 1997a. "Esculturas en miniatura y una maqueta en madera." In Uceda, Mujica, and Morales, eds., 151–176.

———. 1997b. "Introducción a las excavaciones en el Cerro Blanco." In Uceda, Mujica, and Morales, eds., 107.

———. 1997c. "Introducción a las excavaciones en la Huaca de la Luna." In Uceda, Mujica, and Morales, eds., 19–21.

———. 1997d. "El poder y la muerte en la sociedad moche." In Uceda, Mujica, and Morales, eds., 177–188.

———. 2000a. "Dos ceremoniales en Huaca de la Luna: Un análisis de los espacios arquitectónicos." In Uceda, Mujica, and Morales, eds., 205–214.

———. 2000b. "El templo mochica: Rituales y ceremonias." In Makowski et al., 91–101.

———. 2001a. "Investigations at Huaca de la Luna, Moche Valley: An Example of Moche Religious Architecture." In Pillsbury, ed., 47–67.

———. 2001b. "El Nivel Alto de la Plataforma I de Huaca de la Luna: Un Espacio Multifuncional." In Uceda and Morales, eds., 225–242.

———. 2004. "El complejo arquitectónico religioso Moche de Huaca de la Luna: El templo de la Divinidad de las montañas." In Uceda, Mujica, and Morales, eds., 367–375.

———. 2006. "El nivel alto de la Plataforma I de Huaca de la Luna: Un espácio multifuncional." In Uceda, Mujica, and Morales, eds., 225–232.

———. 2008. "The High Priests of the Bicephalic Arc." In Bourget and Jones, eds., 133–178.

Uceda, Santiago, and José Armas. 1998. "An Urban Pottery Workshop at the Site of Moche, North Coast of Peru." In Shimada, ed., 91–110.

Uceda, Santiago, José Armas, and Mario Millones. 2008. "Entierros de dos alfareros en el núcleo urbano de Huaca de la Luna." In Uceda, Mujica, and Morales, eds., 2008b, 209–222.

Uceda, Santiago, and José Canziani Amico. 1993. "Evidencias de Grandes Precipitaciones en Diversas Etapas Constructivas de la Huaca de la Luna, Costa Norte del Perú." *Bulletin de l'Institut Français des Études Andines* 22 (1):313–343.

Uceda, Santiago, Claude Chapdelaine, and John Verano. 2008. "Fechas radiocarbónicas para el Complejo Huacas del Sol y de la Luna: Una primera cronología del sitio." In Uceda, Mujica, y Morales, eds., 2008a, 213–223.

Uceda, Santiago, and Ricardo Morales, eds. 2001. *Proyecto Arqueológico Huaca de la Luna Informe Técnico 2000.* Trujillo: Universidad Nacional de Trujillo, Facultad de Ciencias Sociales.

Uceda, Santiago, Ricardo Morales, José Canziani, and María Montoya. 1994. "Investigaciones sobre la arquitectura y relieves polícromos en la Huaca de la Luna, valle de Moche." In Uceda and Mujica, eds., 251–303.

Uceda, Santiago, and Elías Mujica. 1994. "Moche: Propuestas y perspectivas." In Uceda and Mujica, eds., 11–27.

———. 1997. "Investigaciones en la Huaca de la Luna: A manera de introducción." In Uceda, Mujica, and Morales, 9–15.

———. 1998. "Nuevas evidencias por viejos

problemas: A manera de introducción." In Uceda, Mujica, and Morales, 9–16.

———. 2004. "El Proyecto Arqueológico Huacas del Sol y de la Luna diez años después: A manera de introducción." In Uceda and Mujica, eds., 11–17.

Uceda, Santiago, and Elías Mujica, eds. 1994. *Moche: Propuestas y Perspectivas.* Actas del Primer Coloquio sobre la Cultura Moche. Trujillo: Universidad Nacional de La Libertad.

———. 2003. *Moche hacia el final del milenio.* 2 vols. Trujillo and Lima: Universidad Nacional de Trujillo and Pontificia Universidad Católica del Perú.

Uceda, Santiago, Elías Mujica, and Ricardo Morales, eds. 1996. "Huacas del Sol y de la Luna." Trujillo: Universidad Nacional de la Libertad. Pamphlet with editions in Spanish and in English.

———. 1997. *Investigaciones en la Huaca de la Luna, 1995.* Trujillo: Universidad Nacional de la Libertad, Facultad de Ciencias Sociales.

———. 1998. *Investigaciones en la Huaca de la Luna, 1996.* Trujillo: Universidad Nacional de la Libertad, Facultad de Ciencias Sociales.

———. 2000. *Investigaciones en la Huaca de la Luna, 1997.* Trujillo: Universidad Nacional de Trujillo, Facultad de Ciencias Sociales.

———. 2004. *Investigaciones en la Huaca de la Luna, 1998–1999.* Trujillo: Universidad Nacional de Trujillo, Facultad de Ciencias Sociales.

———. 2006. *Investigaciones en la Huaca de la Luna, 2000.* Trujillo: Universidad Nacional de Trujillo, Facultad de Ciencias Sociales.

———. 2008a. *Investigaciones en la Huaca de la Luna, 2001.* Trujillo: Patronato Huacas del Valle de Moche, Universidad Nacional de Trujillo, Facultad de Ciencias Sociales.

———. 2008b. *Investigaciones en la Huaca de la Luna, 2002.* Trujillo: Patronato Huacas del Valle de Moche, Universidad Nacional de Trujillo, Facultad de Ciencias Sociales.

Uceda, Santiago, and Moisés Tufinio. 2003. "El complejo arquitectónico religioso Moche de Huaca de la Luna: Una aproximación a su dinámica ocupacional." In Uceda and Mujica, eds., vol. 2, 179–228.

Uceda Castillo, Santiago, Henry Gayoso Rullier, and Nadia Gamarra Garranza. 2009. "The Gallinazo at Huacas de Moche: Style or Culture?" In Millaire with Morlion, eds., 105–123.

Urton, Gary. 1981. *At the Crossroads of Earth and Sky: An Andean Cosmology.* Austin: University of Texas Press.

———. 1982. "Astronomy and Calendrics on the Coast of Peru." In *Ethnoastronomy and Archaeoastronomy in the American Tropics,* ed. Anthony F. Aveni and Gary Urton, 231–247. Annals of the New York Academy of Sciences, vol. 385.

———. 1993. "Moieties and Ceremonialism in the Andes: The Ritual Battles of the Carnival Season in Southern Peru." In Millones and Onuki, eds., 117–142.

Valle Álvarez, Luis. 2004. *Desarrollo arqueológico costa norte del Perú.* Trujillo: Ediciones Sian.

Vásquez Sánchez, Víctor F., and Teresa E. Rosales Tham. 1998. "Zooarqueológia de la zona urbana Moche." In Uceda, Mujica, and Morales, eds., 173–193.

———. 2004. "Arqueozoología y arqueobotánica de la Huaca de la Luna, 1998–1999." In Uceda, Mujica, and Morales, eds., 337–366.

———. 2008. "Análisis del material orgánico de los conjuntos arquitectónicos CA30 y CA35, núcleo urbano Moche, Huaca de la Luna." In Ucedea, Mujica, and Morales, eds., 2008b, 169–183.

Vásquez Sánchez, Victor F., Teresa E. Rosales Tham, Arturo Morales Muñiz, Eufrasia Roselló Izquierdo. 2003. "Zooarqueología de la zona urbana Moche, Complejo Huacas del Sol y la Luna, Valle de Moche." In Uceda and Mujica, eds., vol. 2, 33–63.

Vázquez de Espinosa, Antonio. 1948 [1616]. *Compendium and Description of the West Indies.* Trans. Charles Upton Clark. Smithsonian Miscellaneous Collections, vol. 102, pub. 3646.

Vélez Diéguez, Juan. 1980. "Peces marinos." Boletín de Lima no. 9:1–16.

Verano, John W. 1995. "Where Do They Rest? The Treatment of Human Offerings and Trophies in Ancient Peru." In Dillehay, ed., 189–227.

———. 1997. "Physical Characteristics and Skeletal Biology of the Moche Population at Pacatnamu." In Donnan and Cock, eds., 189–214.

———. 1998. "Sacrificios humanos, desmembramientos y modificaciones culturales en restos osteológicos: Evidencias de las temporadas de investigación 1995–96 en Huaca de la Luna." In Uceda, Mujica, and Morales, eds., 159–171.

———. 2001a. "Human Sacrifice at the Pyramid of the Moon, Northern Peru: Report on the 2001 Field Season." Report submitted to the National Geographic Society's Committee on Research and Exploration.

———. 2001b. "The Physical Evidence of Human Sacrifice in Ancient Peru." In Benson and Cook, eds., 165–184.

———. 2001c. "War and Death in the Moche World: Osteological Evidence and Visual Discourse." In Pillsbury, ed., 111–125.

———. 2003. "Avances en la bioantropología de los Moche." In Uceda and Mujica, eds., vol. 2, 15–32.

———. 2008. "Community and Diversity in Moche Human Sacrifice." In Bourget and Jones, eds., 195–213.

Verano, John W., Moisés Tufinio, and Mellisa Lund Valle. 2008. "Esqueletos humanos de la Plaza 3C de Huaca de la Luna." In Uceda, Mujica, and Morales, eds., 2008a, 225–254.

Vergara, Enrique. 1990. "La conception de la sexualité au Perou ancien." In *Inca—Peru: 3000 Ans d'Histoire*, ed. Sergio Purin, 400–411. 2 vols. Brussels: Musées Royaux d'Art y d'Histoire.

Vogt, Evon Z. 1969. *Zinacantán: A Maya Community in the Highlands of Chiapas.* Cambridge, MA: Belknap Press of Harvard University.

Vreeland, James M., Jr. 1992a. "Day of the Dead." *Archaeology* 45 (6):43.

———. 1992b. "Preliminary Report on Native Cotton Collection and Cultivation in Northern Peru." *Willay* 37/38:20–23.

Wassén, S. Henry. 1979. "Was 'Espingo' (*Ispincu*) of Psychotropic and Intoxicating Importance for the Shamans in Peru?" In Browman and Schwarz, eds., 55–62.

Weiss, Pedro. 1961. "La asociación de la uta y verruga peruana en los mitos de la papa, figurados en la cerámica mochica y chimu." *Revista del Museo Nacional* 30:65–77. Lima.

Willey, Gordon R. 1953. *Prehistoric Settlement Patterns in the Virú Valley, Peru.* Bureau of American Ethnology Bulletin 155. Washington, DC: Smithsonian Institution.

Williams, A. R. 2006. "Mystery of the Tattooed Mummy." *National Geographic* 209 (6):70–83.

Wilson, David J. 1988. Settlement Patterns in the Lower Santa Valley, Peru: A Regional Perspective on the Origins and Development of Complex North Coast Society. Washington, DC: Smithsonian Institution Press.

Wing, Elizabeth. 1989. "Human Use of Canids in the Central Andes." *Advances in Neotropical Mammalogy*, 265–278.

Zevallos Quiñones, Jorge. 1946. "Un diccionario yunga." *Revista del Museo Nacional* 15:163–188. Lima.

———. 1989. "Area y fases de la cultura moche." In Lavalle, ed., 96–126. Lima: Banco de Credito del Peru en la Cultura.

———. 1994. *Huacas y huaqueros en Trujillo durante el Virreynato (1535–1835).* Trujillo: Editora Normas Legales S.A.

———. 1995. "La prehistoria de Trujillo." In *Trujillo Precolombino*, 221–243. Lima: Odebrecht.

Zighelboim, Ari. 1995. "Mountain Scenes of Human Sacrifice in Moche Ceramic Iconography." *Journal of the Steward Anthropological Society* 23 (1 & 2):153–188.

Zuidema, R. Tom. 1992. "Inca Cosmos in Andean Context." In *Andean Cosmologies Through Time*, ed. Robert V. H. Dover, Katharine E. Seibold, and John H. McDowell, 17–45. Bloomington and Indianapolis: Indiana University Press.

INDEX